AF249135

DON LI-LEGER

PAINTINGS

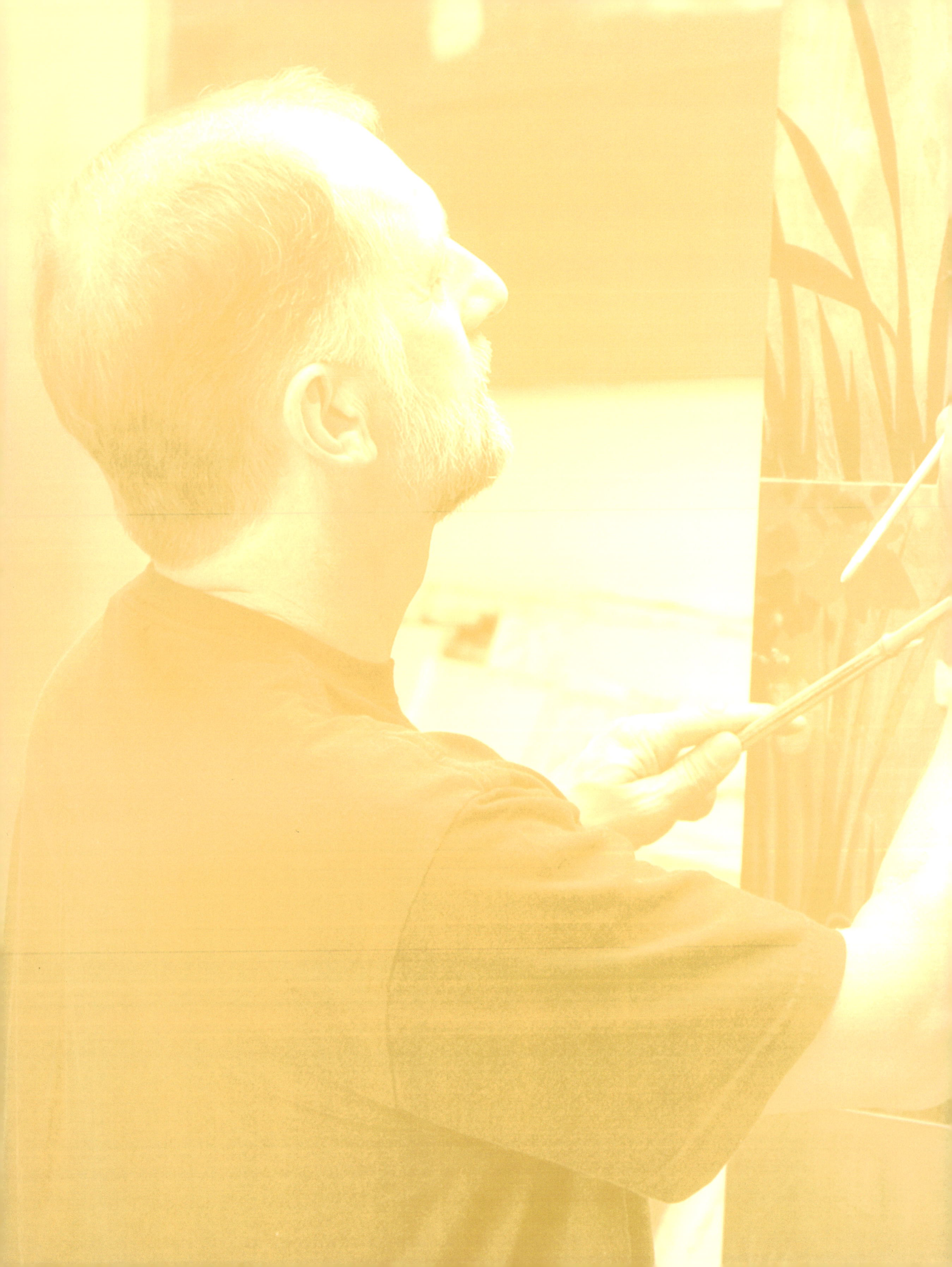

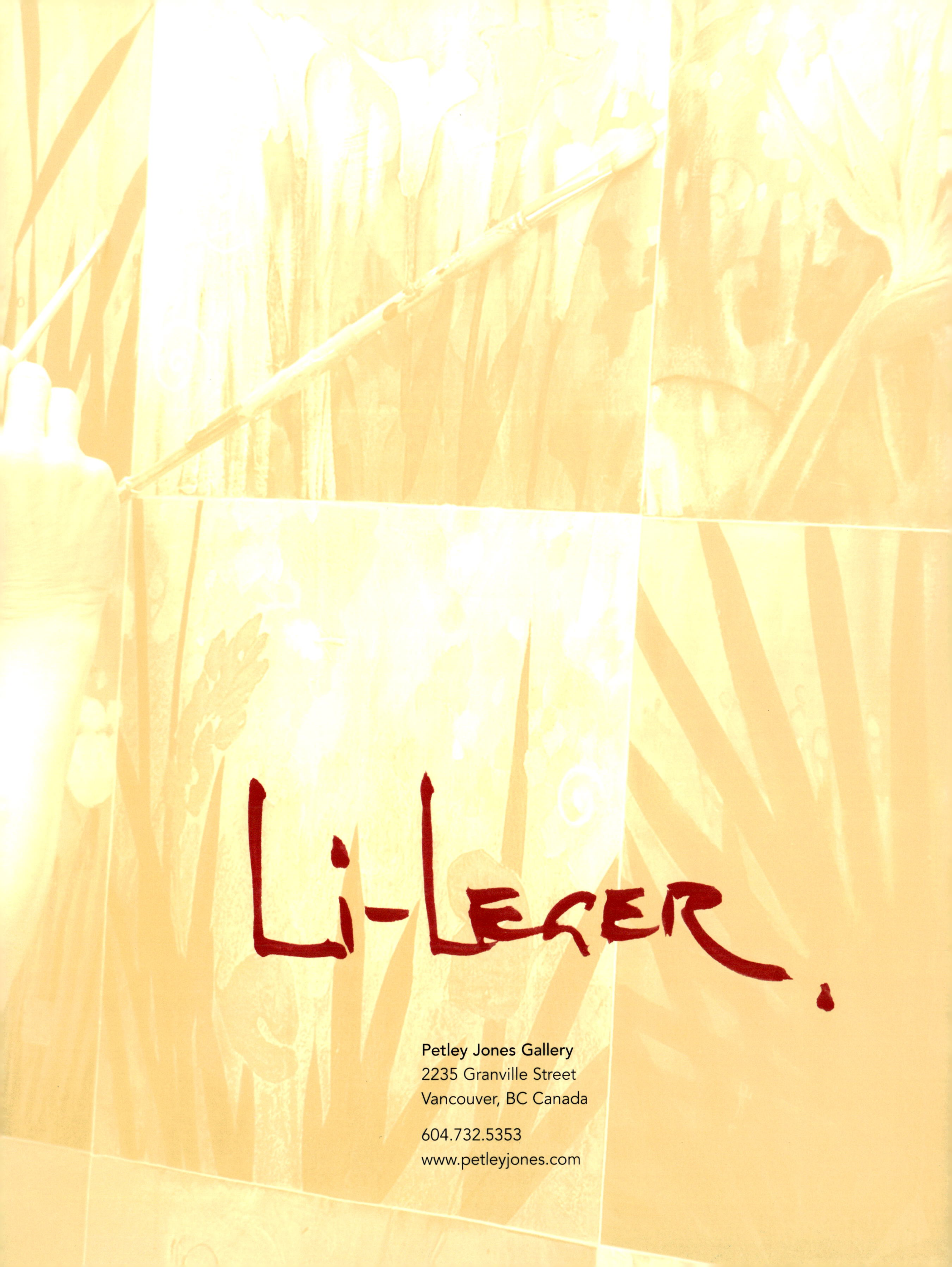

Petley Jones Gallery
2235 Granville Street
Vancouver, BC Canada

604.732.5353
www.petleyjones.com

CREDITS
STUDIO PHOTOGRAPHY: Eric Milner Photography
GARDEN PHOTOGRAPHY: Don Li-Leger
PAINTING PHOTOGRAPHY: Roman Skotnicki Photo Design
BOOK DESIGN: Sage Design, Vancouver, BC
PRINTER: Metropolitan Fine Printers, Vancouver, BC

LIBRARY AND ARCHIVES CANADA
CATALOGUING IN PUBLICATION

Li-Leger, Don
  Don Li-Leger paintings.

Essay by Carol Prokop; introduction by Matt Petley-Jones ;
  tribute by Peter Ohler.
ISBN 0-9737709-0-2

 I. Prokop, Carol Ann, 1951-   II. Petley-Jones, Matt
III. Ohler, Peter   IV. Petley Jones Gallery.   V. Title.

ND249.L448A4 2005   759.11   C2005-903623-0

ACKNOWLEDGEMENTS
This book would not have been possible without the dedicated support of some very special people. They are Cora, Noah and Erica Li-Leger; Pam Hudson, Jessica and Rick at the Petley Jones Gallery; Peter Ohler; Carol Prokop; Gina Chase; the staff at Canadian Art Prints, in particular, Hal, Niki, Lisa, Jeff and Jocelyn. Thanks also to Barb, Eric and Gail at Canada House Gallery, Banff, Alberta; Peter, Dennie, Nikol and Francis at The White Rock Gallery, White Rock, BC; Aimee, Patti and Jamie at Winn Devon Art Group Ltd., Seattle, Washington.

DON LI-LEGER'S PAINTINGS CAN BE VIEWED AT THE FOLLOWING
Petley Jones Gallery, Vancouver, BC   http://petleyjones.com/lileger.html
Canada House Gallery, Banff, Alberta   http://www.canadahouse.com/dynamic/artists/Don_Li_Leger.asp
The White Rock Gallery, White Rock, BC   http://www.whiterockgallery.com/LiLeger.htm
Hambleton Galleries, Kelowna, BC   http://www.hambletongalleries.com/dynamic/artists/Li-LegerDon_public.htm
Don Li-Leger   http://www.li-leger.ca
Galerie d'Art Michel Bigué, St-Sauveur, QC
Winn Devon Art Group Ltd., Seattle, Washington   http://www.winndevon.com

INTRODUCTION

The Petley Jones Gallery is proud to be the publisher of this exciting new book on the work of Don Li-Leger. The Gallery has represented and exhibited Don's work since 1988, and throughout that time we have witnessed his evolution into one of the most creative personalities in the Canadian art scene.

The fertility of his creative imagination has been transformed through his painting into wondrous visions of colour-field gardens, texture and harmony. Long overdue, this book is a stunning overview of his accomplishments over the past five years. The colour plates, informative essay, chronology and bibliography represent the depth of Don's creativity and commitment to his work. It offers a glimpse of his universe, a narrative on the intricate textures of his inner world. The love of his garden is transformed into graphic chromatic structures of atmosphere and life. This book will reveal to you his love of life, colour, nature and his insatiable spirit that brings it all together. It is our hope that this book will give you an insight into Don's work and, ultimately, the pleasure that it has given me over the last seventeen years. ■

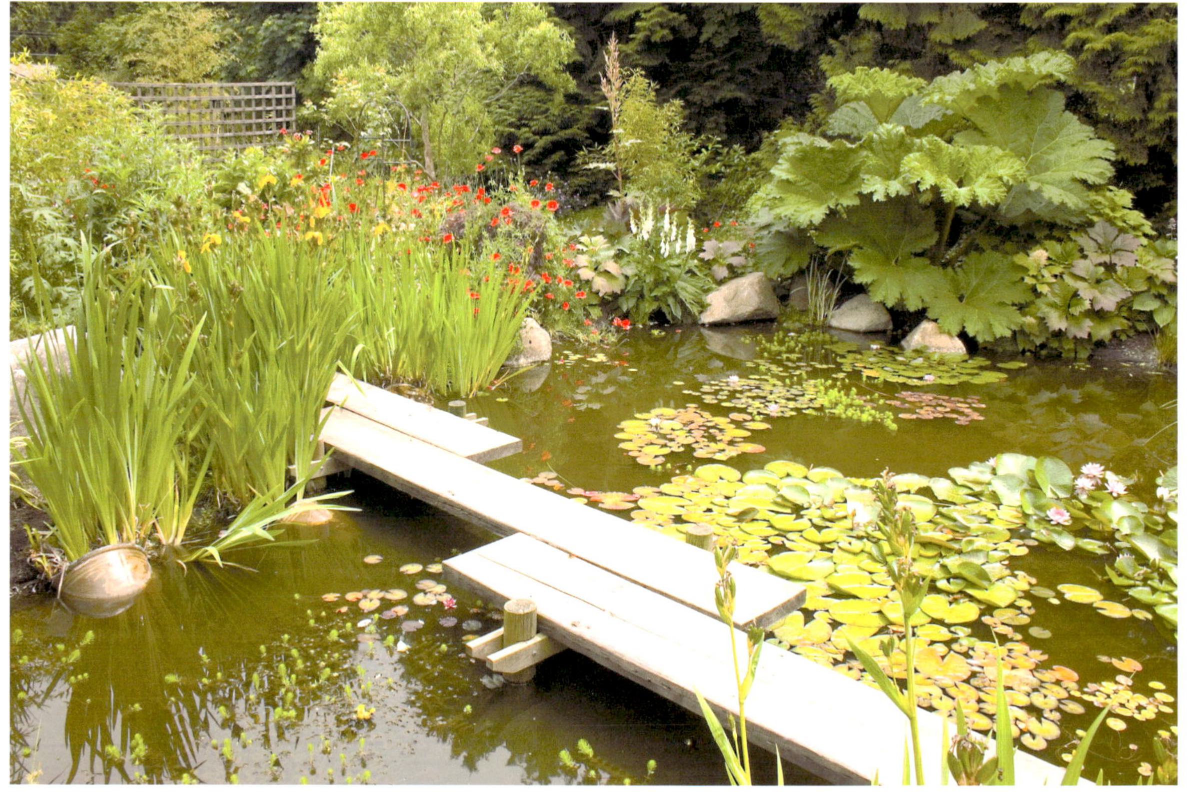

Over the past decade, I have watched the paintings of Don Li-Leger reflect dramatically his personal artistic maturation and creative growth.

From his earlier craftsman-like renderings of birds, flowers and other varied subject matter, Don has invented a way to infuse his art with energy and visual impact.

Collage, colour, interpretive block-like angles all intermingle with controlled expressive brushwork and personal emotional honesty.

It is rare when a young painter progresses quickly and discovers his true voice. Rarer yet, when his technical expertise is equal to the challenges of moving forward in a meaningful and substantive way.

Don Li-Leger is, in my opinion, an artist poised to be fully recognized as a Canadian artist with a big future. ▪

— PETER OHLER SR.
Vancouver, B.C.
April 25th, 2005

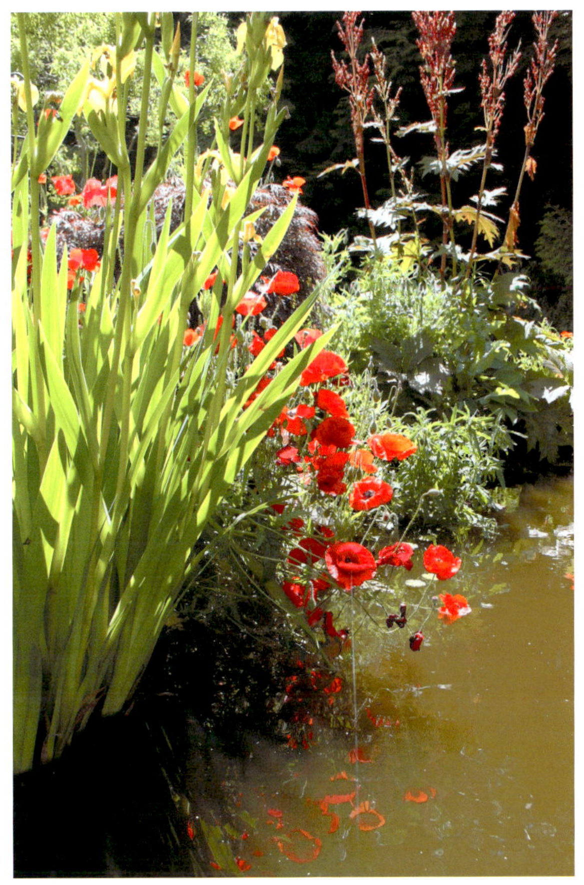

Art will never be able to exist without nature.

— PIERRE BONNARD

DON LI-LEGER A PORTRAIT IN PAINTING

This book presents the first comprehensive survey of paintings created by Don Li-Leger between 1999 and 2005. The paintings reproduced here mark a different and distinct phase in Li-Leger's career. Li-Leger moved away from his widely-appreciated nature painting based on observation and representation to concentrate on semi-abstract and abstract painting focused on colour, geometry and limited subject matter. Expressed simply, Li-Leger's artistic production was transformed from an almost scientific engagement with the visible world, where details and specificity were critical, to a more personal, selective response to external stimuli, where contemplation and interpretation became more important. The paintings represented in this book range from small canvases measuring 18 inches by 18 inches to large panels measuring 45 inches by 78 inches and are, for the most part, executed in acrylic paints and gels on canvas.

The transformation of Li-Leger's practice from realistic to abstract painting did not occur overnight. He had painted abstract works early in his career [*Untitled 1978*] and had admired the works of Wassily Kandinsky, Mark Rothko, Piet Mondrian and Richard Diebenkorn, particularly the spiritual and metaphysical aspects of their art. Li-Leger had also developed a deep appreciation of Asian art and Eastern philosophy and an interest in writings on art theory and art therapy. Peter London's *No More Second Hand Art* was a significant influence, as were Rollo May's *The Courage to Create*, Shaun McNiff's *Trust the Process* and Chang Chung-yuan's *Creativity and Taoism.*

Li-Leger's return to abstraction also evolved from his practice of making monoprints. A monoprint is an image created by pressing a piece of paper against a painted or inked metal or glass plate and then passing the plate and paper through a high pressure press. The resultant image on the paper is a mirror impression of that on the plate. Li-Leger began making monoprints in 1997 and was impressed by the creative possibilities of the medium. He found the medium liberating and was inspired by its spontaneity and serendipity – a quality he characterized as "happy accidents". He began to experiment with colour and brushwork and to collage leaves and other natural materials from his own garden onto the plates. *Collections* is an example of a monoprint using that collage process. Initially the monoprints were both representational and non-representational, but gradually they became more and more abstract.

Inspired by the freshness of the monoprinting, Li-Leger began painting canvases with colour-saturated, rigorously simplified images, using Chinese and Western bristle brushes, that

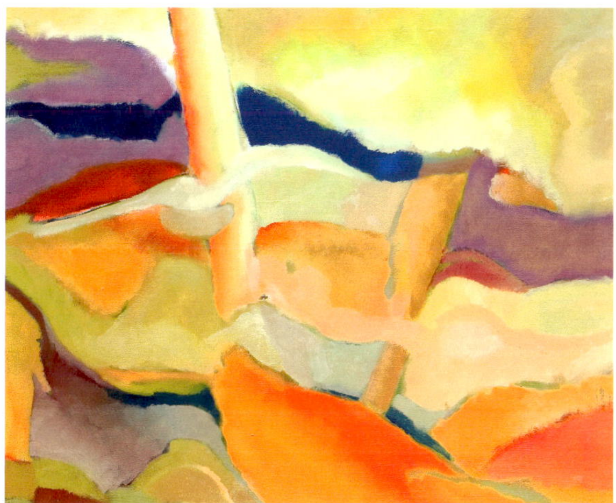

Untitled, oil on canvas, 26" x 32", 1978

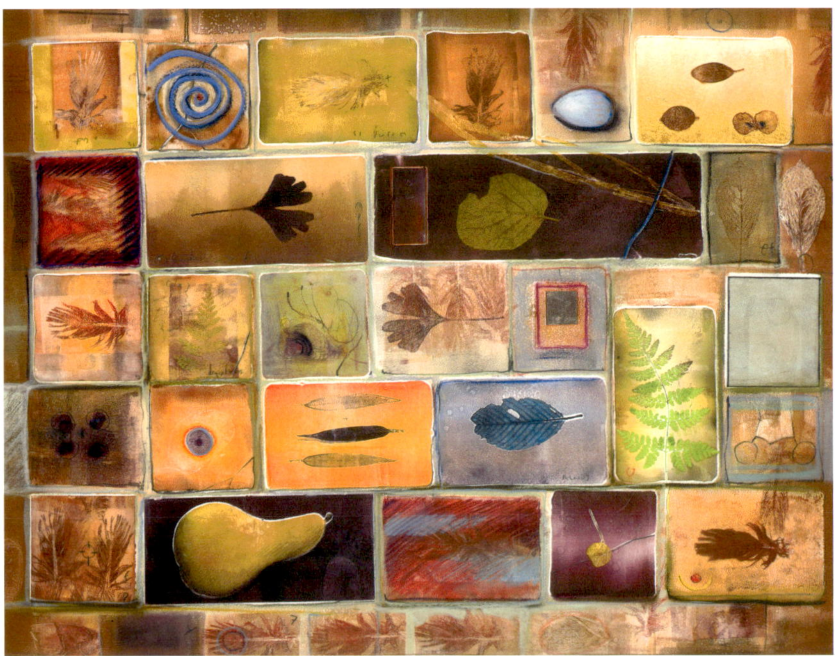

Collections, monoprint on paper, 20" x 32", 1998

combined elements of geometry, natural phenomena, calligraphy and collage. Li-Leger often painted in series, and over time he built up an anthology of visual elements that became the fundamental building blocks of individual paintings. Those building blocks or formal characteristics include Li-Leger's use of specific *compositional formats*, his exploitation of *recurring motifs* and his distinctive *colour palette*.

Compositionally, the paintings fall into two main formal arrangements. They are either edged on three sides by bands of colour that function like frames or architectural components (*Sanctuary, Terra Cotta Garden, Garden Gateway*) or are spatially divided into grids (*Water Garden II, Iris Nine Patch II*). Both formats are essentially classical in nature and feature prominently in antique antecedents. In the first instance, the frames function as borders to confine areas or direct the viewer's gaze. In some cases, they almost dominate the space (*Bamboo Garden, Hollyhock Garden*). The frames are also surfaces for script or calligraphy and function like literary sidebars inscribed with Buddhist words meaning "compassion" or

"still mind." In other images, the frames contain plants, such as bamboo stalks or reeds. Li-Leger has likened these images to "…gateways, openings, windows and porticos. One can be looking out of a room into another space, another world, framed by pillars and architectural elements." *After the Hammam*, with its evocative archways, is an obvious example. Despite Li-Leger's reference to windows and apertures, there is no real attempt at perspective; however, as there is usually no border along the top edge of the works, there is the suggestion of space beyond the surface of the paintings.

The grid paintings, on the other hand, make no allusion to space beyond the painted surface. Their flat two-dimensionality is reminiscent of the textile arts of quilting and weaving and of patterns such as checks and plaids. Some of these works are completely abstract (*Intention, Joie de Vie*) while others are reminiscent of Li-Leger's own carefully laid out garden (*42 Views of my Garden, Tropical Nine Patch*).

Whether semi-abstract or abstract, the frame and grid paintings share a repertoire of *recurring motifs*. This characteristic is perhaps most readily apparent in Li-Leger's paintings of irises, poppies, lilies and bamboo (*The Heavenly Art of Gardening, 42 Views of my Garden*). All of these plants flourish in Li-Leger's garden, and the iris and the bamboo, in particular, are plants that Li-Leger returns to again and again.

In the abstract paintings spirals, calligraphic symbols and square and rectangular medallion-like panels frequently appear like punctuation marks or musical notes across the surfaces. *Water Garden I* and *Water Garden II* both feature spirals and small square panels as well as traces of text. The spiral pattern is an ancient symbol in many cultures and has been associated with water, growth and evolution. It appears in a myriad of forms, from whirlpools to snail shells. The square and rectangle panels, on the other hand, are based on the "chop" or "seal", a feature of traditional printmaking often used in Oriental prints as a form of identification or "trade mark" by artists, collectors and even viewers.

Although the compositional format and the recurring motifs in Li-Leger's paintings are both important components of his oeuvre, his *restrained colour palette* is the lynch pin. Golds and burgundies, which Li-Leger relates to as the traditional Tibetan Buddhist colours of wisdom and compassion, suffuse his paintings, while blues and greens play supporting roles. For Li-Leger, "Colour is intuitive and infinite, and each colour changes according to its adjacent colours." Colour also dictates the level of tension in the composition and guides the viewer's visceral response. In *Luncheon on the Grass*, for example, the golden background is so strong, the poppies almost pop out of the picture plane. Without the green band at the base, the composition might fly off the canvas. By contrast, the poppies in *Mystic Journey* seem composed and tranquil, set against the cool blue background.

While Li-Leger's current artworks are a departure from his earlier paintings and prints, there are still many resonances with previous work. At the same time, exposure to new influences has inspired renewal and rejuvenation in his artwork. "What is really important to me is the notion of exploration and discovery leading to inspiration. I once did a workshop with a Taos, New Mexico, artist named Ciel Bergman. We talked a lot about preparing your mental state, how important it was to create a special place in your studio – to set it up as a site of experimentation, a special place for creativity. It's all about getting the creative juices flowing, doing automatic painting, doing whatever it takes to get the right side of the brain going. Art is so much more than decoration. It's the meditative aspect of turning your logical brain off and responding to what's there. When you don't worry about mistakes and just focus on what's before you,

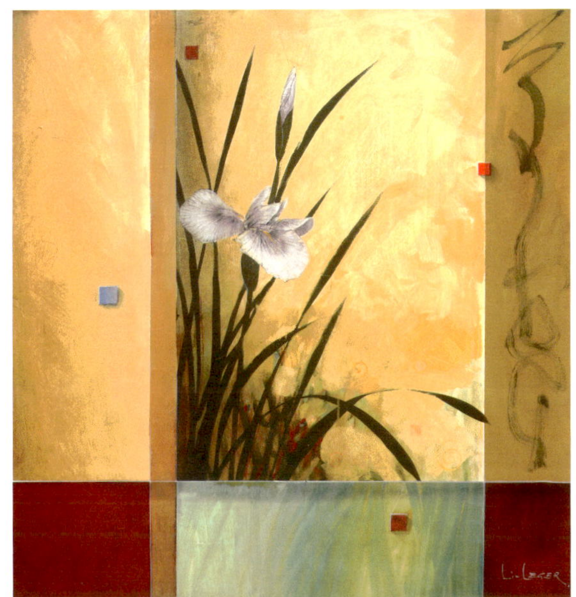

Sanctuary, acrylic on canvas, 40" x 40", 2002

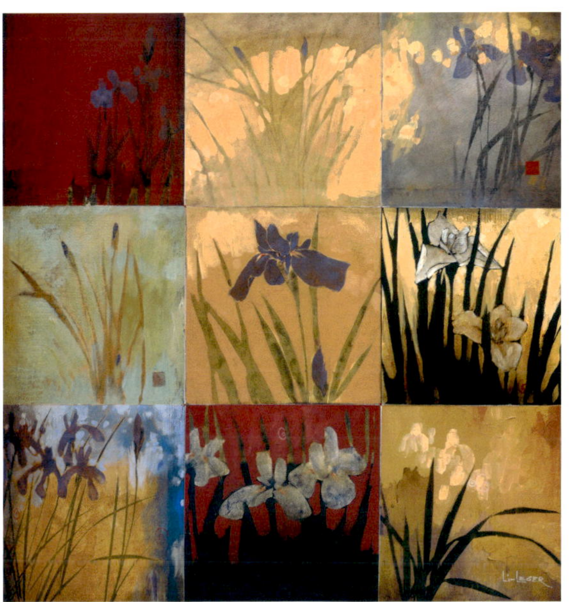

Iris Nine Patch II, acrylic on canvas, 40" x 40", 2003

you can enter a pure state of consciousness and experience a sense of free expression."

In the final analysis, the real key to Li-Leger's art transcends the boundaries of career phases and stylistic definitions. Instead, it can be found in his deep appreciation of the natural world, his receptivity to different forms of cultural expression and, perhaps most importantly, his fascination with the creative process itself. ■

Carol Prokop has a BFA in Art History from Concordia University and an MA in Art History from the University of British Columbia. She has written over 30 newspaper and magazines articles on art and other topics. She resides with her husband and son in Surrey, British Columbia.

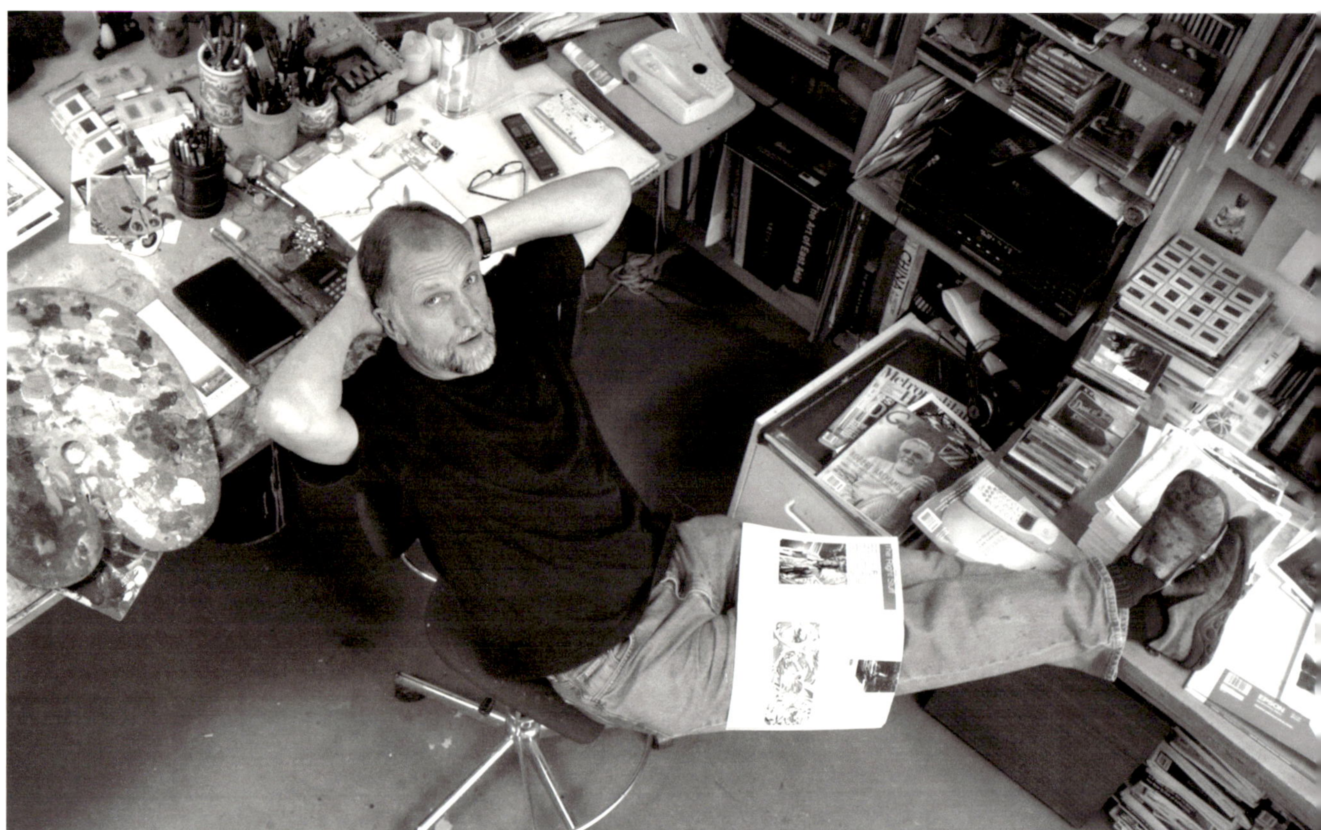

Don Li-Leger

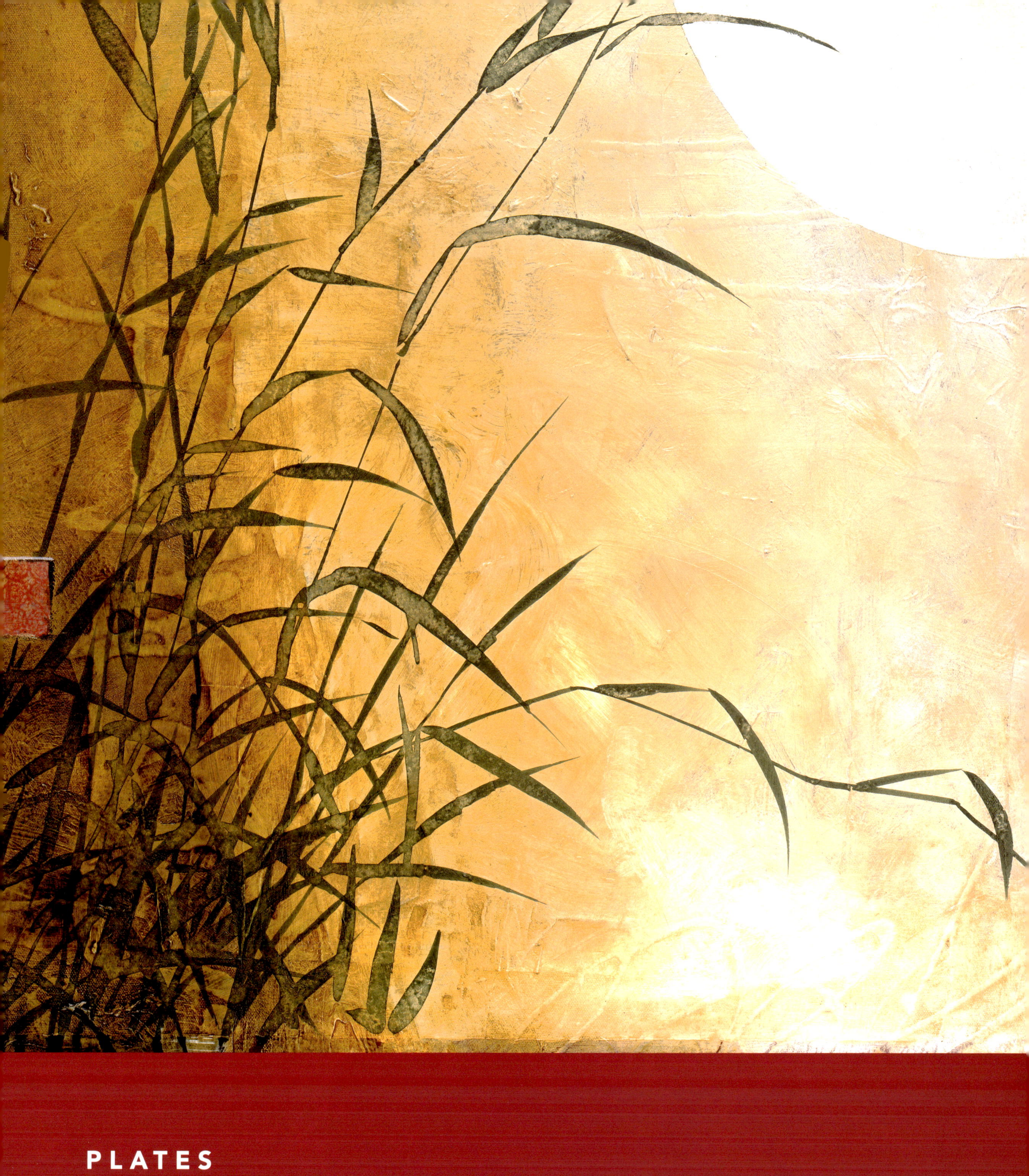
PLATES

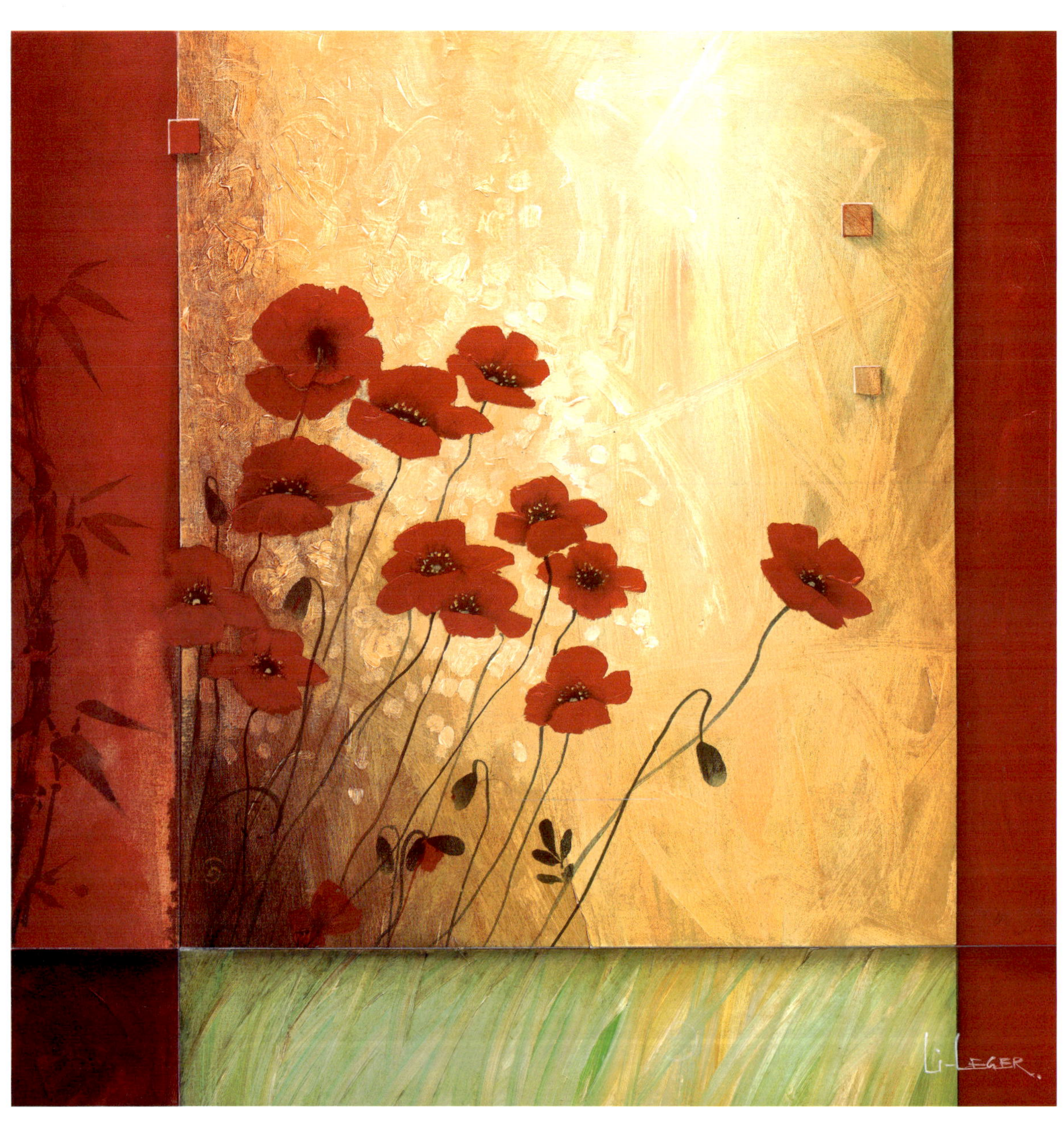

Into the Light II
Acrylic on canvas
36" x 36", 2004
Private Collection

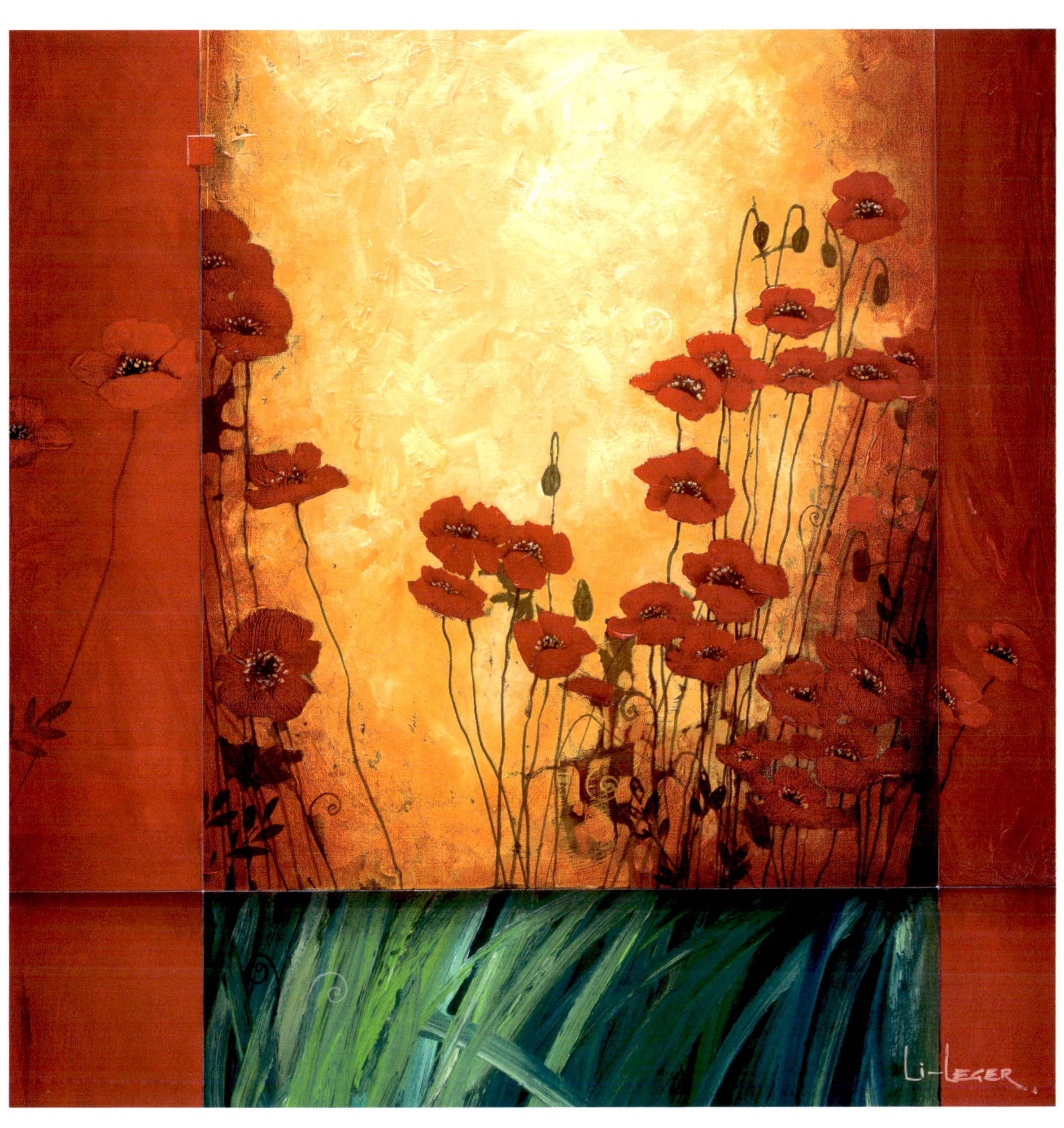

Luncheon on the Grass
Acrylic on canvas
36" x 36", 2004
Collection of
Sandra R. Bruce

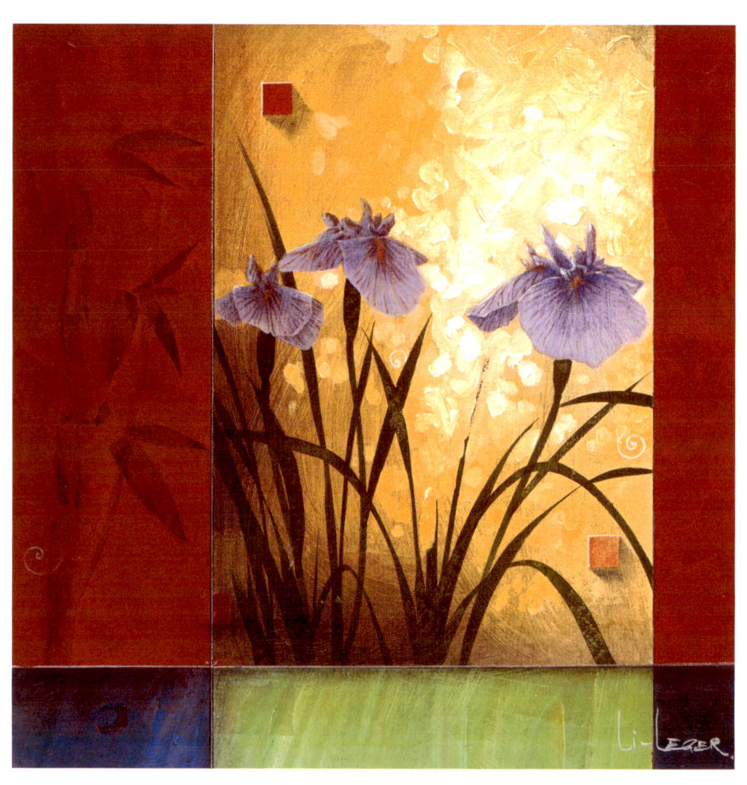

Garden Notes
Acrylic on canvas
24" x 24", 2003
Private Collection

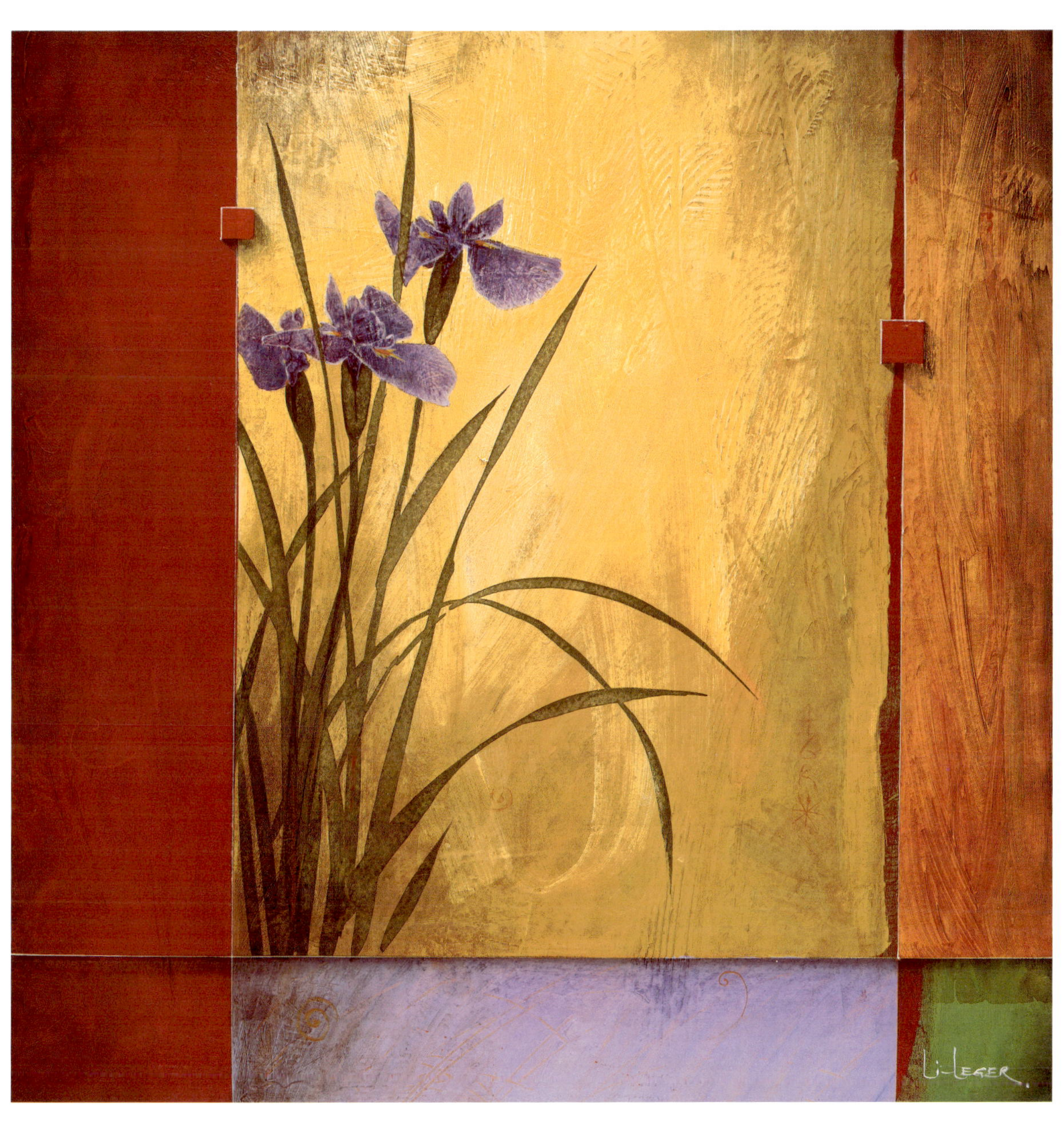

Iris Siesta
Acrylic on canvas
32" x 32", 2002
Private Collection

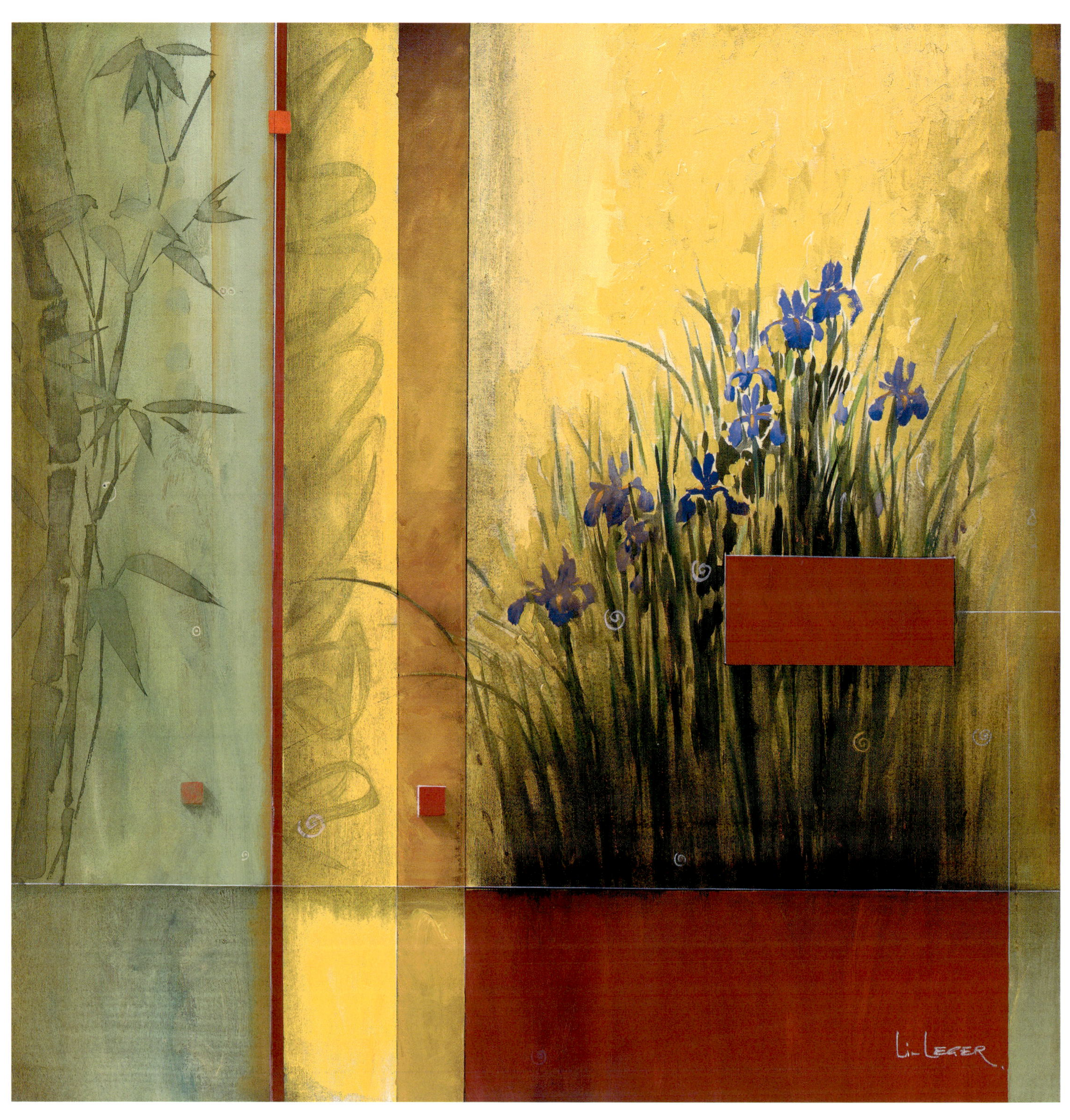

Terrazzo Garden
Acrylic on canvas
40" x 40", 2002
Private Collection

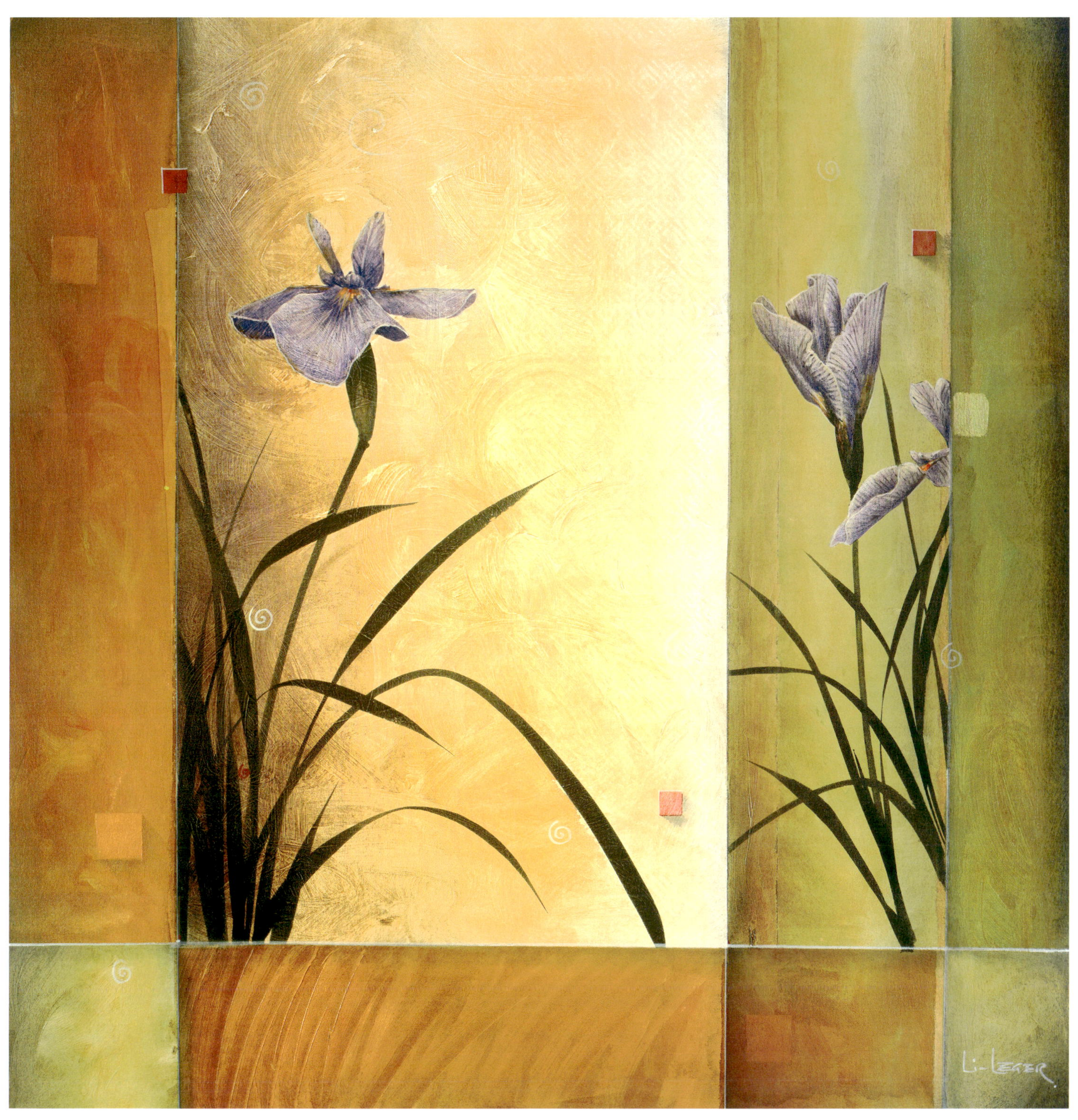

Terra Cotta Garden
Acrylic on canvas
40" x 40", 2003
Private Collection

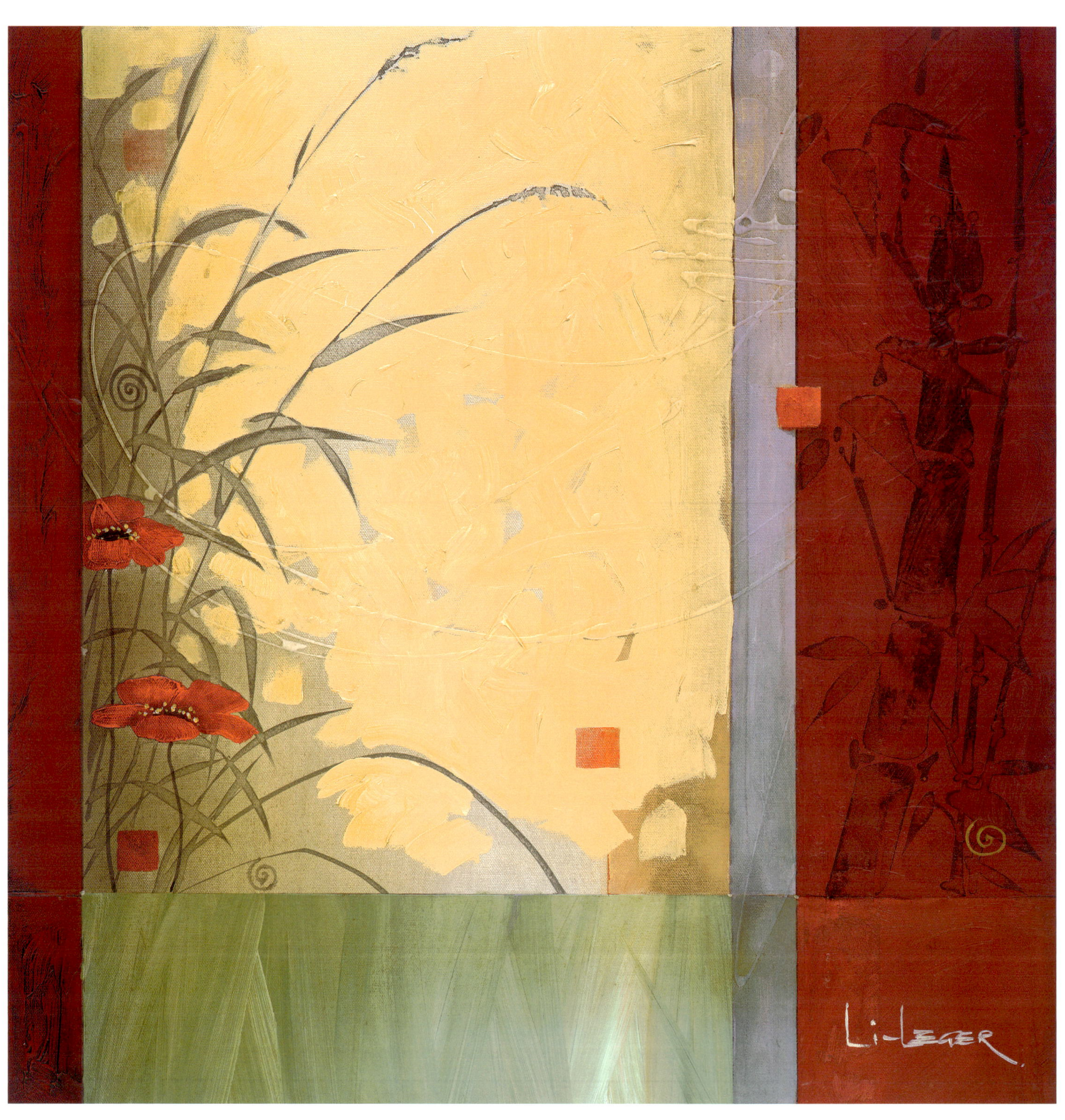

Dancing the Wind
Acrylic on canvas
40" x 40", 2002
Private Collection

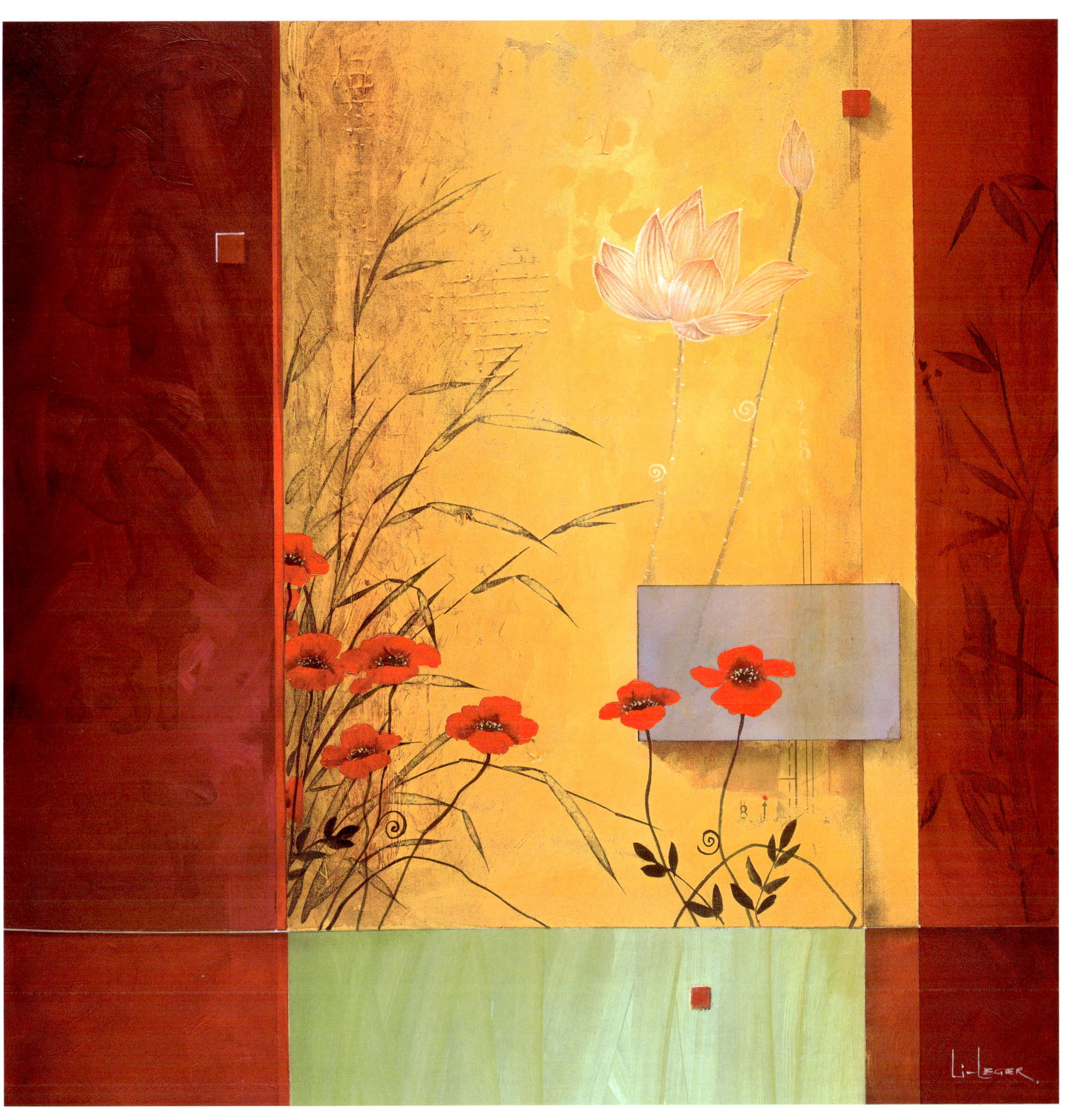

Meditative Journey
Acrylic on canvas
40" x 40", 2003
Private Collection

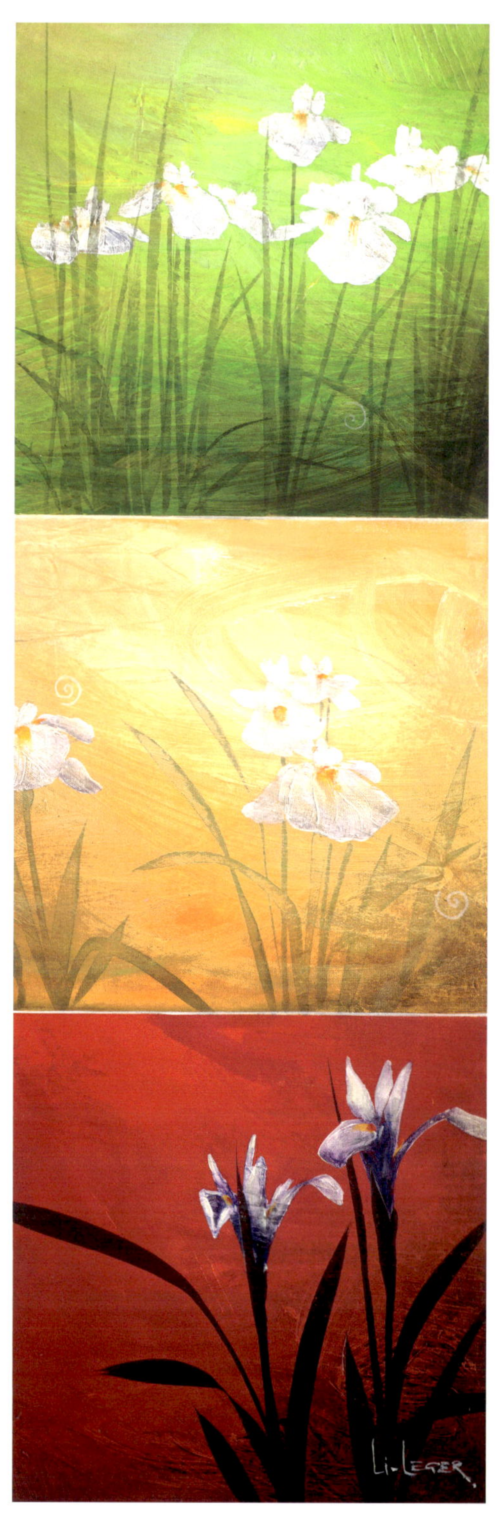

Spring Trio
Acrylic on canvas
48" x 16", 2003
Private Collection

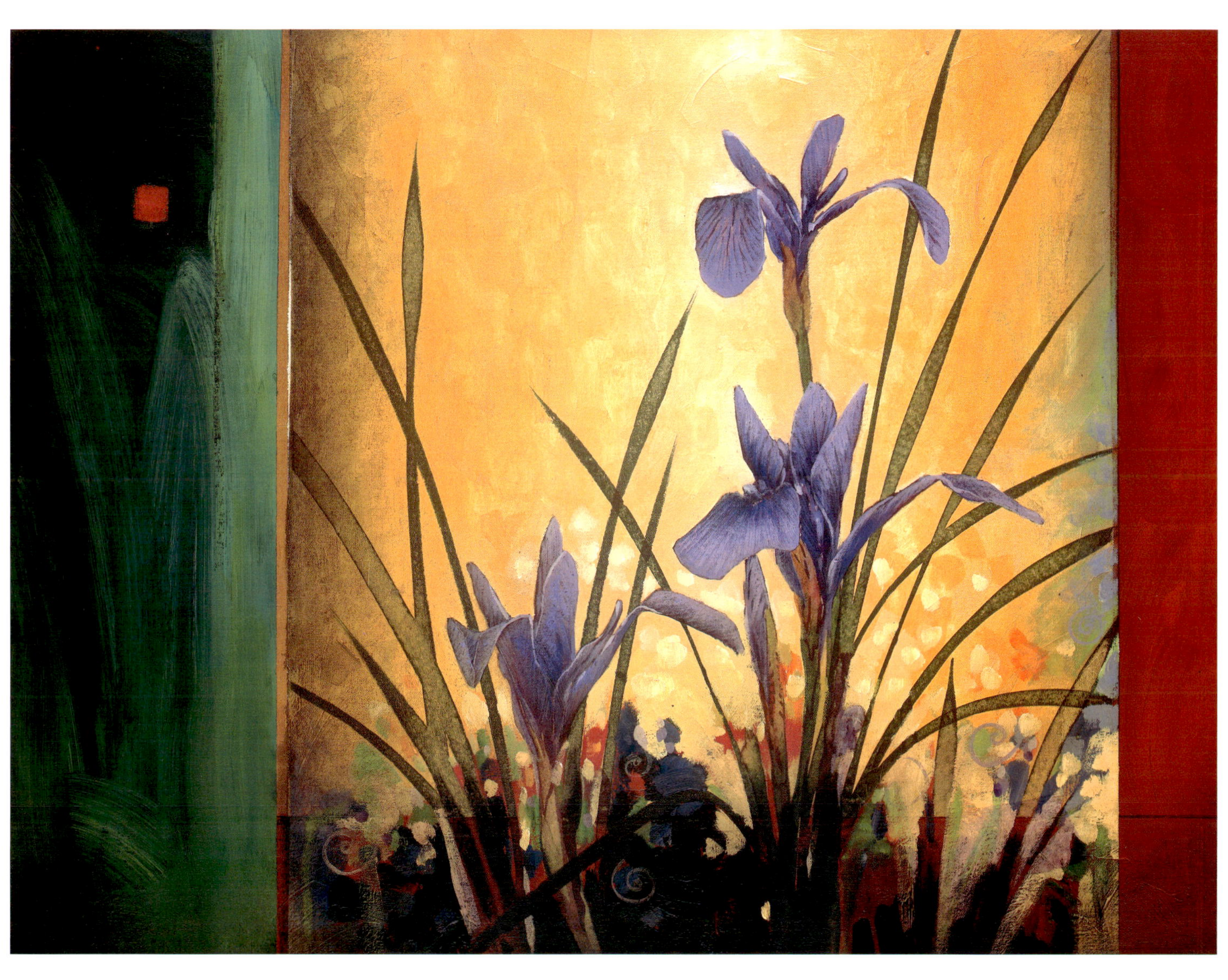

Iris Garden
Acrylic on canvas
30" x 40", 2002
Private Collection

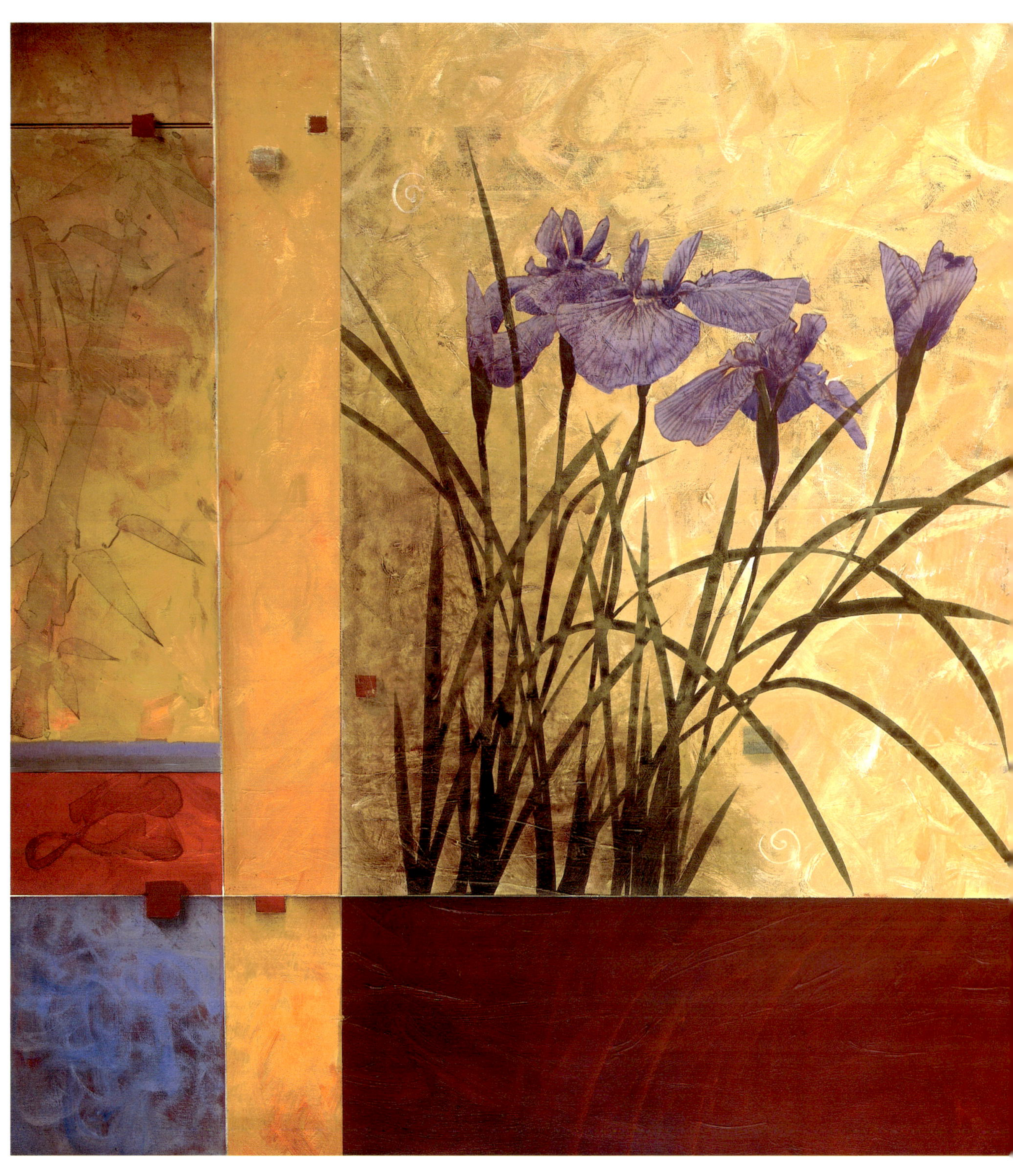

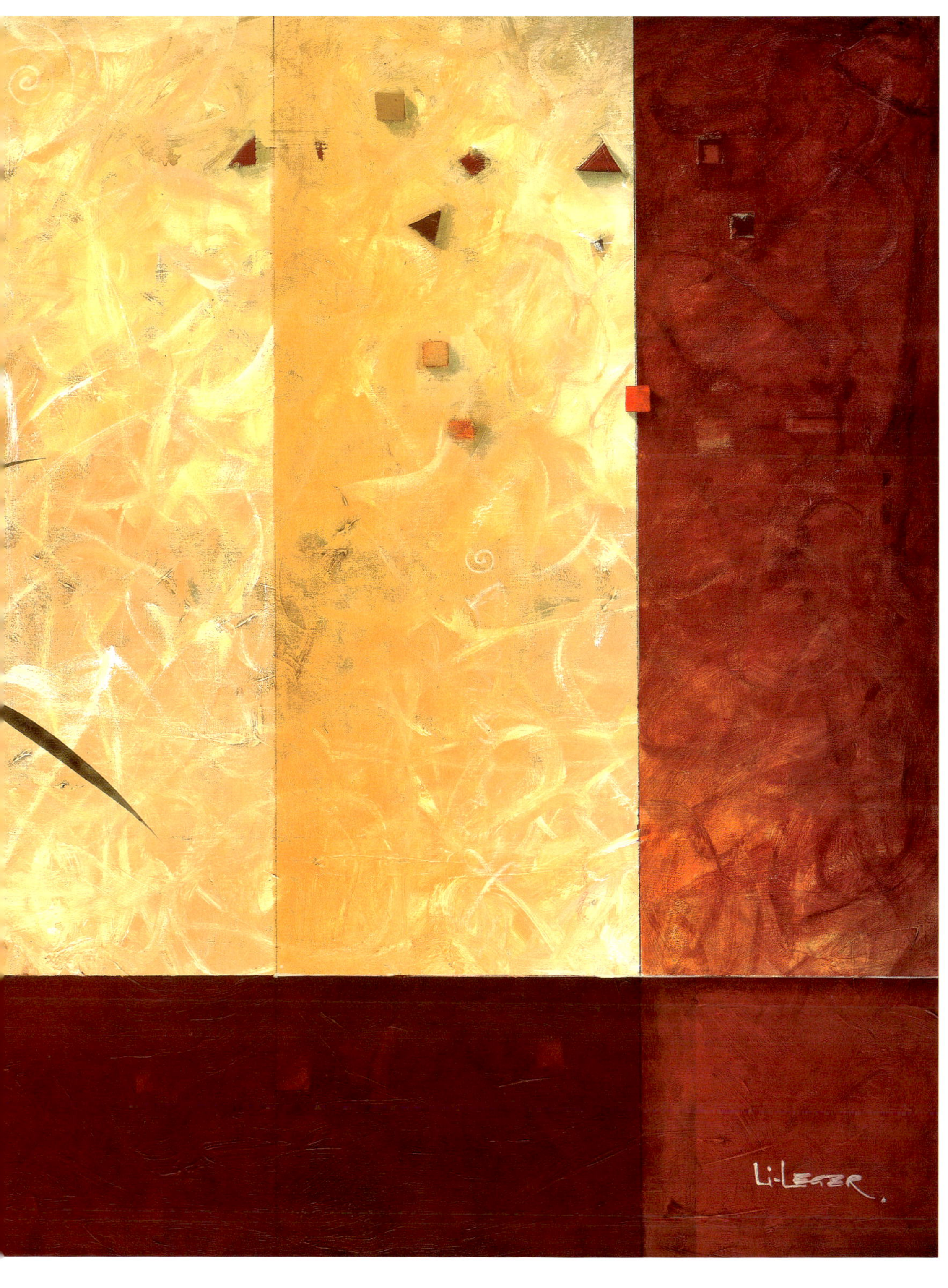

The Iris Dance
Acrylic on canvas
45" x 78", 2002
Private Collection

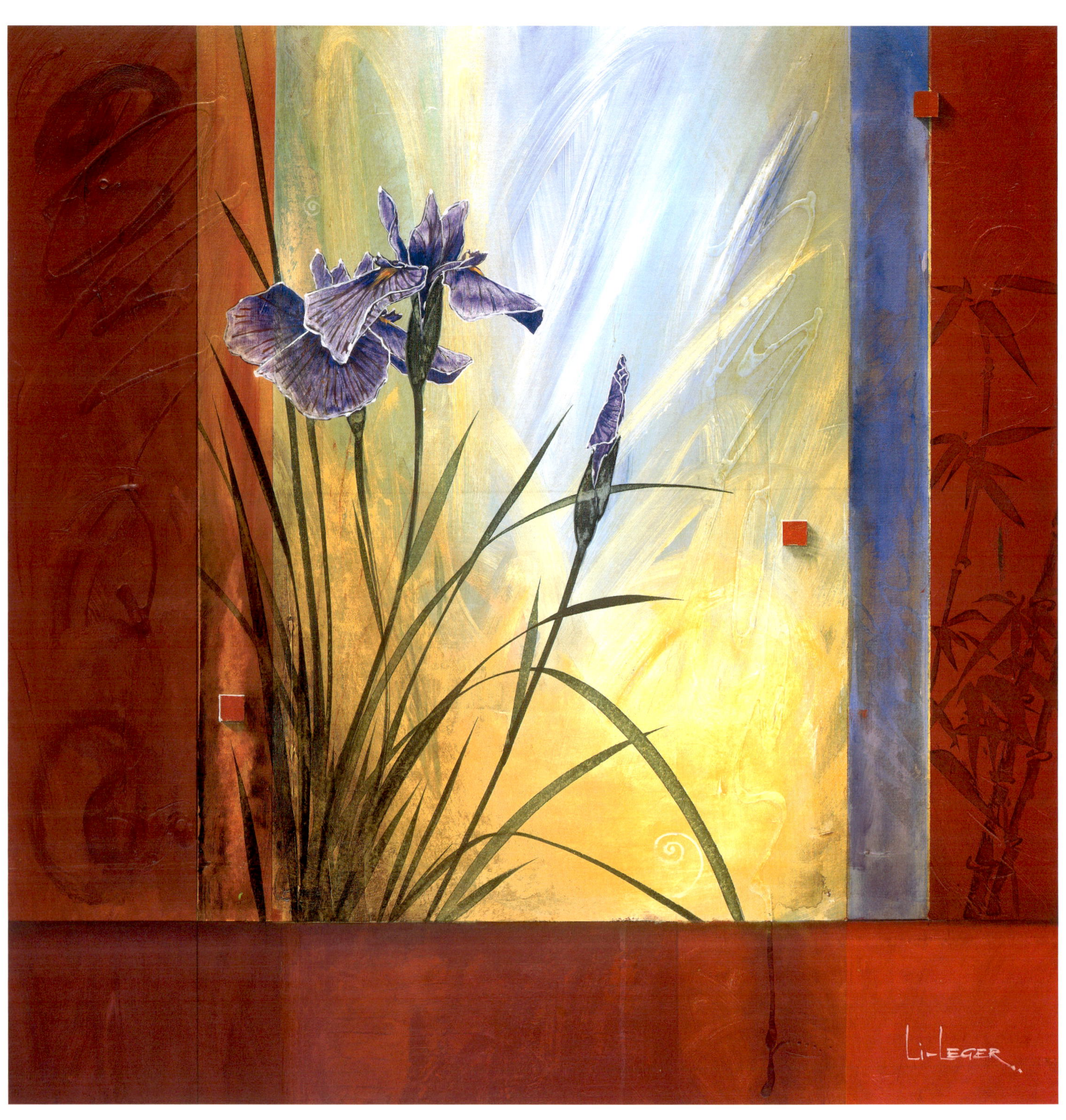

L'Esprit du Printemps
Acrylic on canvas
40" x 40", 2004
Private Collection

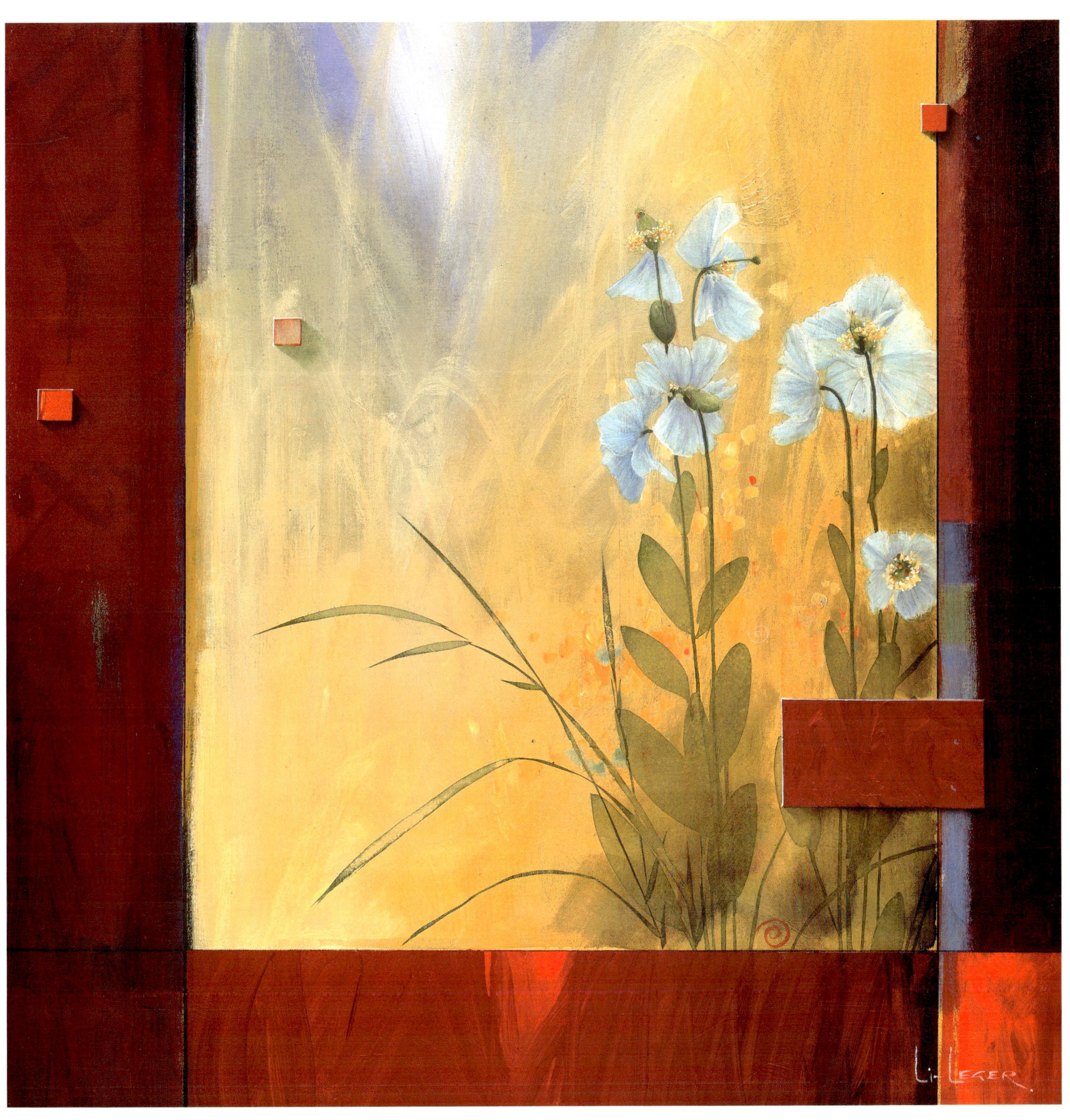

La Découverte du Jardin
Acrylic on canvas
40" x 40", 2004
Collection of the Artist

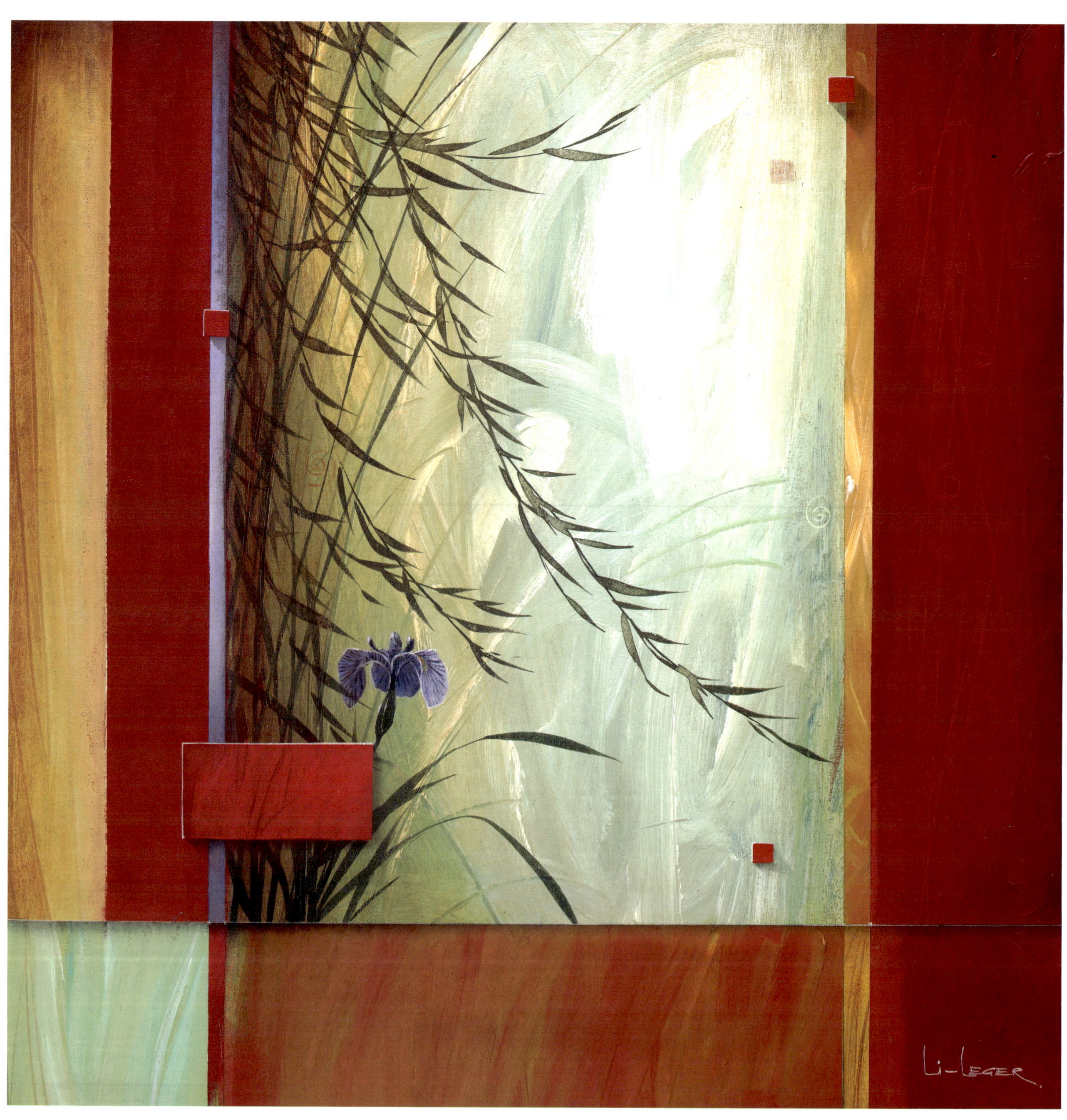

Wind in the Willows
with Iris
Acrylic on canvas
40" x 40", 2003
Private Collection

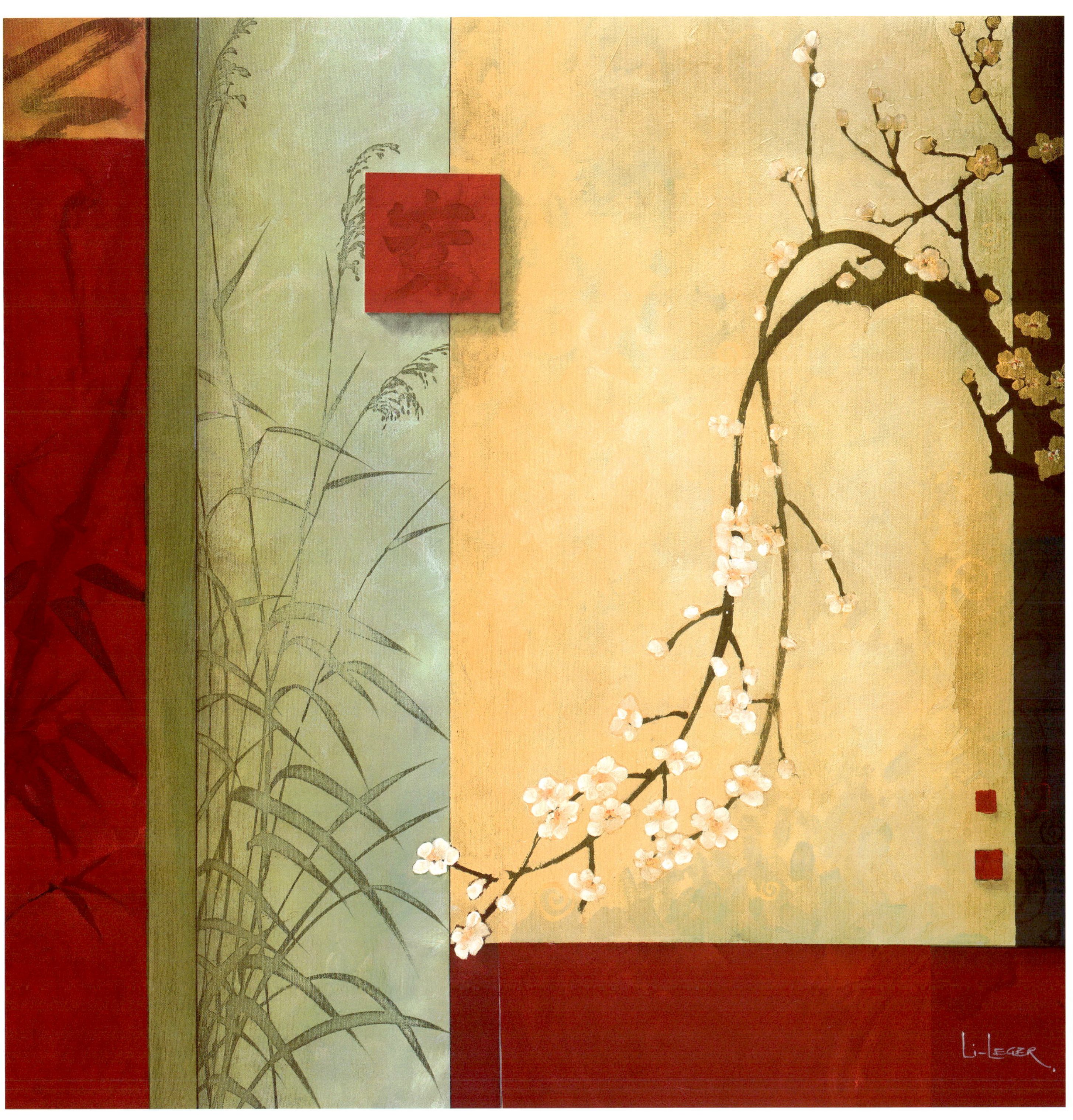

Spring Chorus
Acrylic on canvas
40" x 40", 2003
Private Collection

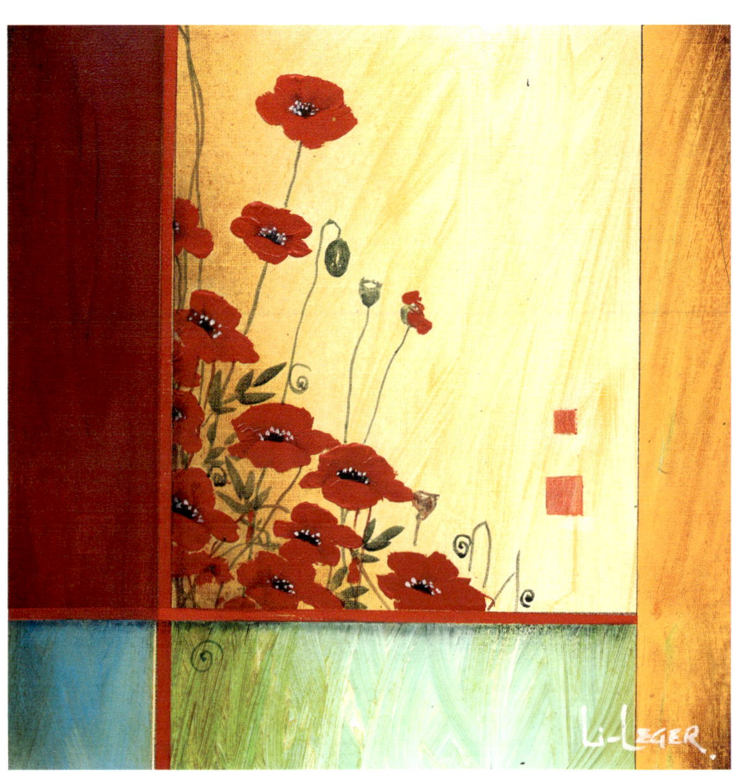

Along the Garden Wall II
Acrylic on canvas
18" x 18", 2005
Private Collection

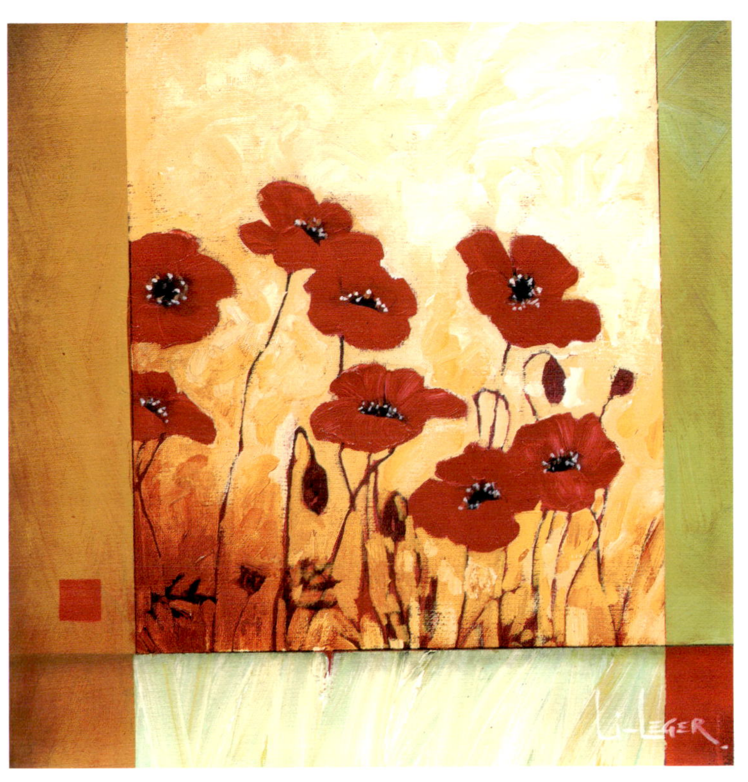

Gentle Garden
Acrylic on canvas
16" x 16", 2005
Private Collection

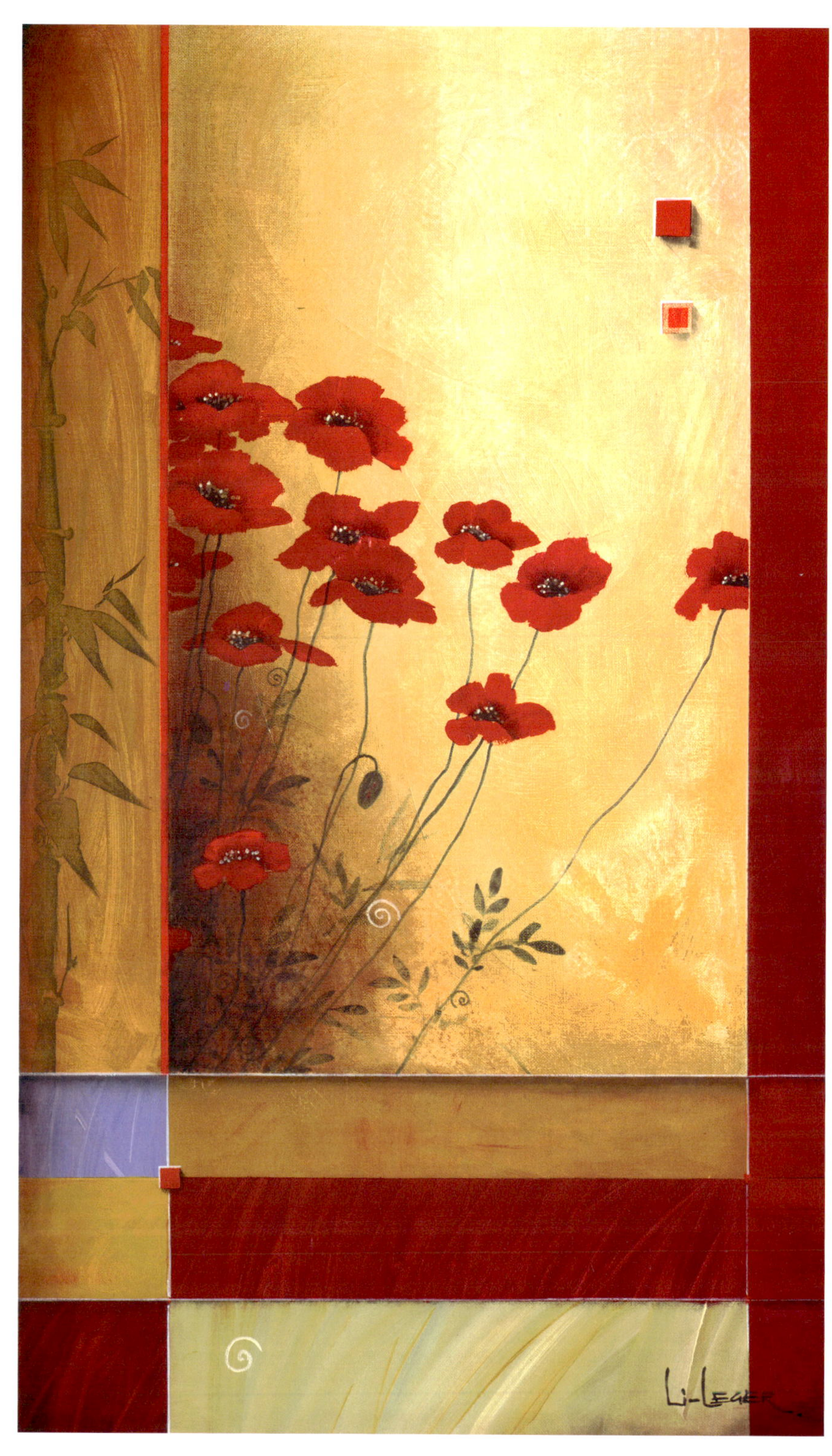

Parallel Dreams
Acrylic on canvas
40" x 24", 2005
Private Collection

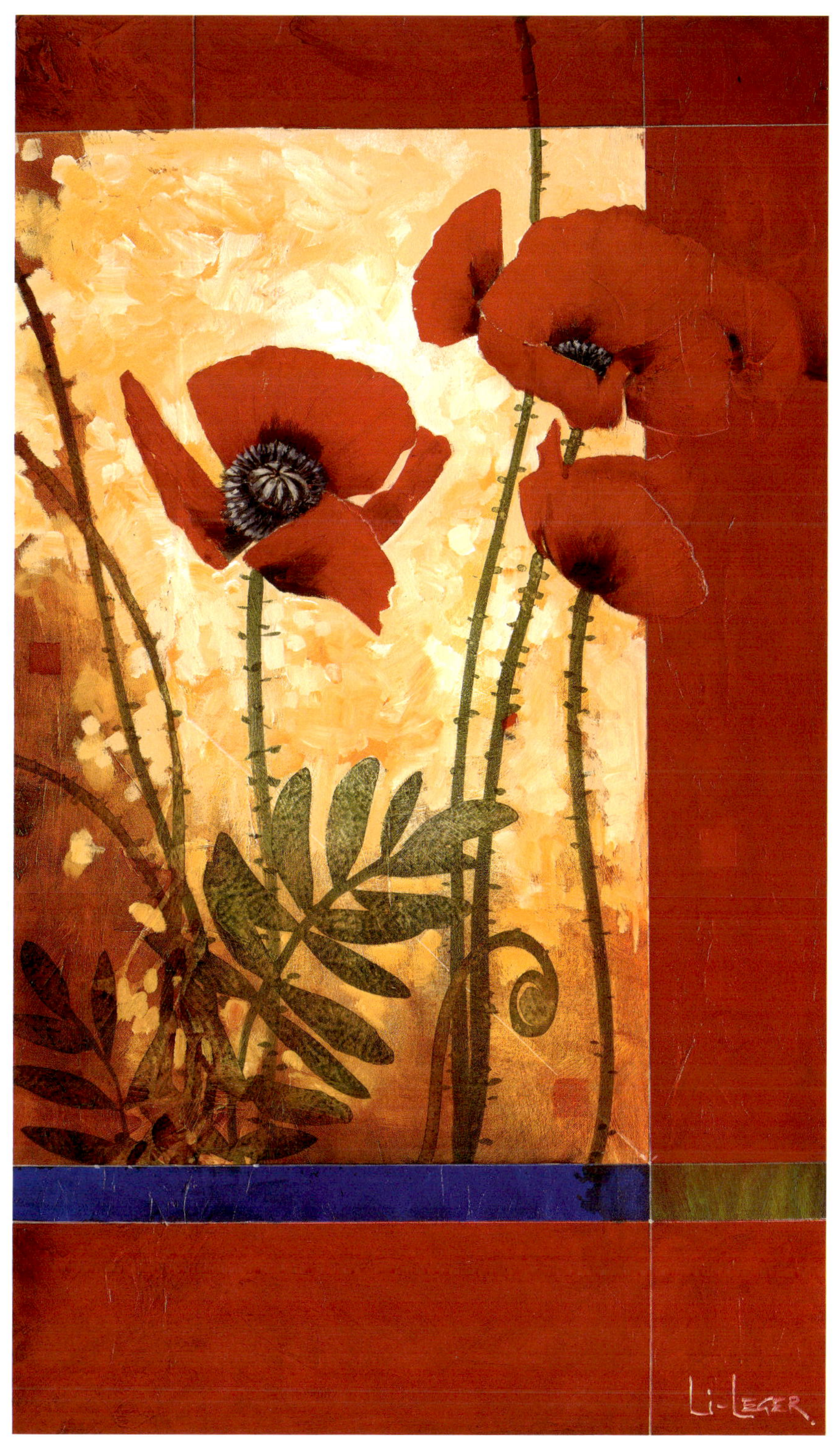

Dancing in the Light
Acrylic on canvas
40" x 24", 2005
Courtesy of
Canada House Gallery

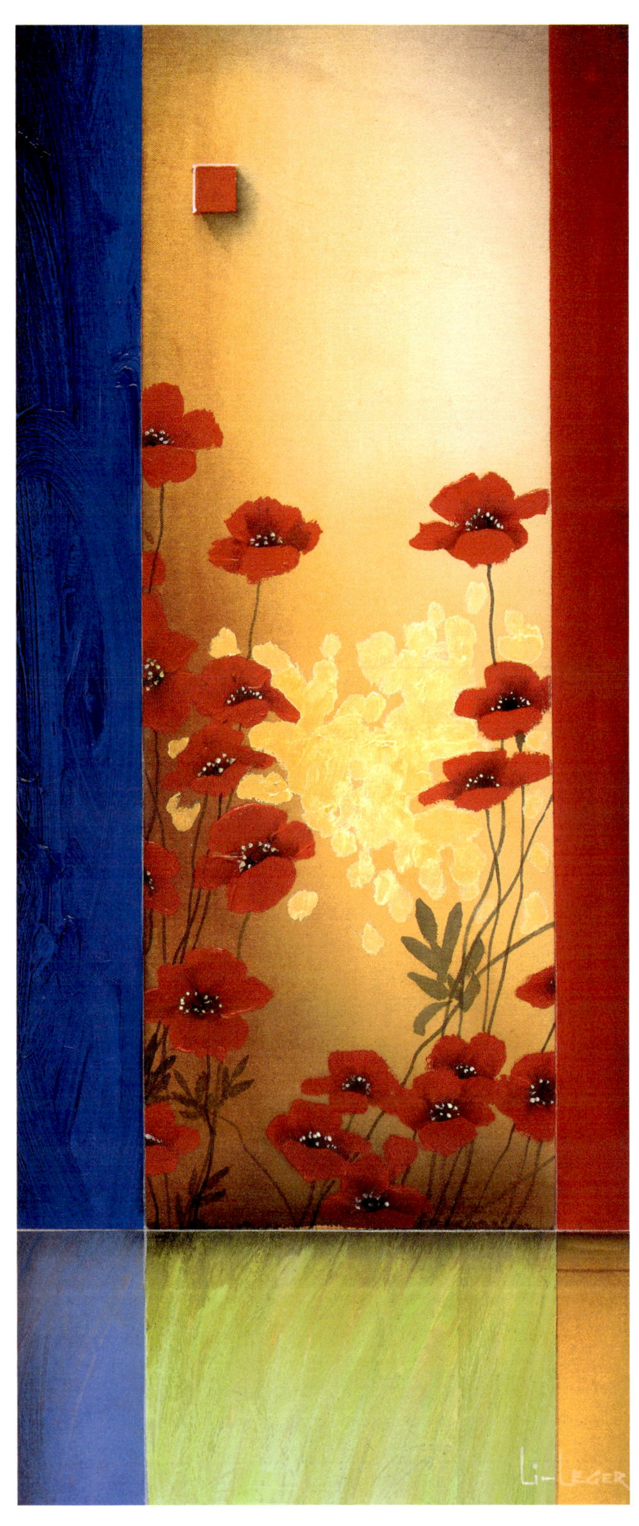

Painter's Garden II
Acrylic on canvas
36" x 16", 2004
Collection of Fiona and
Robert Prince-Wright

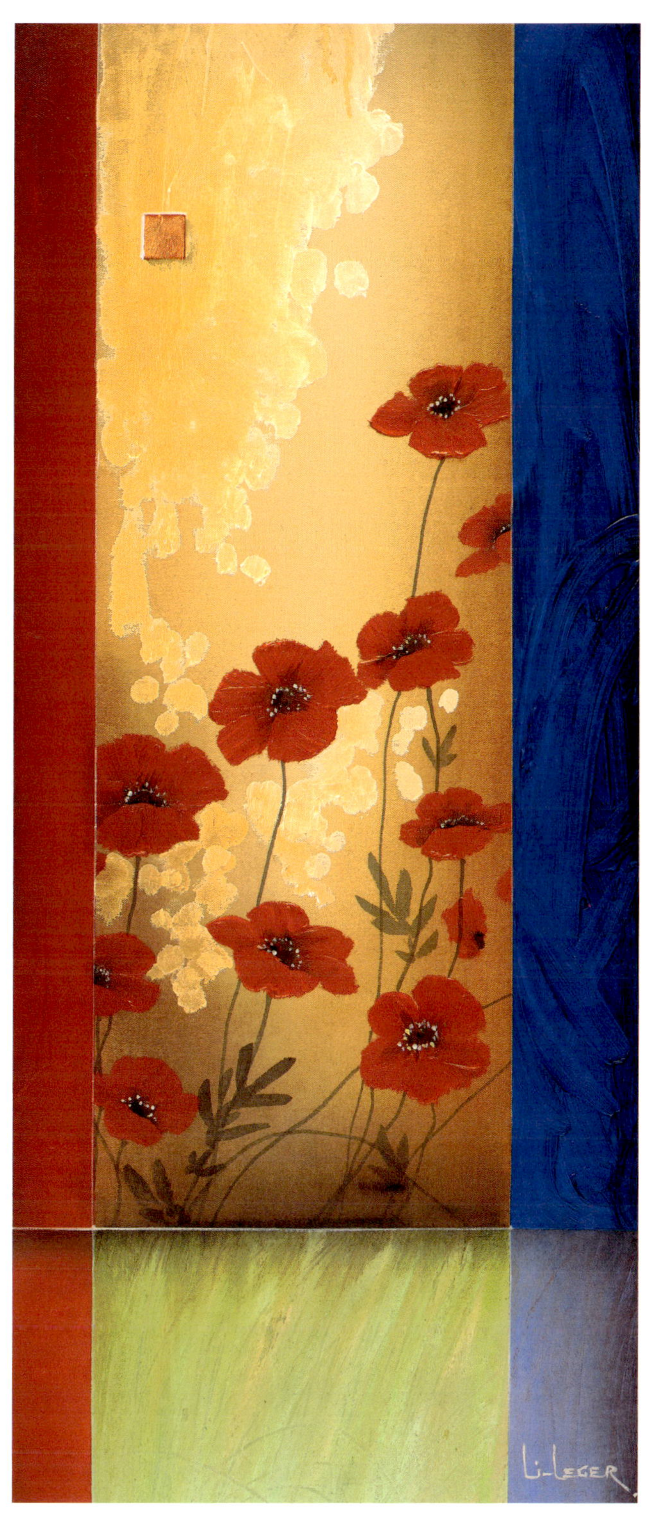

Painter's Garden I
Acrylic on canvas
36" x 16", 2004
Private Collection

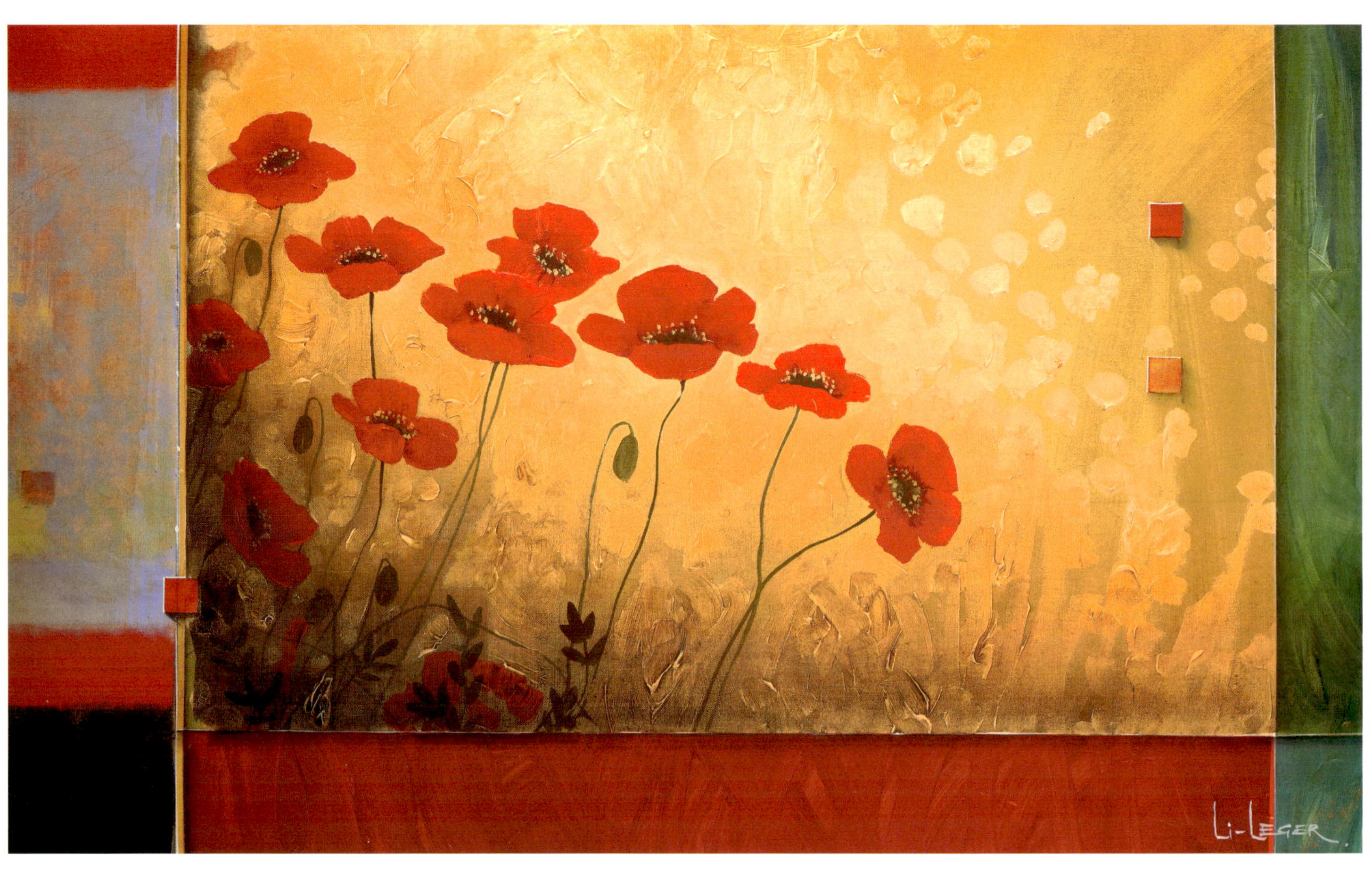

Walking in Eden
Acrylic on canvas
24" x 40", 2004
Private Collection

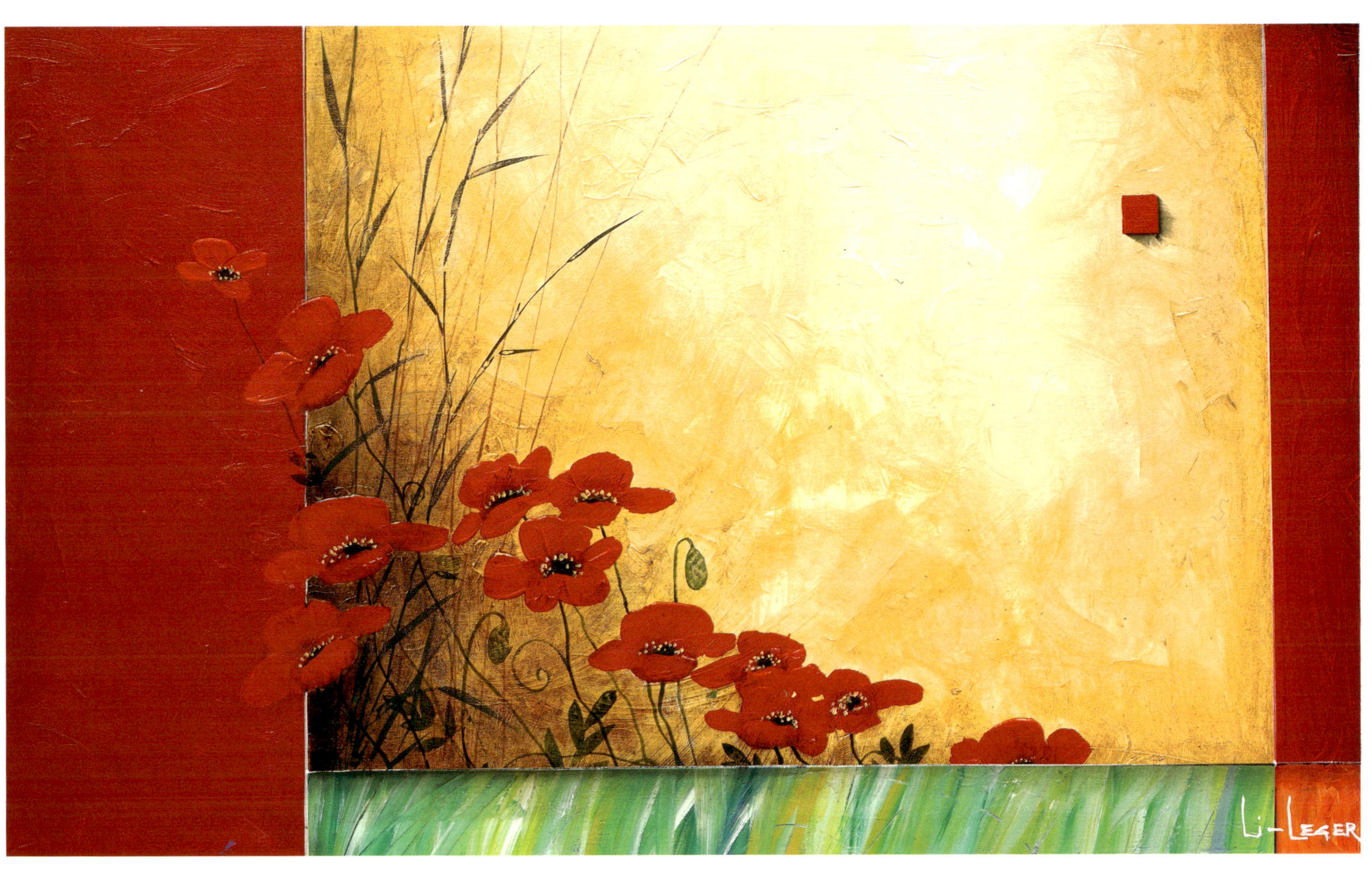

Tuscan Sun
Acrylic on canvas
24" x 40", 2004
Private Collection

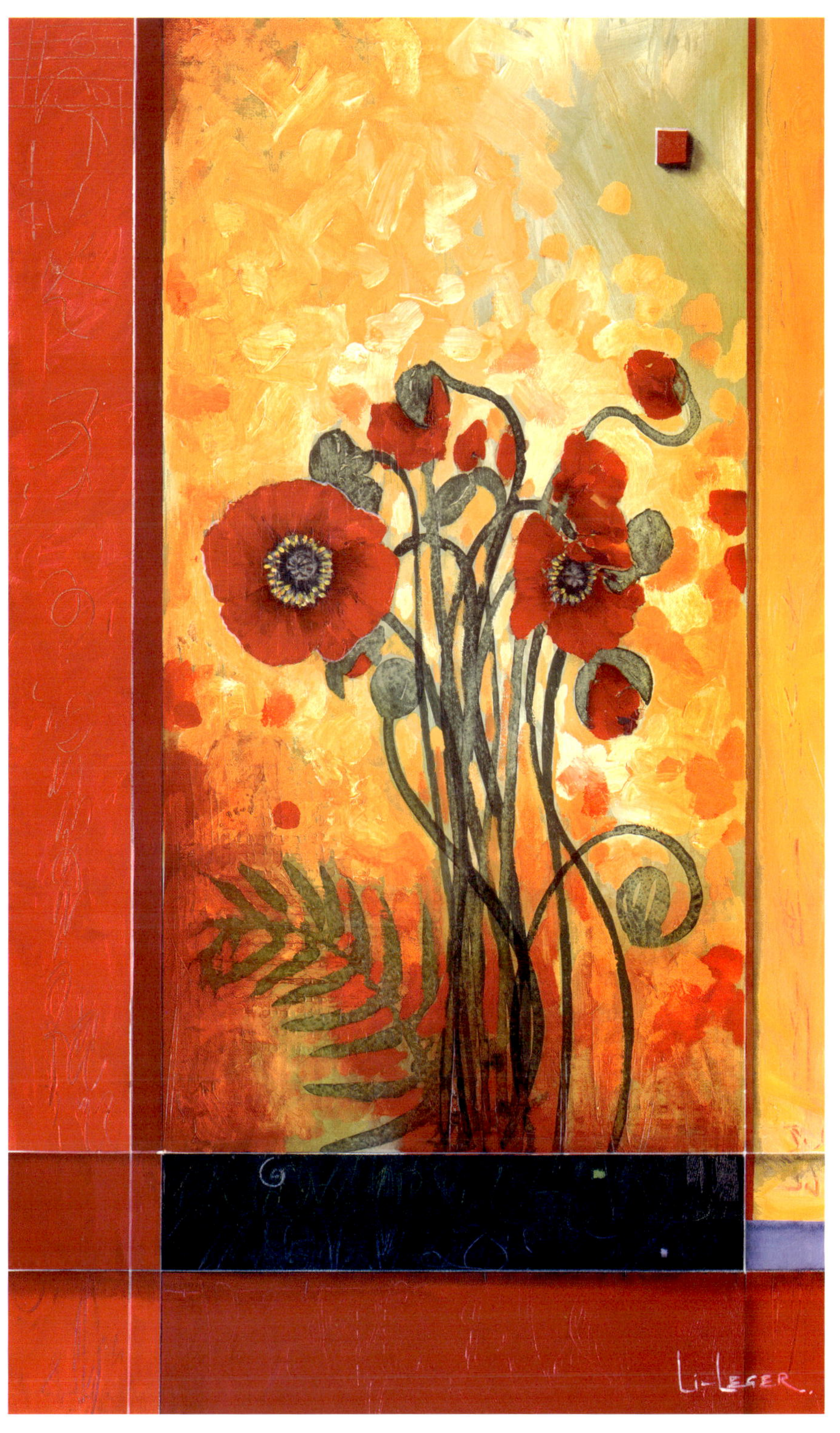

Poet's Garden V
Acrylic on canvas
40" x 24", 2005
Courtesy of
Canada House Gallery

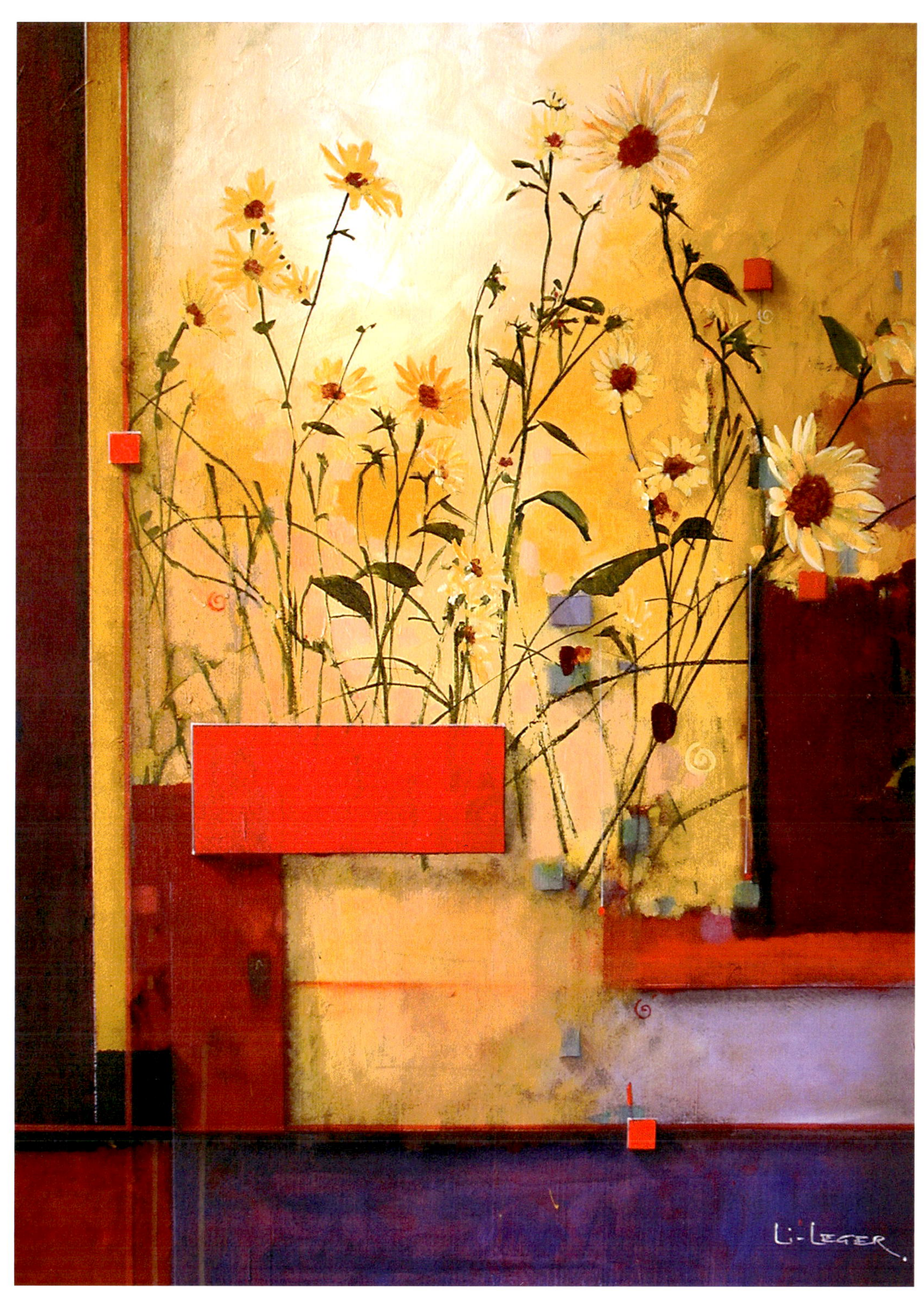

Sonoran Garden
Acrylic on canvas
40" x 30", 2003
Private Collection

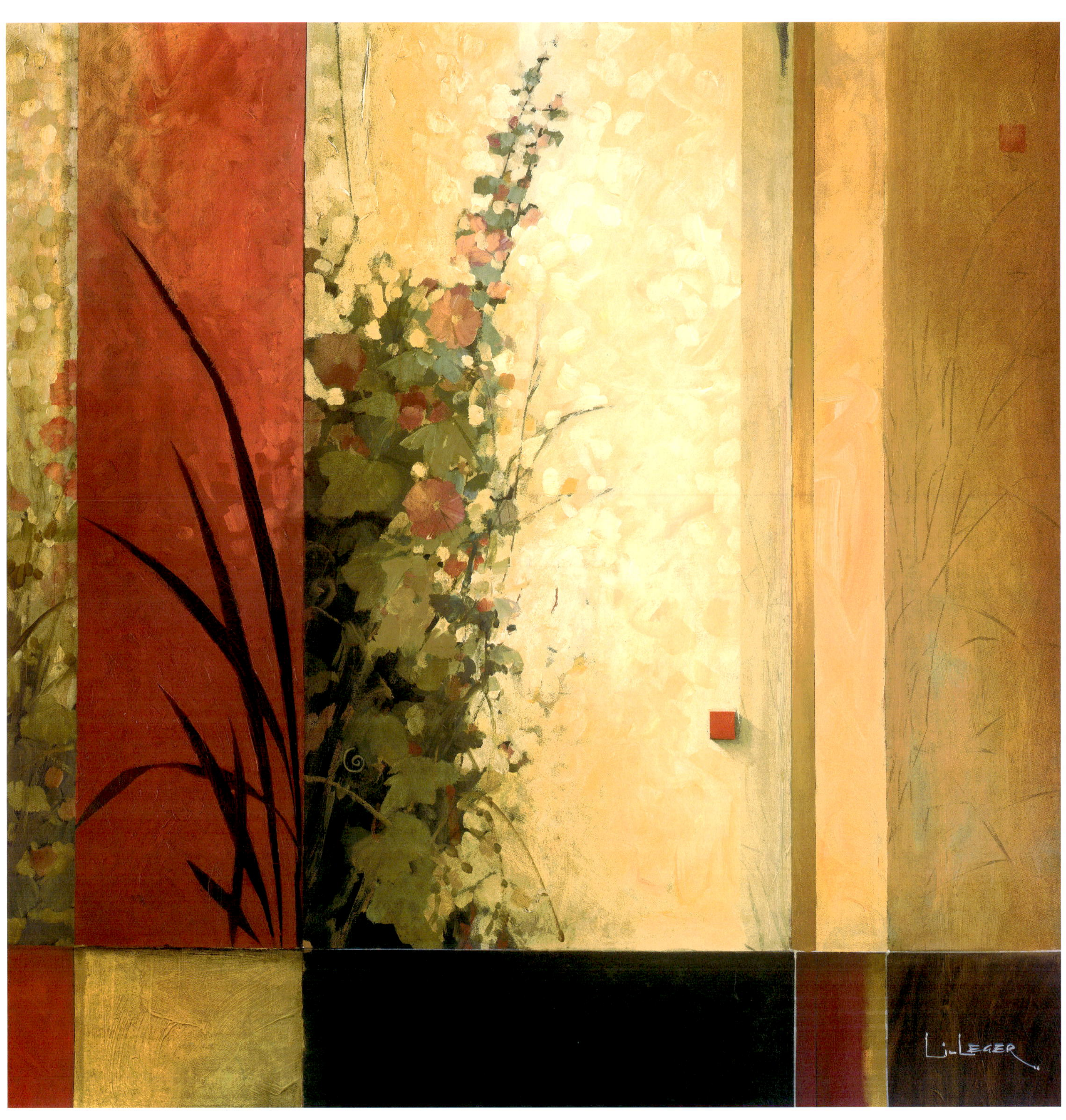

Hollyhock Garden
Acrylic on canvas
40" x 40", 2002
Private Collection

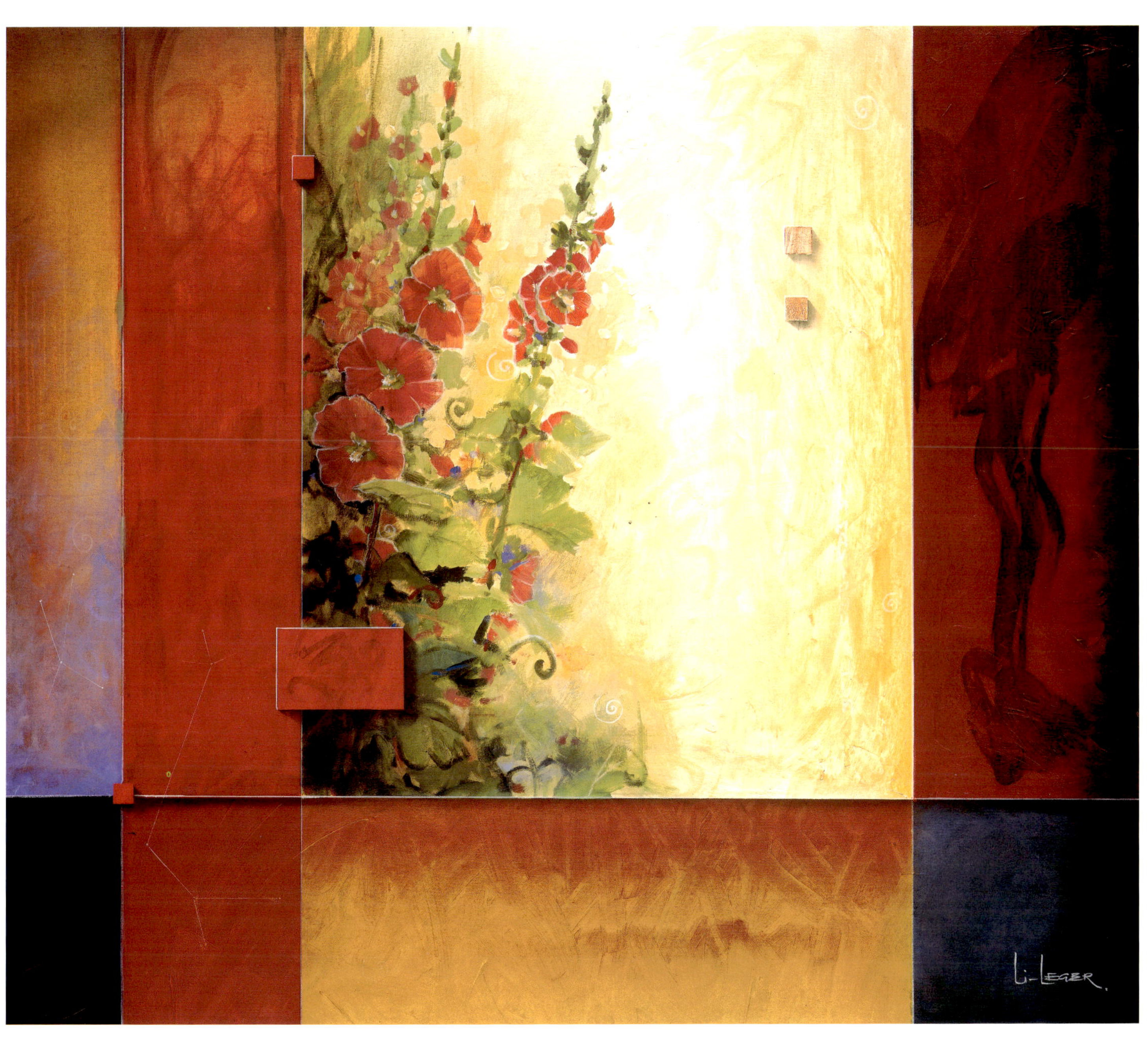

Hollyhock Garden II
Acrylic on canvas
30" x 40", 2003
Private Collection

*Study nature, love nature, stay close
to nature. It will never fail you.*

— FRANK LLOYD WRIGHT

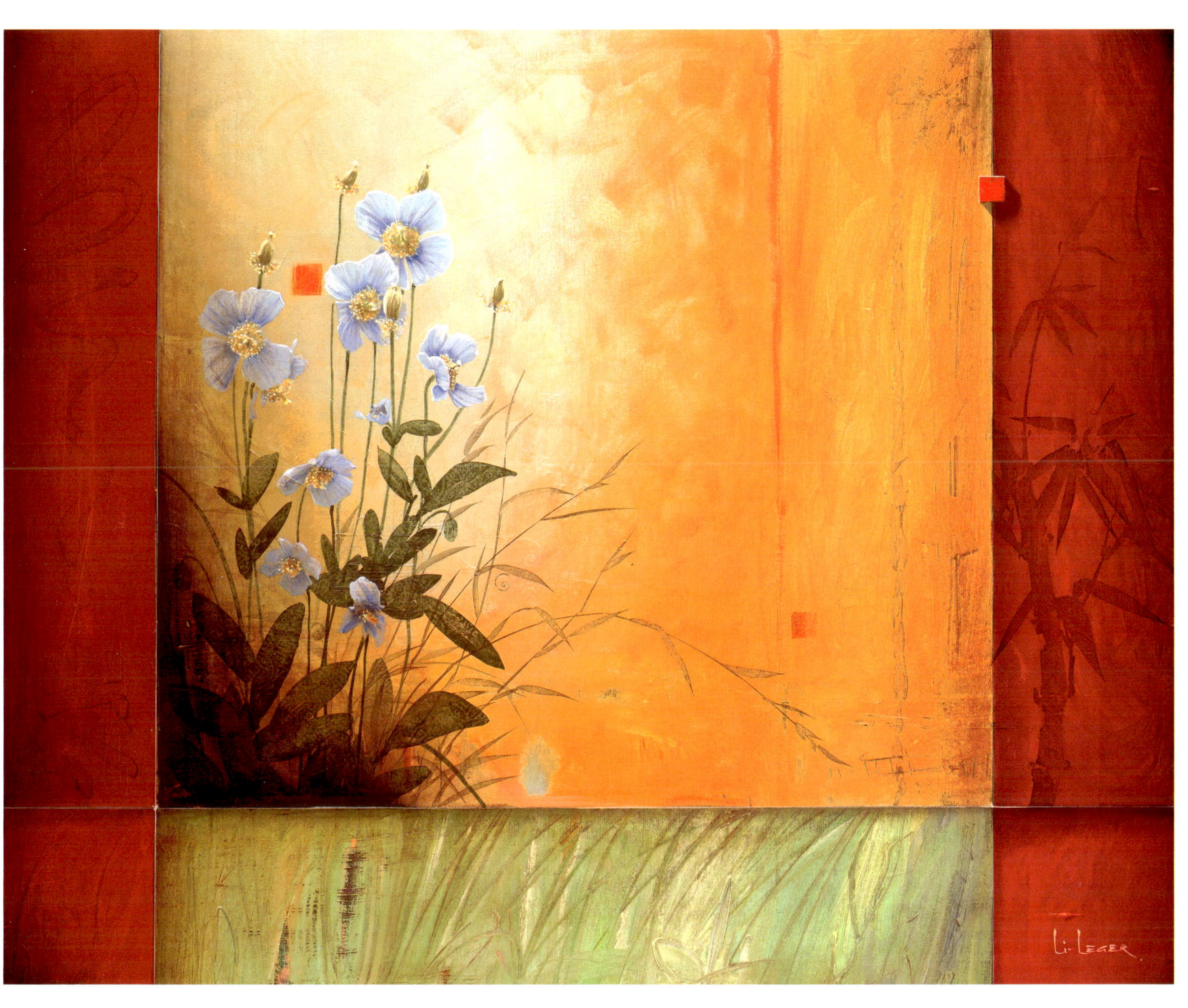

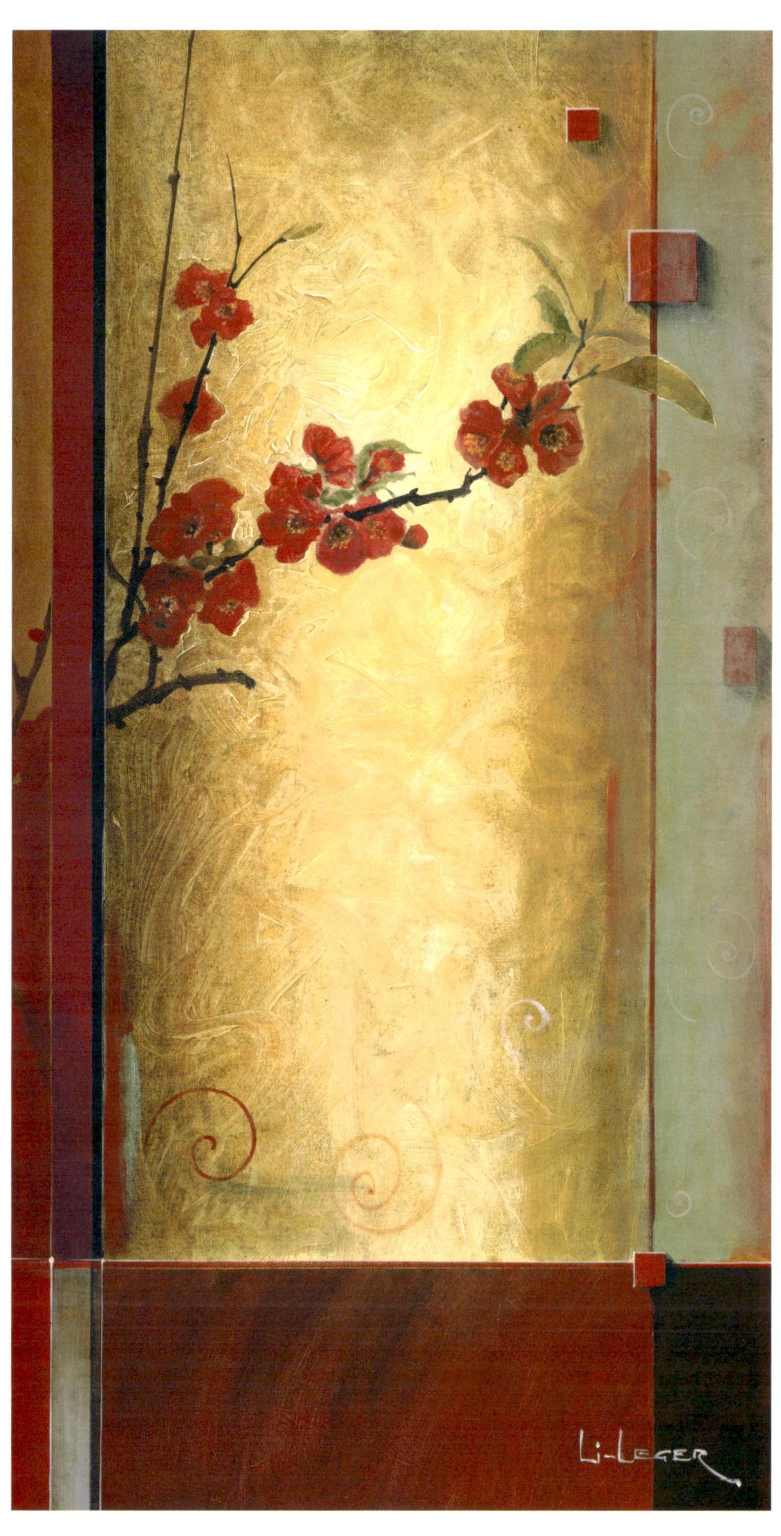

Morning Light Quince
Acrylic on canvas
40" x 24", 2002
Private Collection

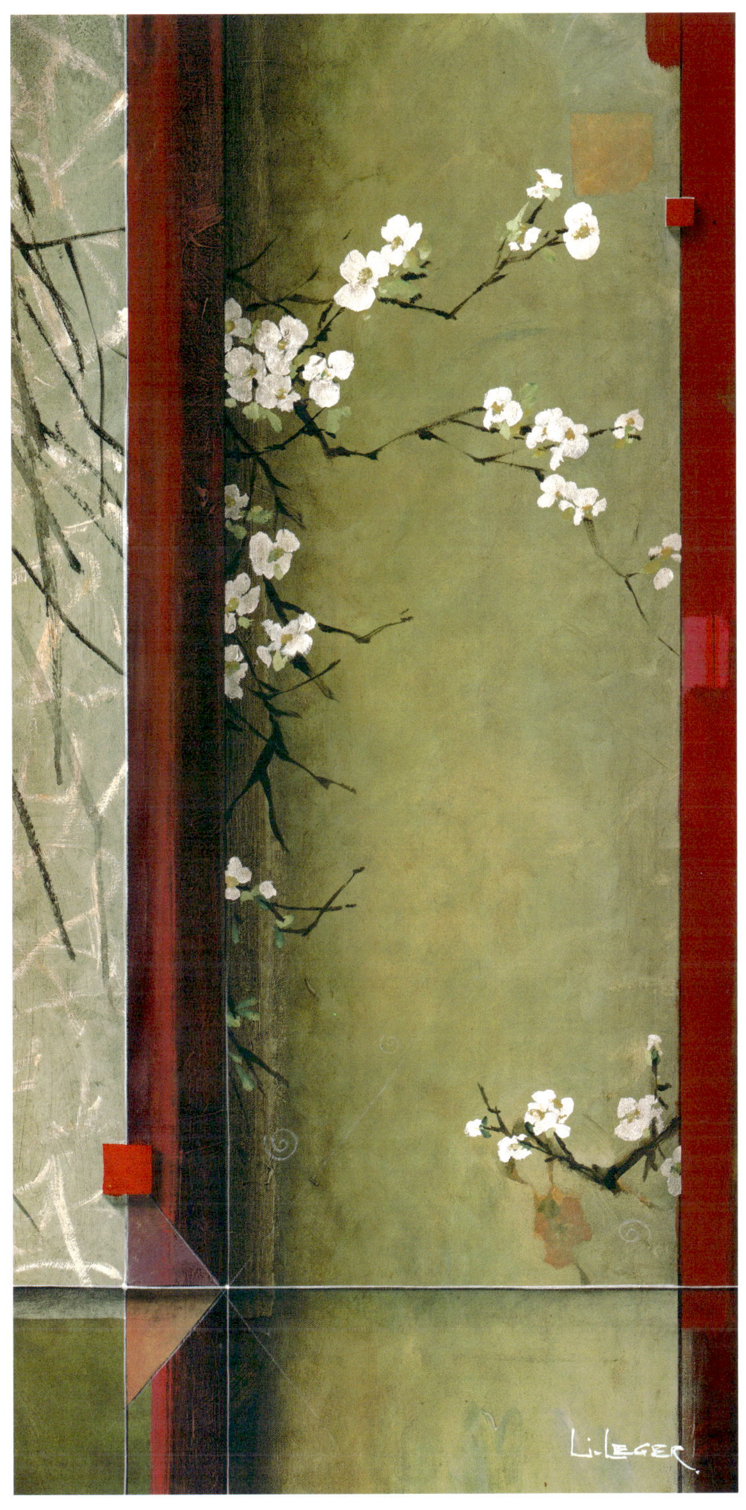

The Tea House Garden
Acrylic on canvas
40" x 24", 2003
Collection of Andrea
and Michael Roberts

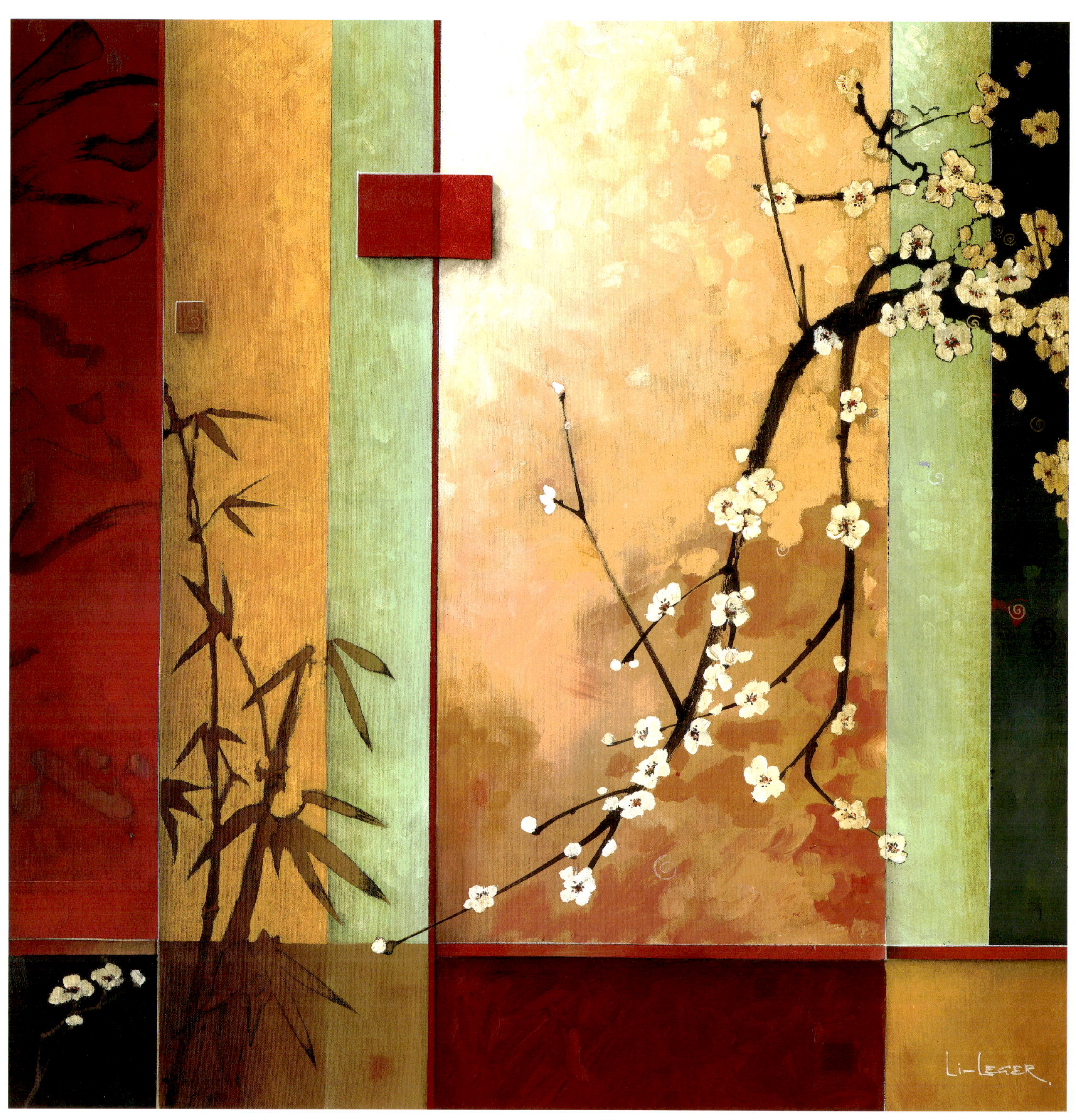

Cherry Blossoms II
(Blossom Garden)
Acrylic on canvas
40" x 40", 2003
Collection of
Gregg Karawan

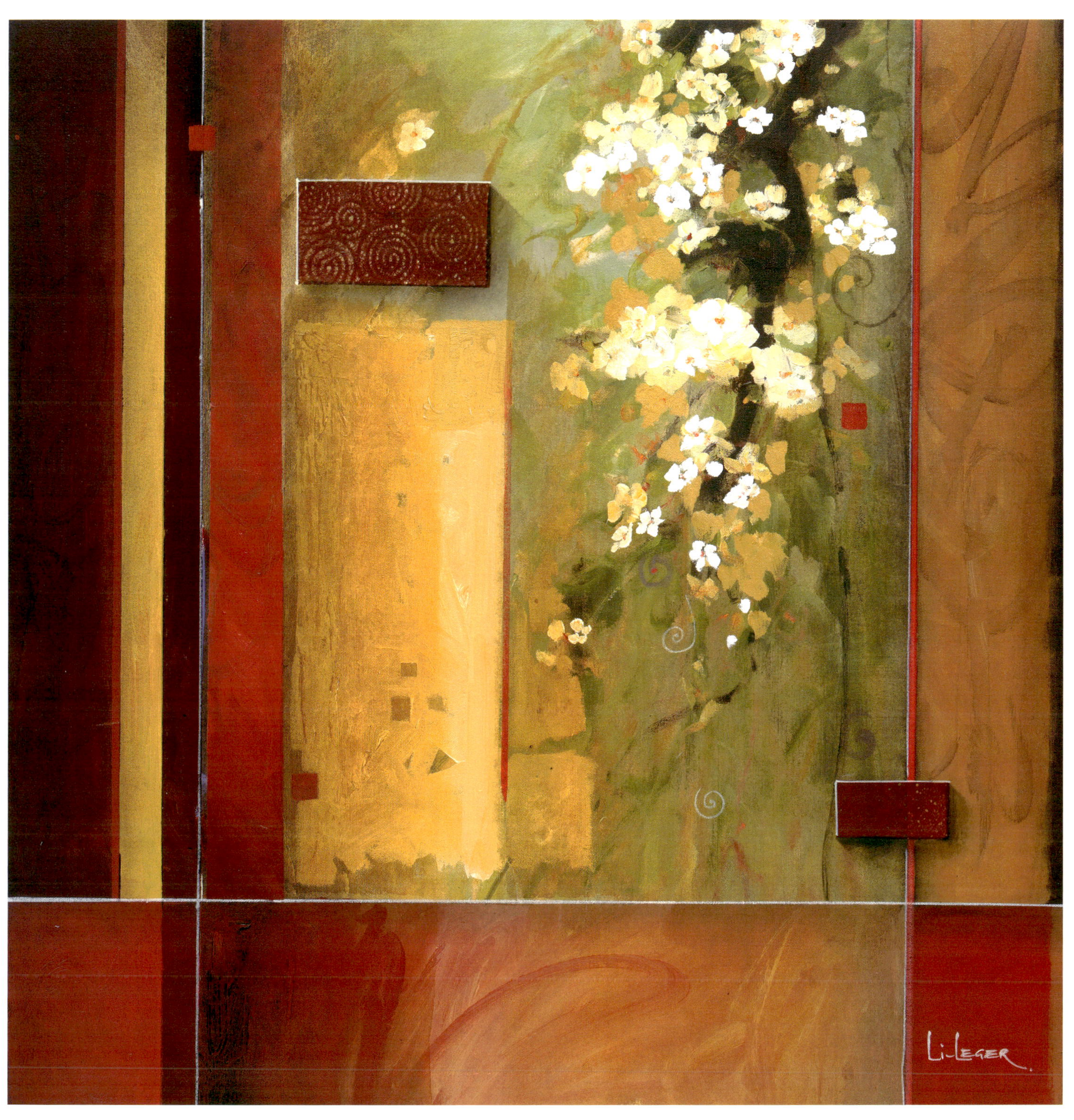

Summer Bloom
Acrylic on canvas
40" x 40", 2002
Private Collection

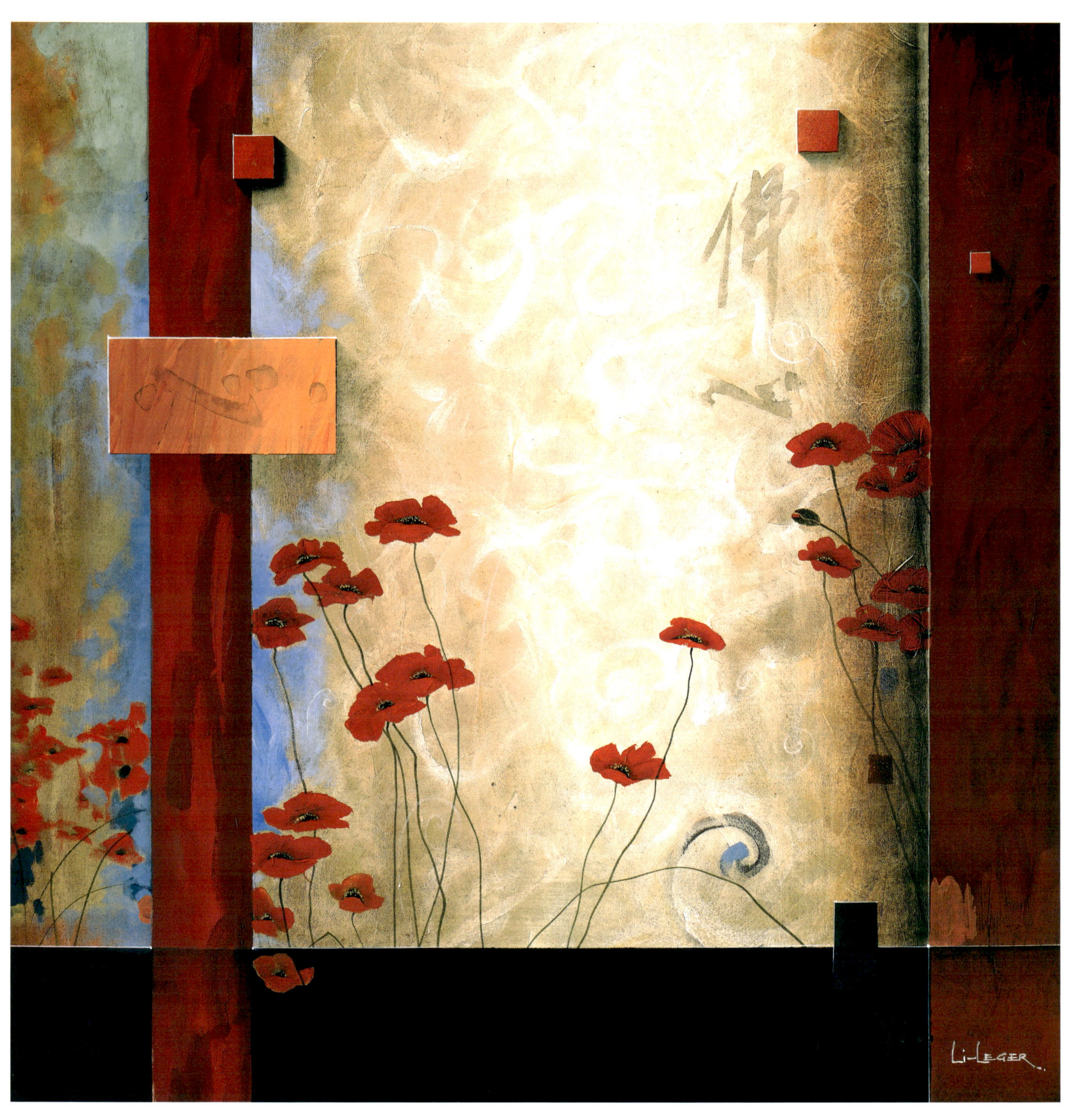

Edge of Blue
Acrylic on canvas
40" x 40", 2002
Private Collection

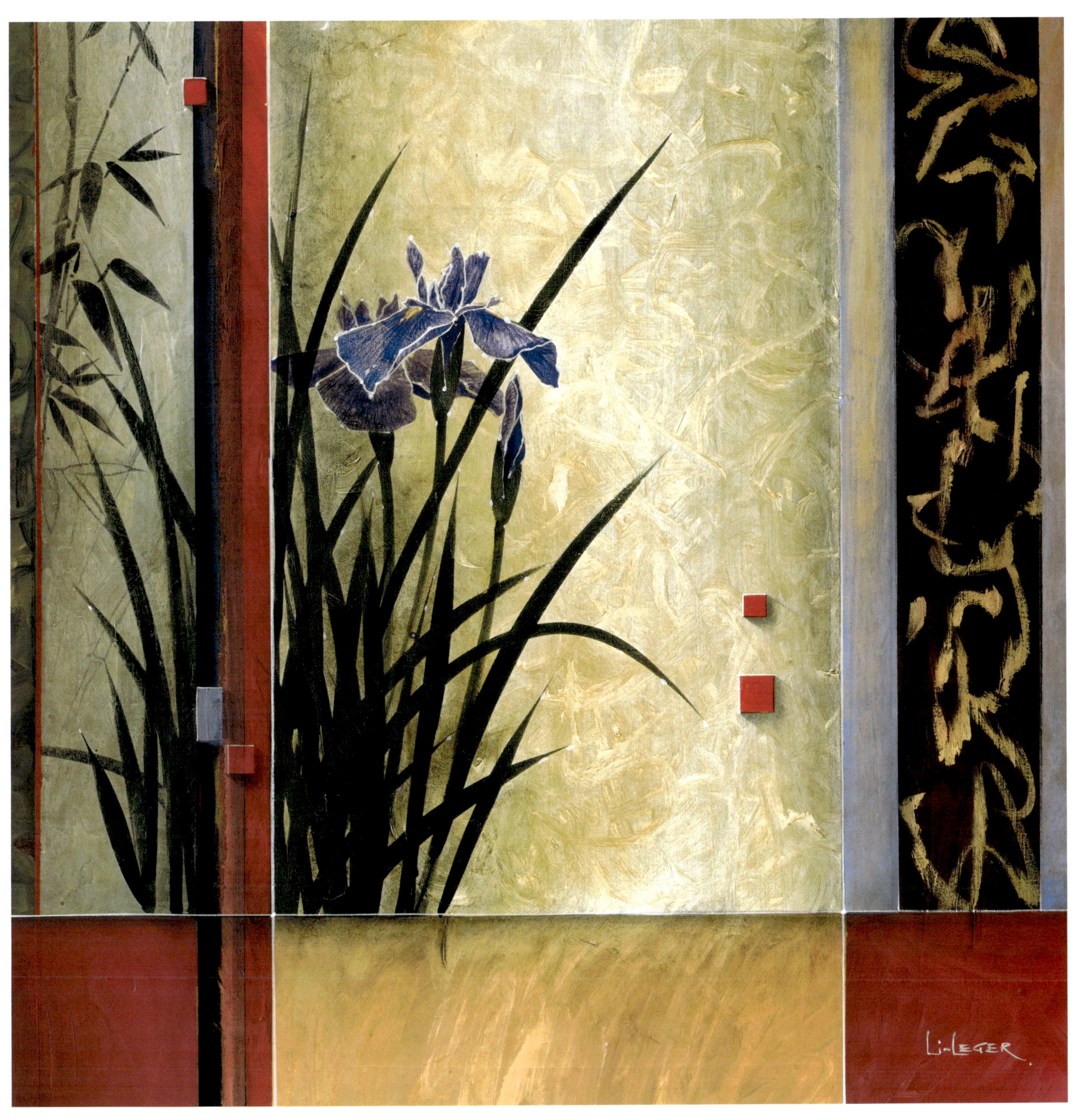

Garden Gateway
Acrylic on canvas
40" x 40", 2002
Private Collection

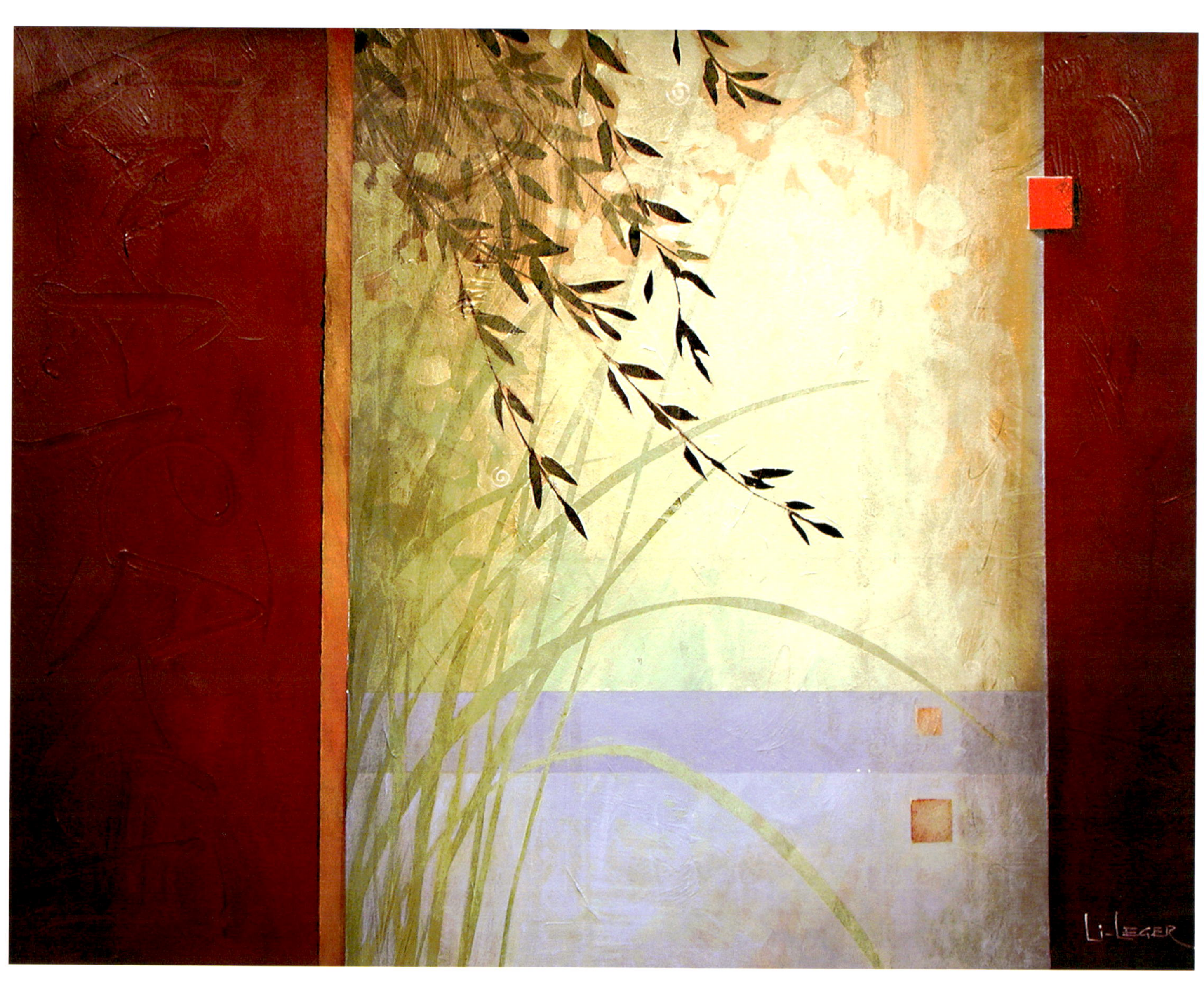

Whispering Willows
Acrylic on canvas
30" x 40", 2003
Private Collection

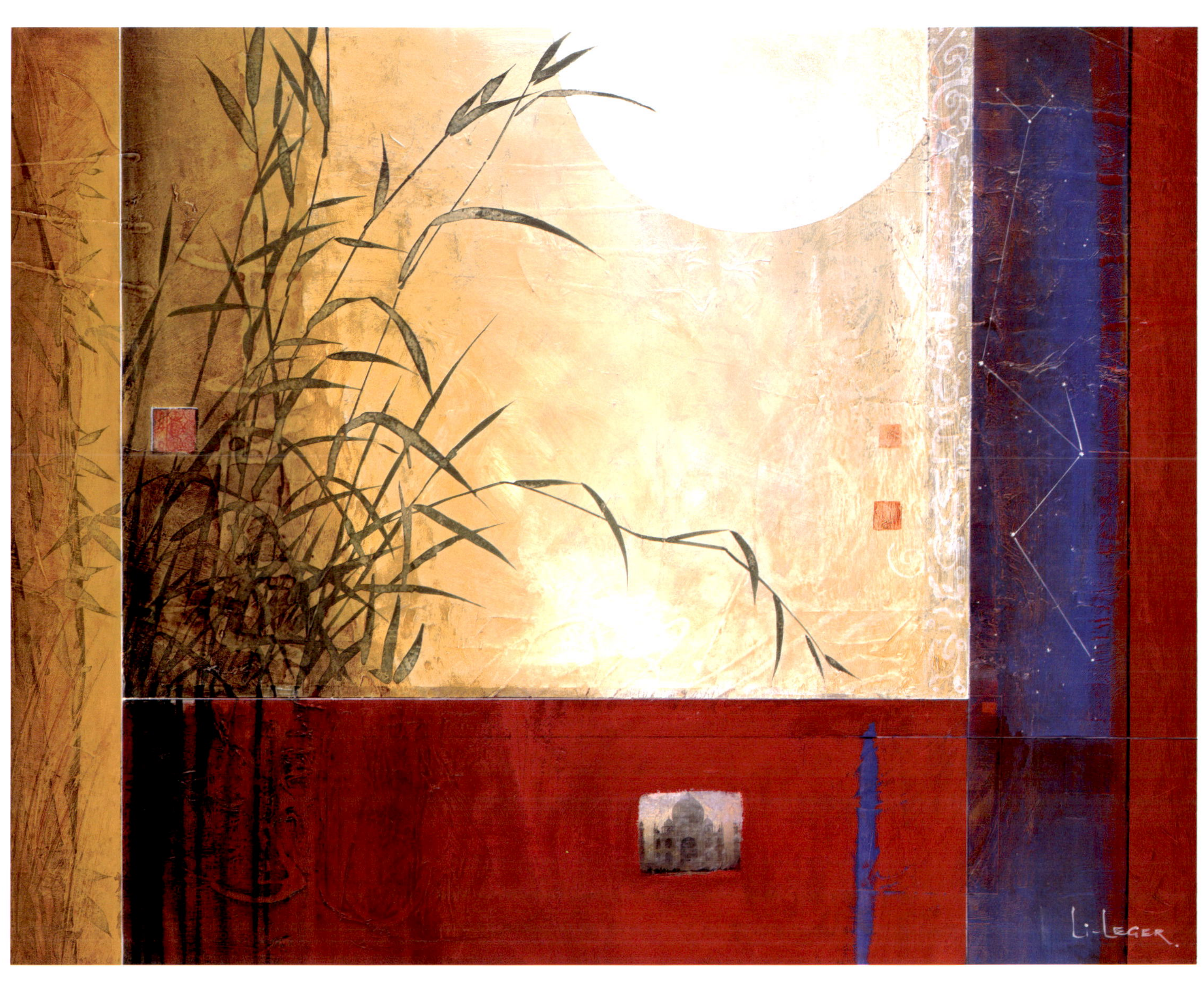

Moon Viewing, Grasses,
Taj Mahal
Acrylic on canvas
33" x 40", 2004
Collection of the Artist

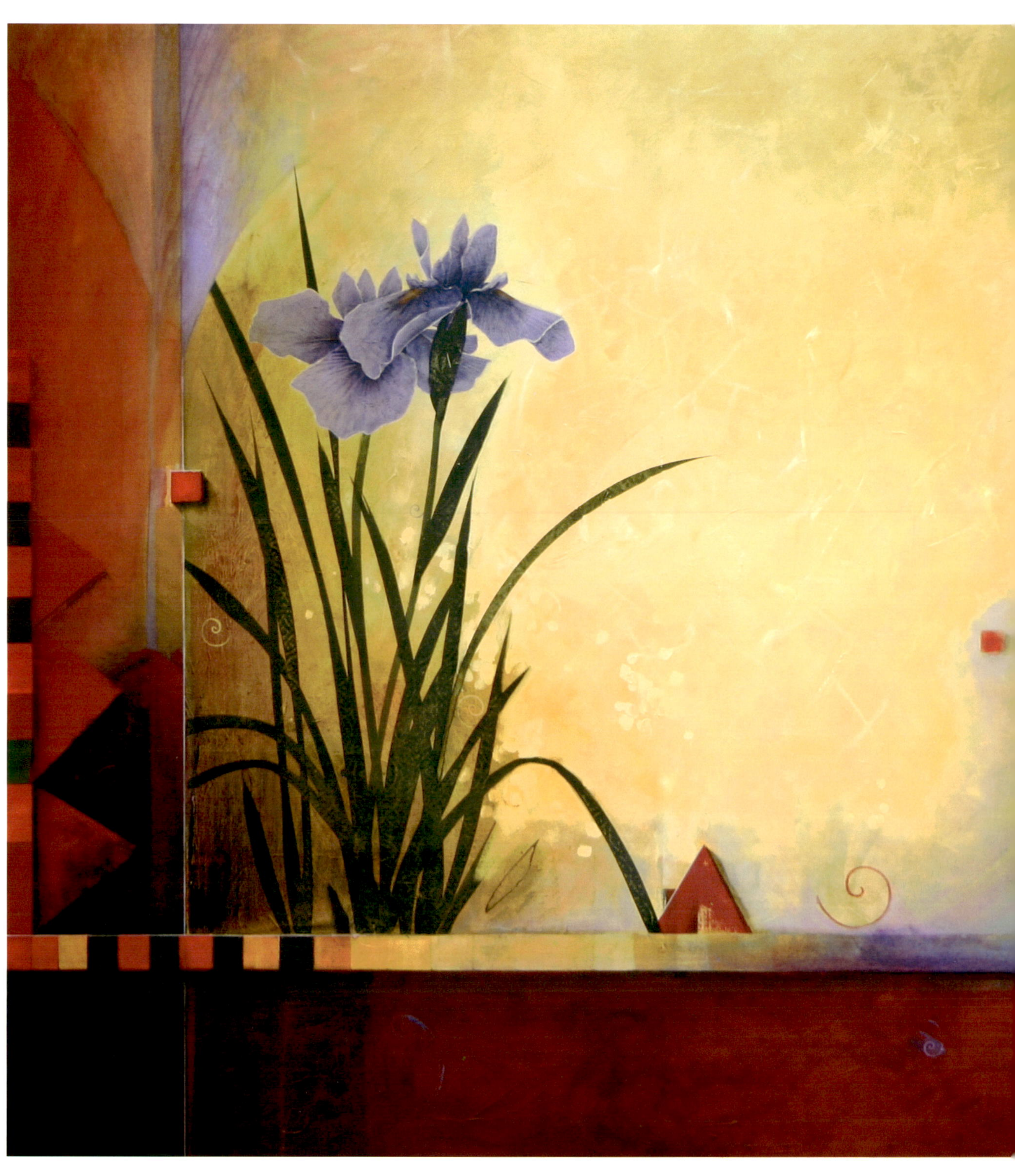

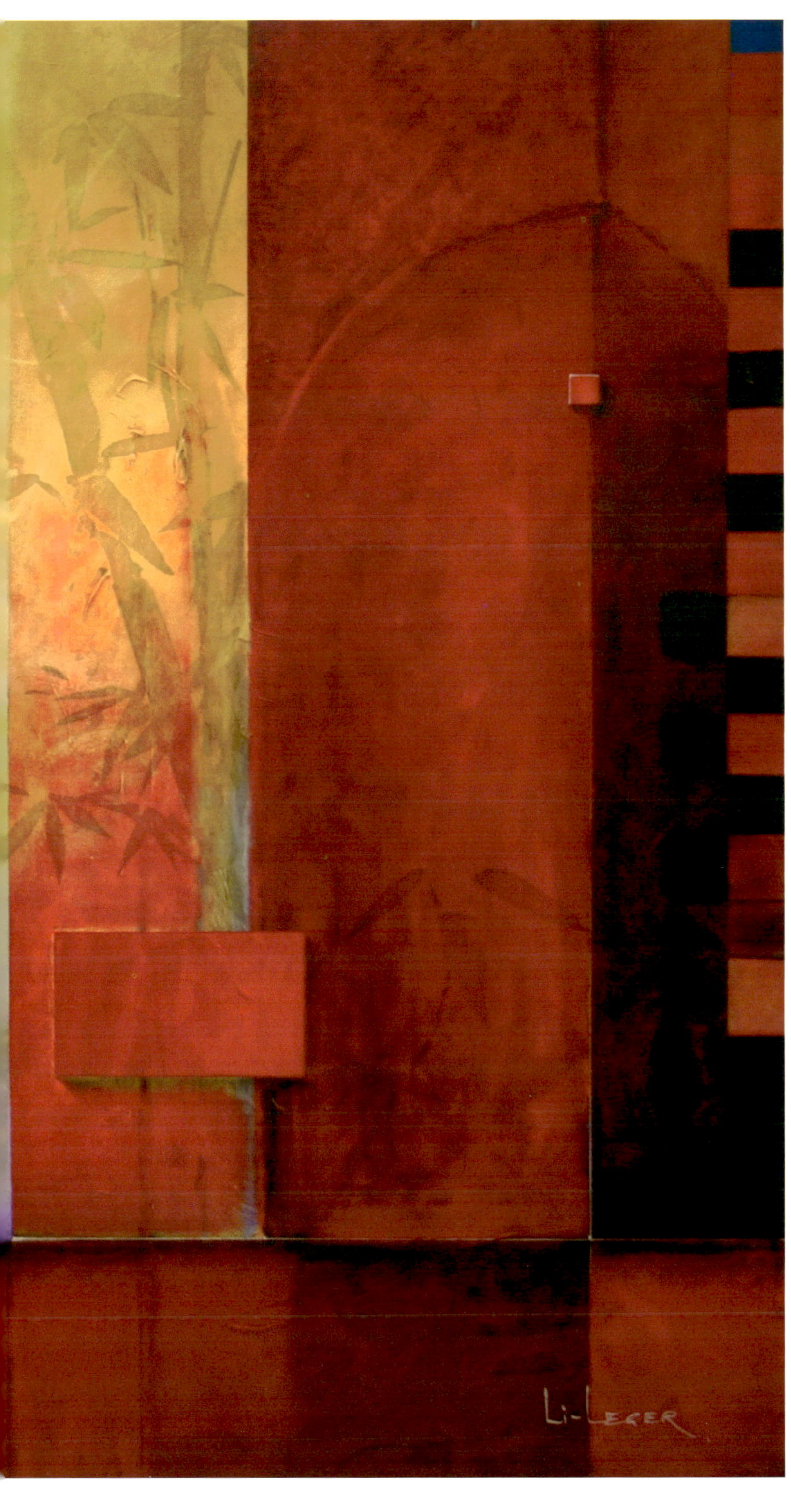

Jardin Exotique
Acrylic on canvas
48" x 72", 2004
Collection of Glen and
Ann Sather, New York

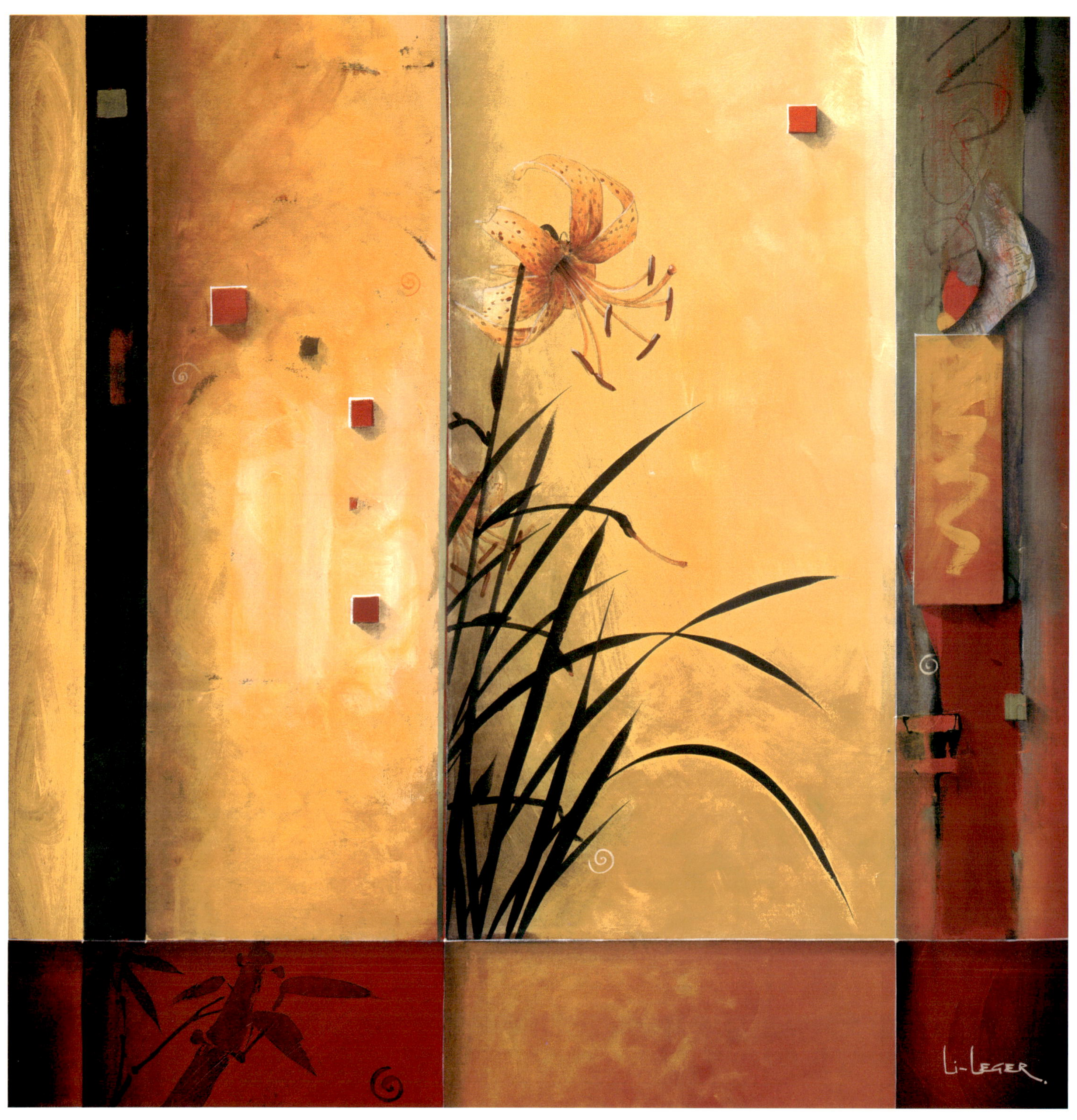

Poet's Garden
with Tiger Lily
Acrylic on canvas
40" x 40", 2002
Private Collection

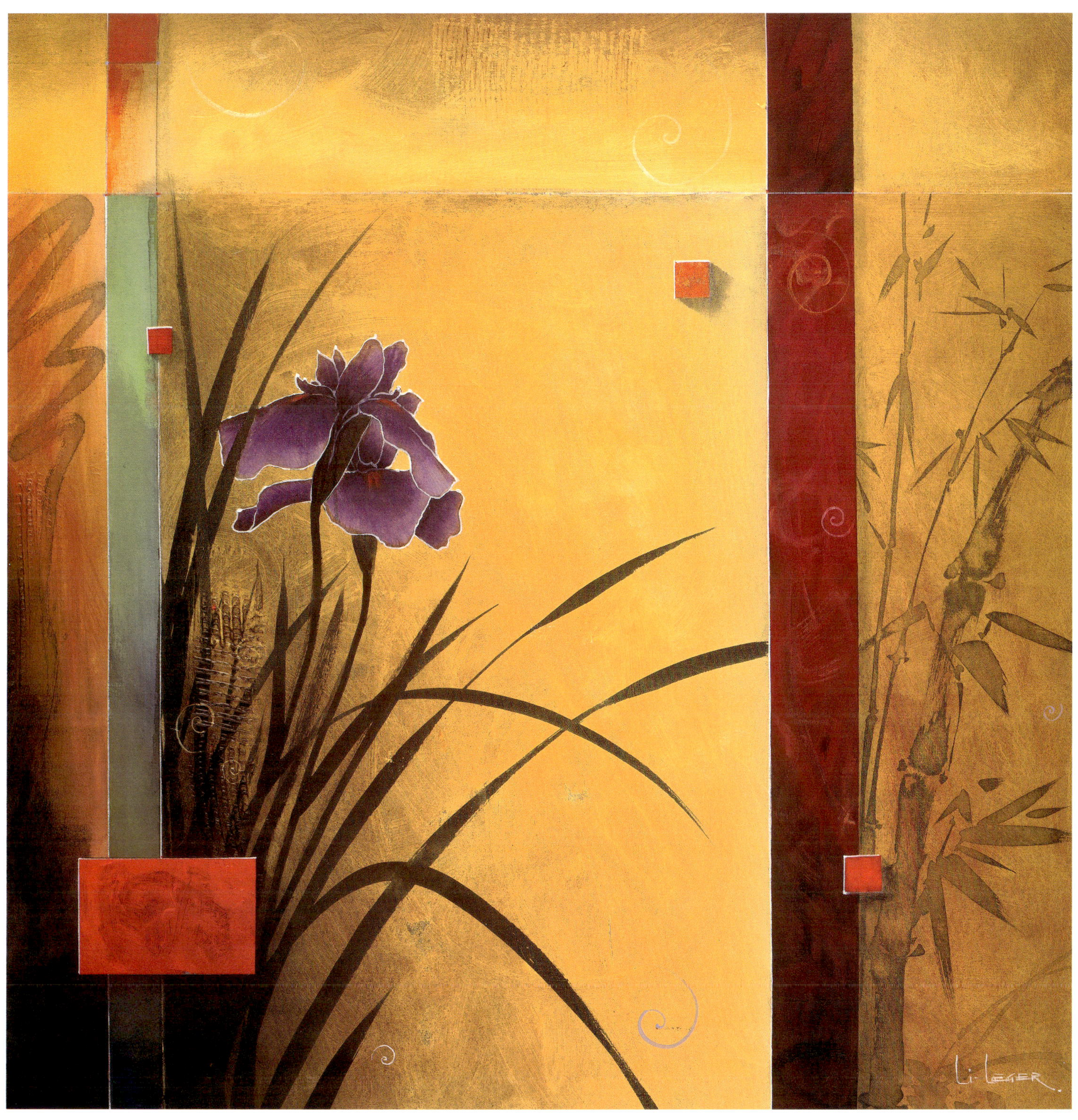

Jardin Bohême
Acrylic on canvas
40" x 40", 2004
Courtesy of
Petley Jones Gallery

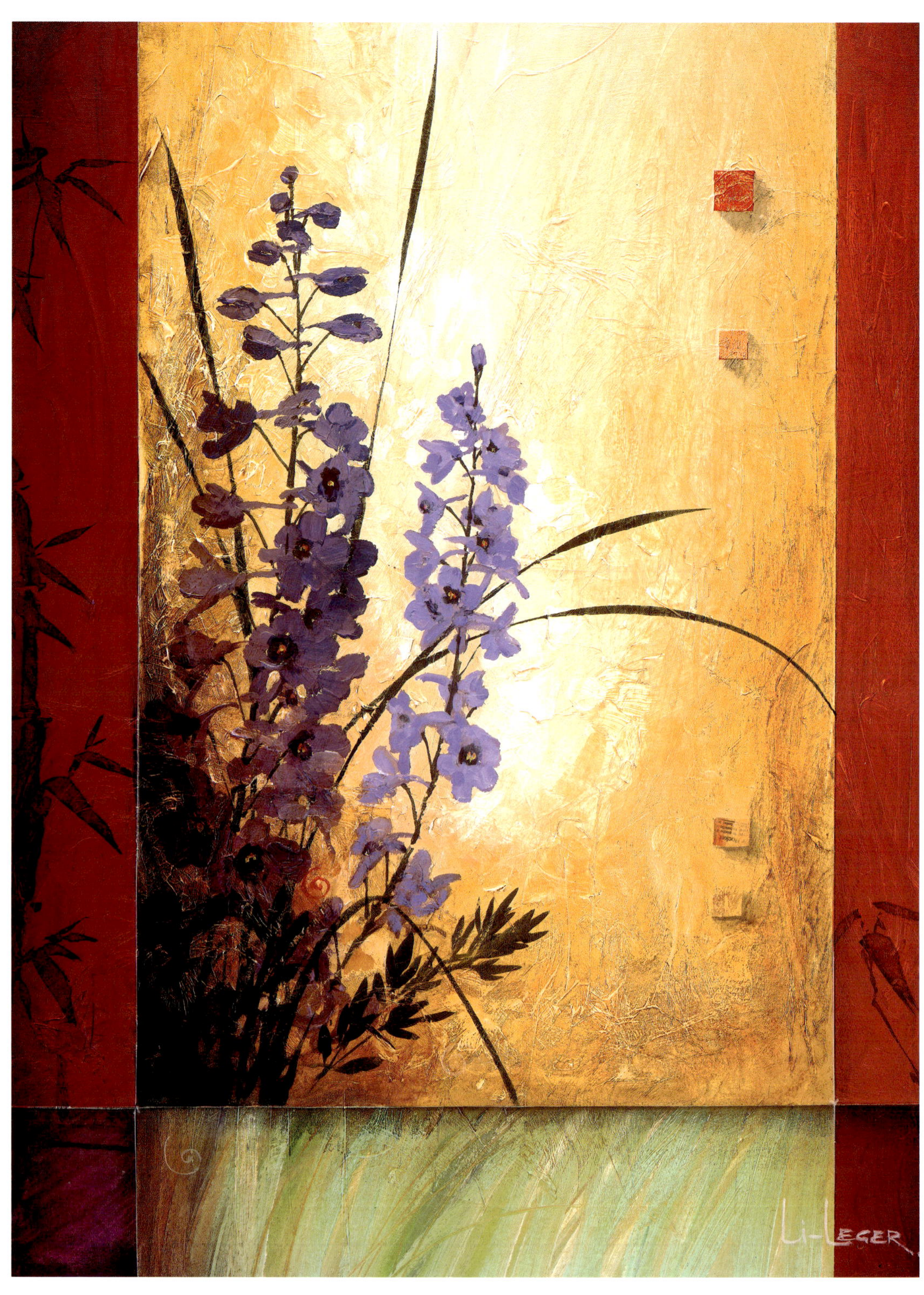

Garden's Edge
Acrylic on canvas
40" x 30", 2004
Private Collection

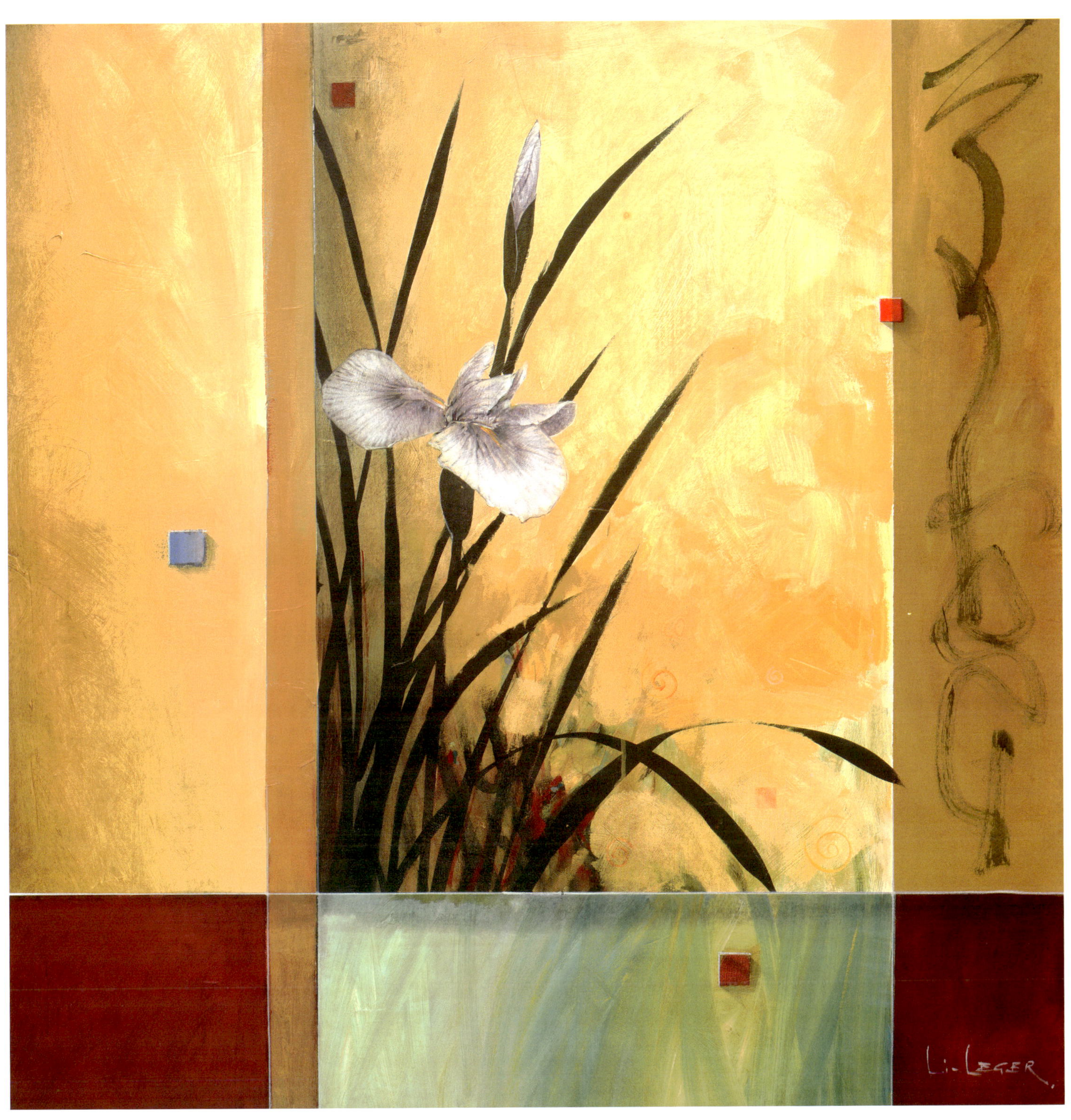

Sanctuary
acrylic on canvas
40" x 40", 2002
Private Collection

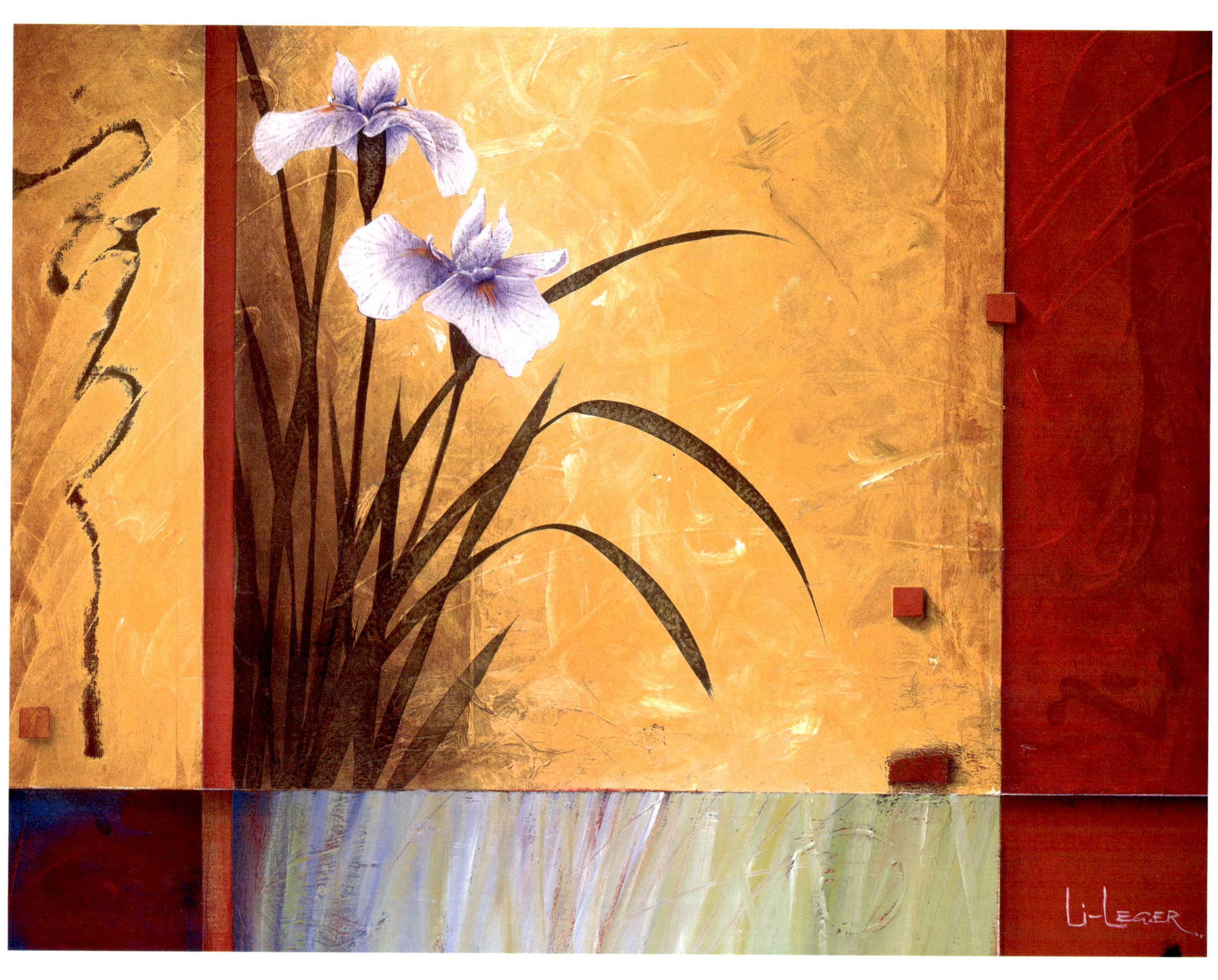

The Calm of the Day
Acrylic on canvas
30" x 40", 2004
Courtesy of
Canada House Gallery

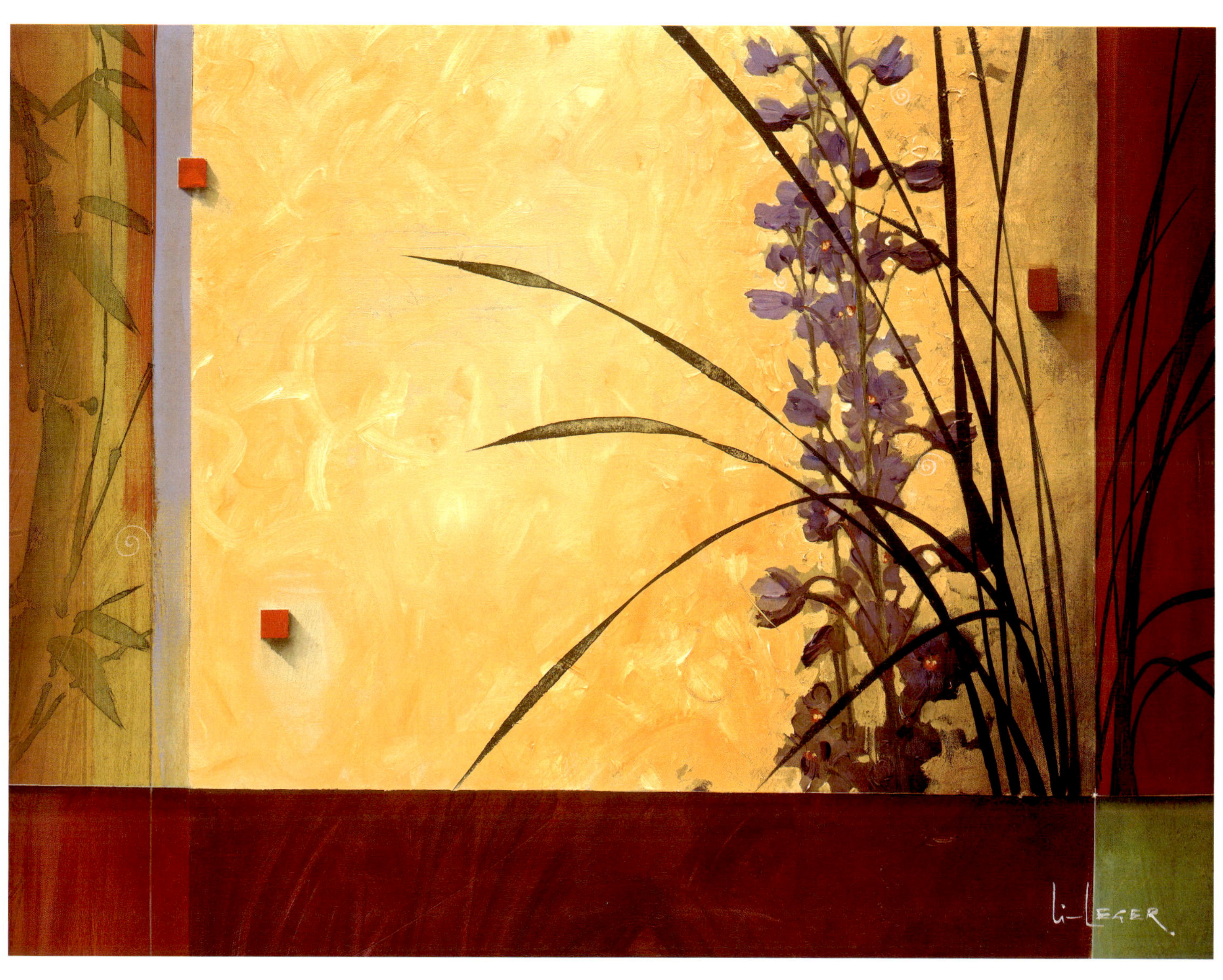

Poet's Garden II
Acrylic on canvas
40" x 30", 2003
Collection of Nancy
and Alan Wasserkrug

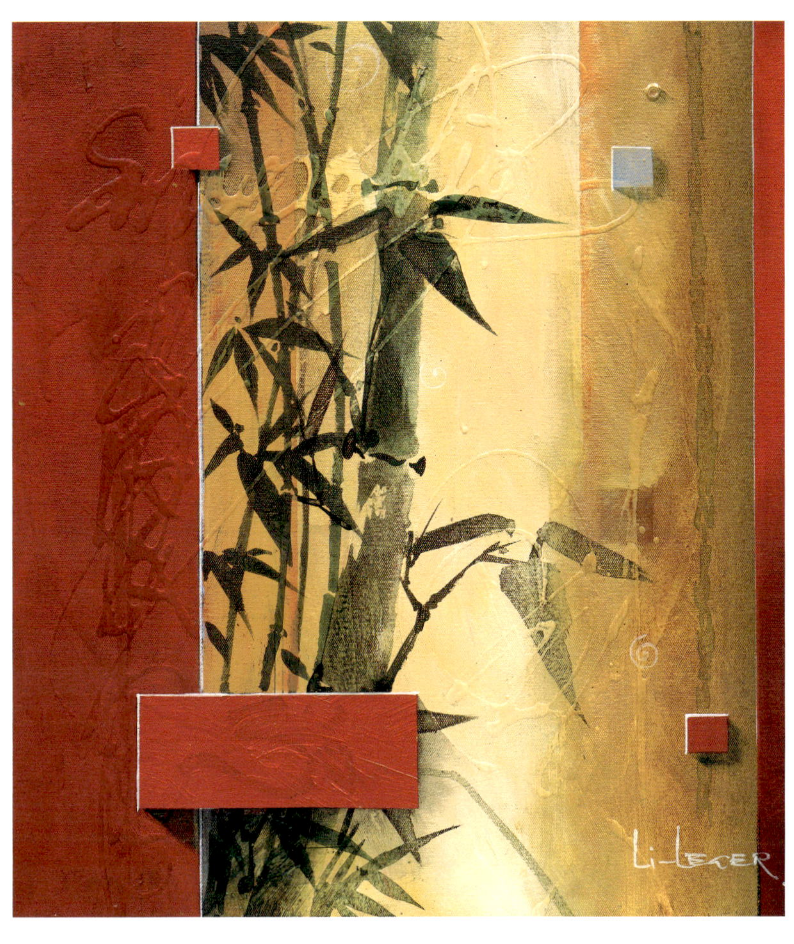

Bamboo Garden II
Acrylic on canvas
18" x 20", 2004
Private Collection

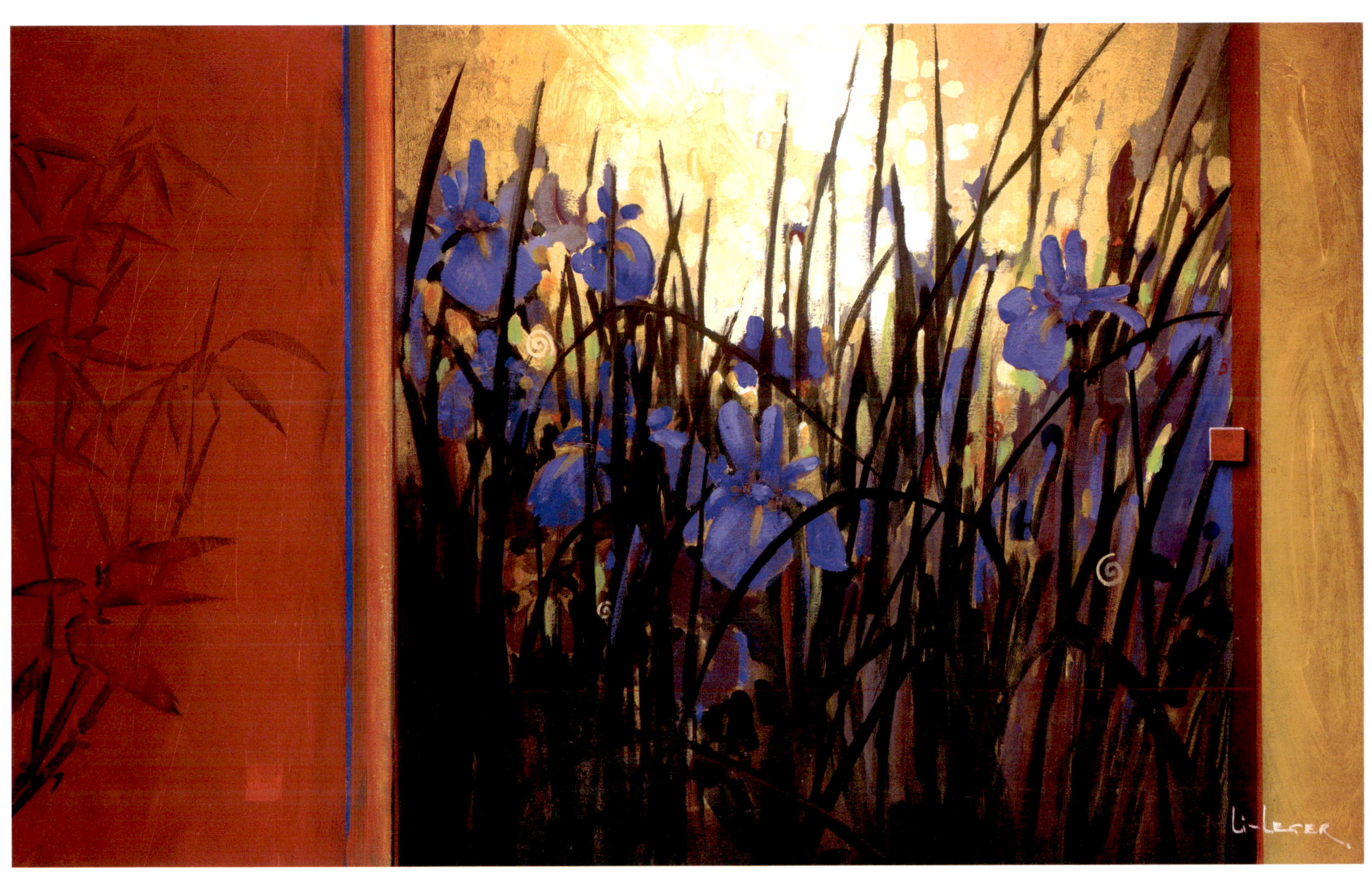

Iris Bed
Acrylic on canvas
24" x 40", 2004
Courtesy of
Petley Jones Gallery

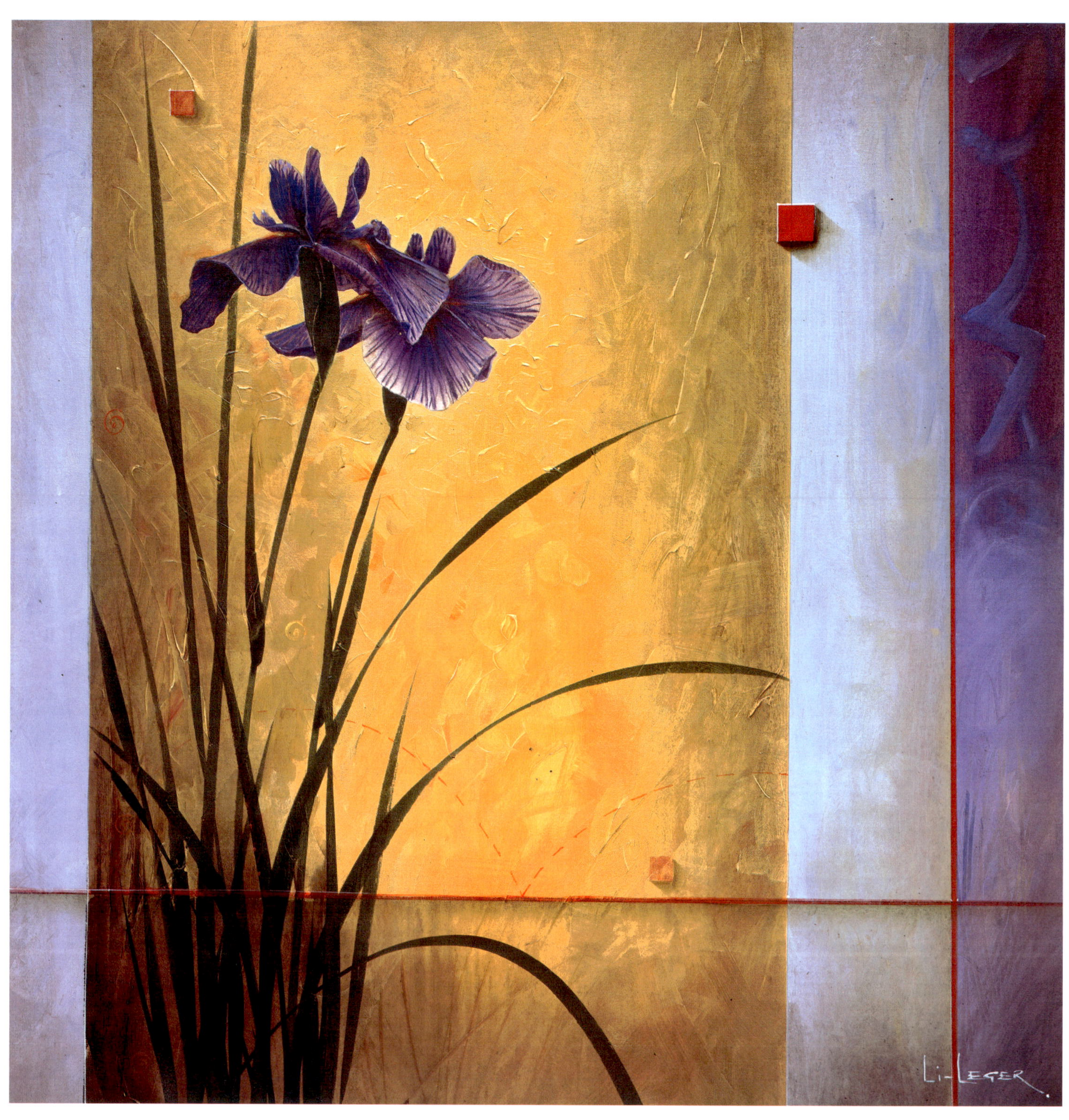

Sanctuary II
(Japanese Iris)
Acrylic on canvas
40" x 40", 2002
Private Collection

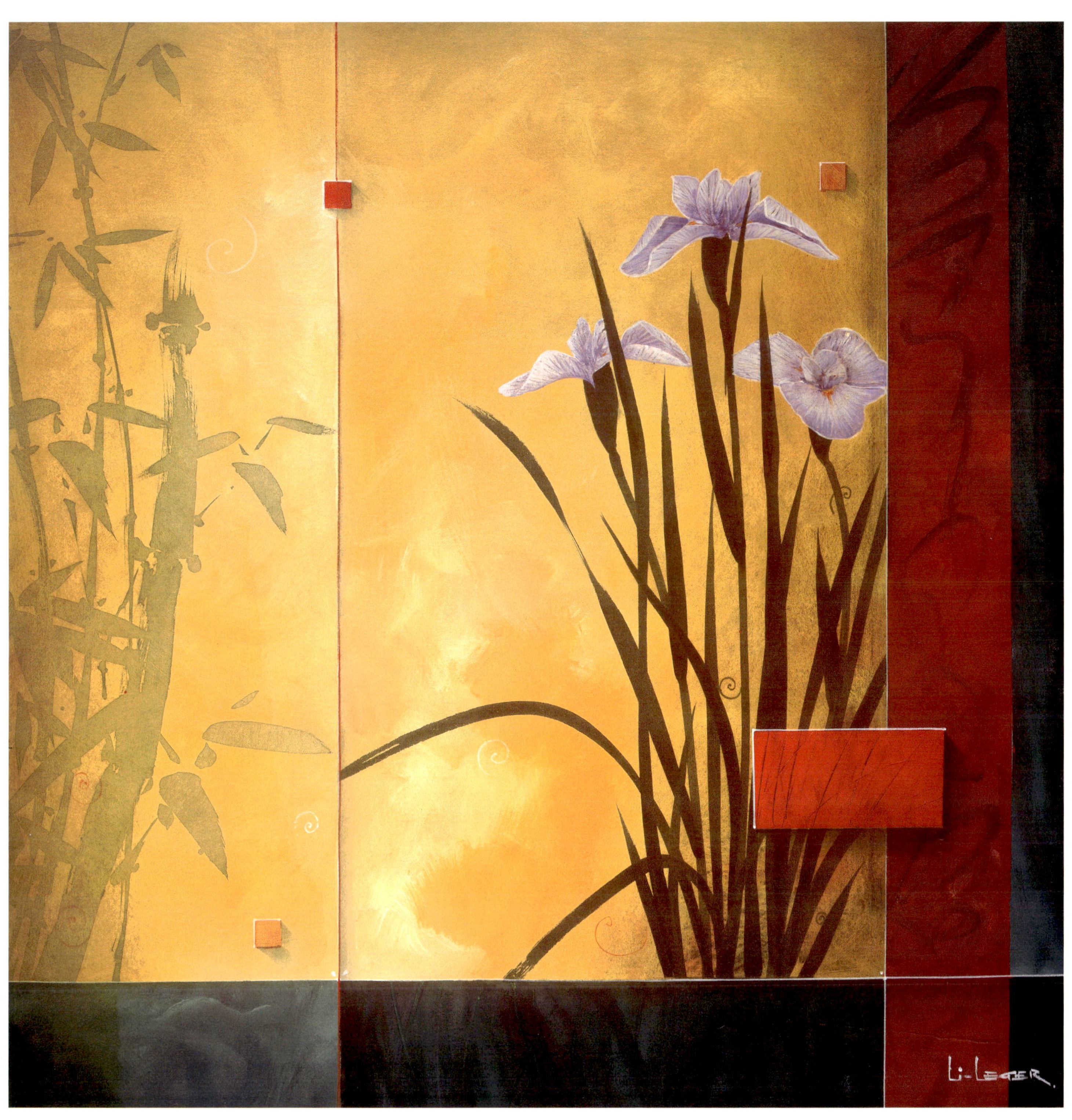

Jardin Mystique II
Acrylic on canvas
40" x 40", 2003
Collection of the Artist

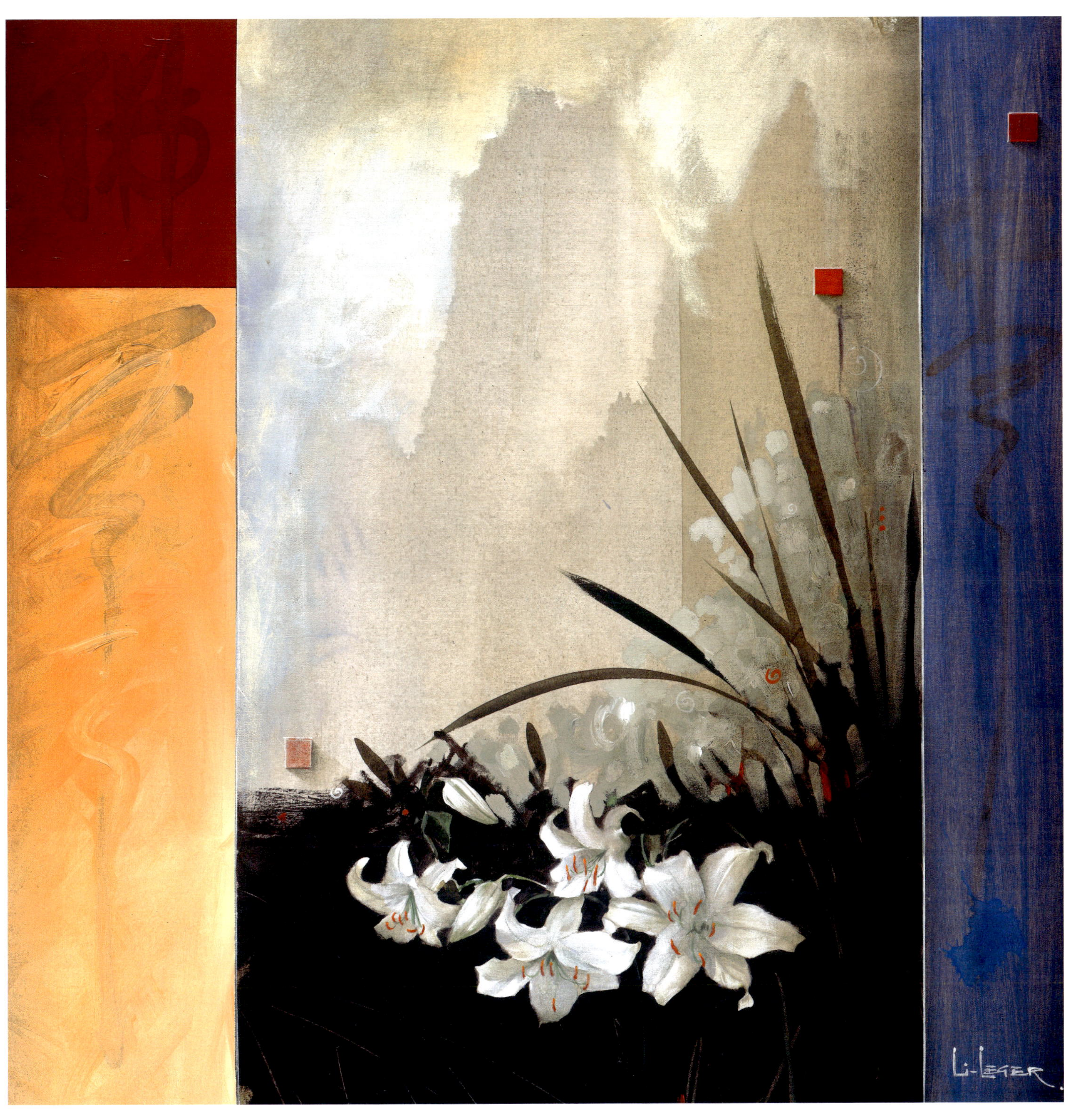

The Long Trek
Acrylic on canvas
40" x 40", 2003
Private Collection

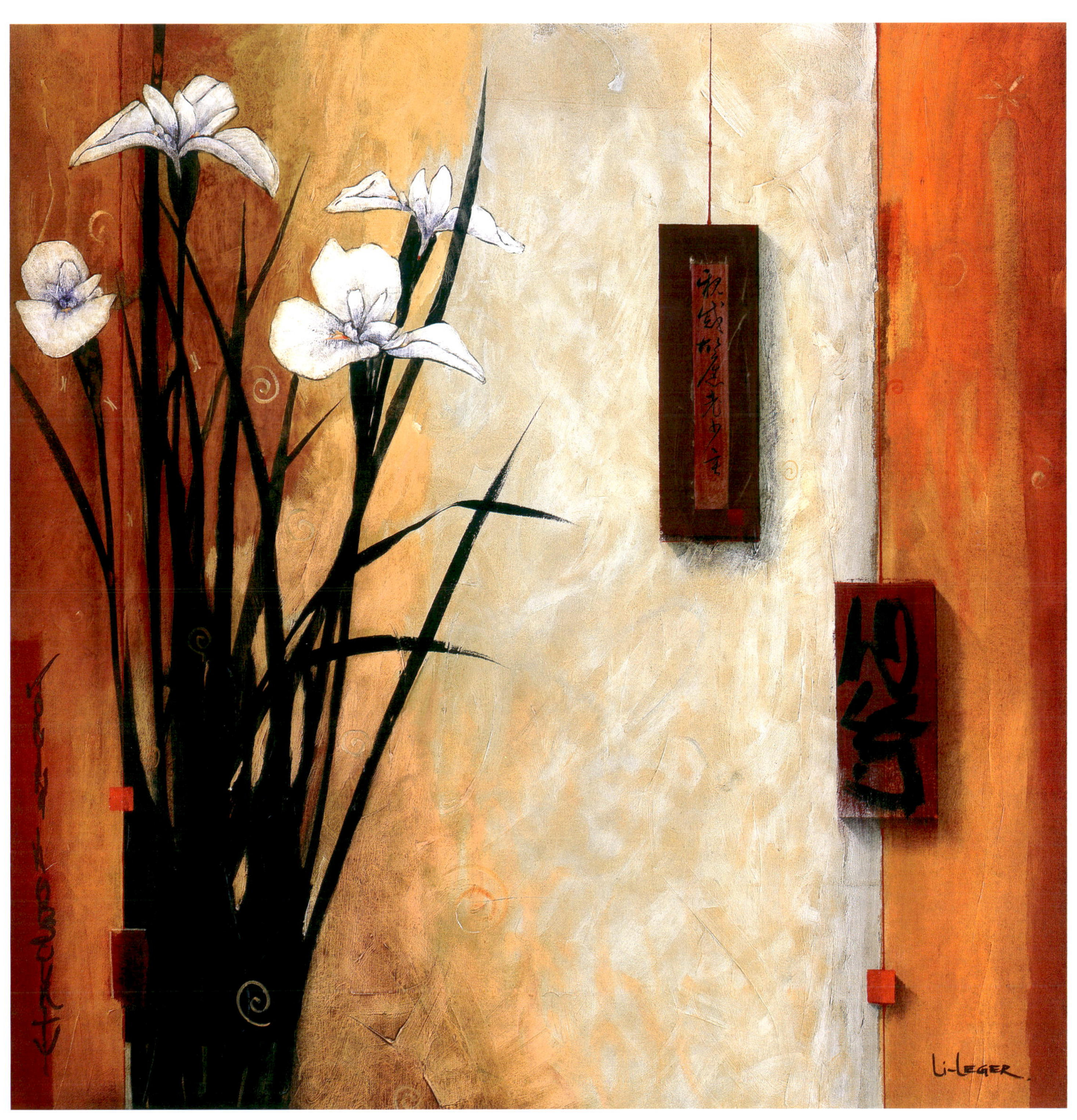

Mountain Travel
Acrylic on canvas
40" x 40", 2003
Private Collection

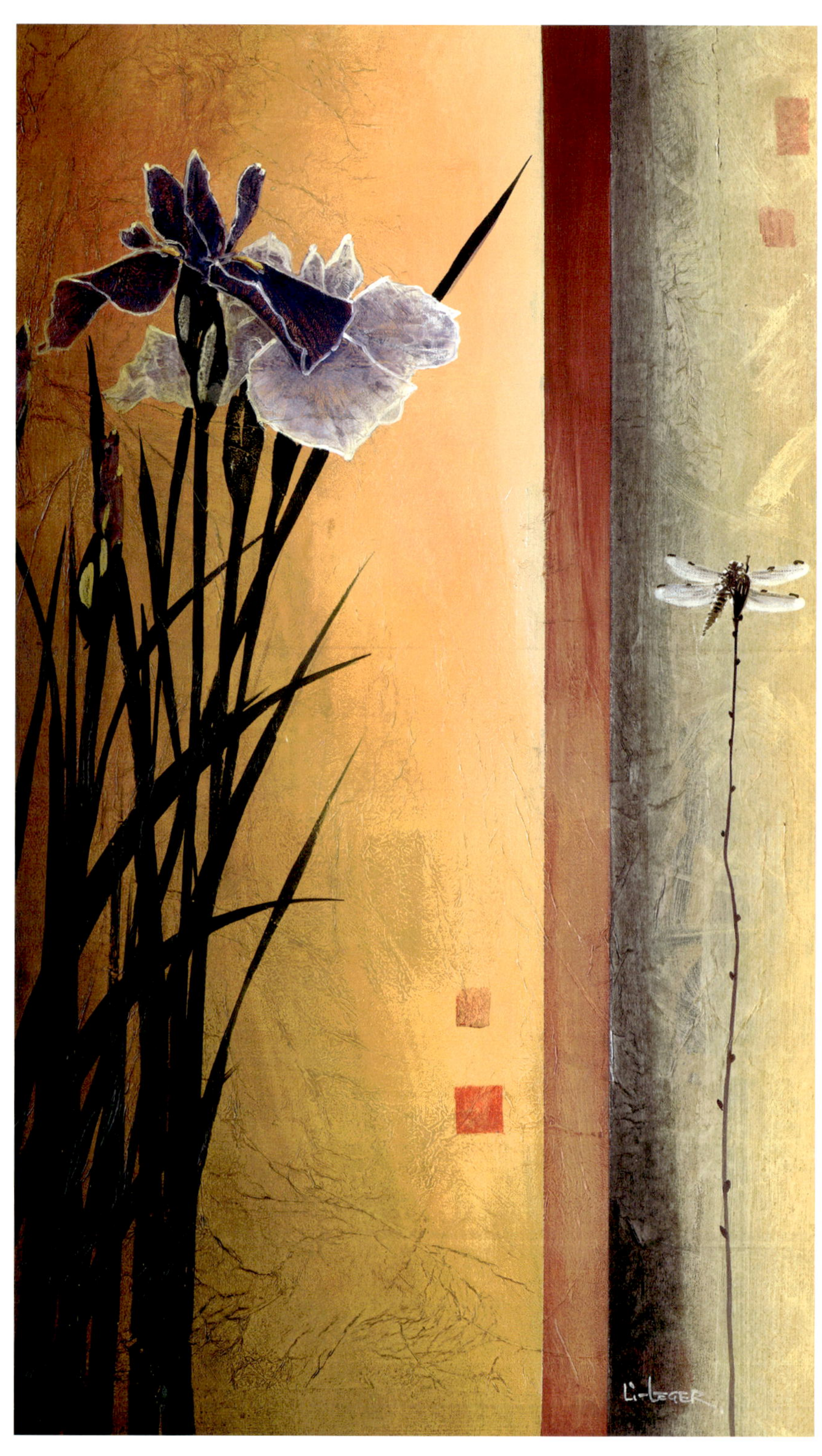

Waiting
Acrylic on canvas
40" x 24", 2002
Private Collection

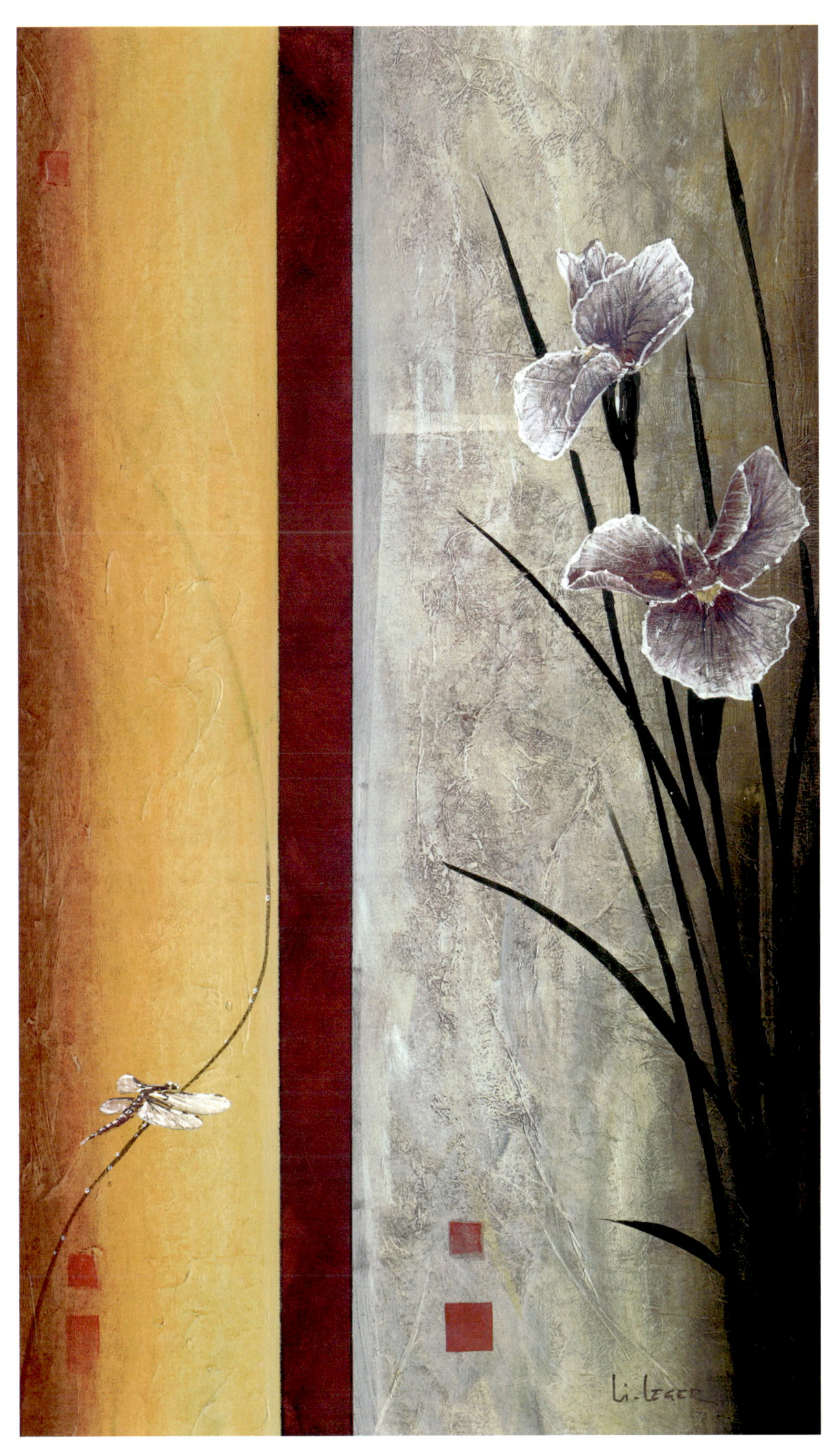

Rising
Acrylic on canvas
40" x 24", 2002
Private Collection

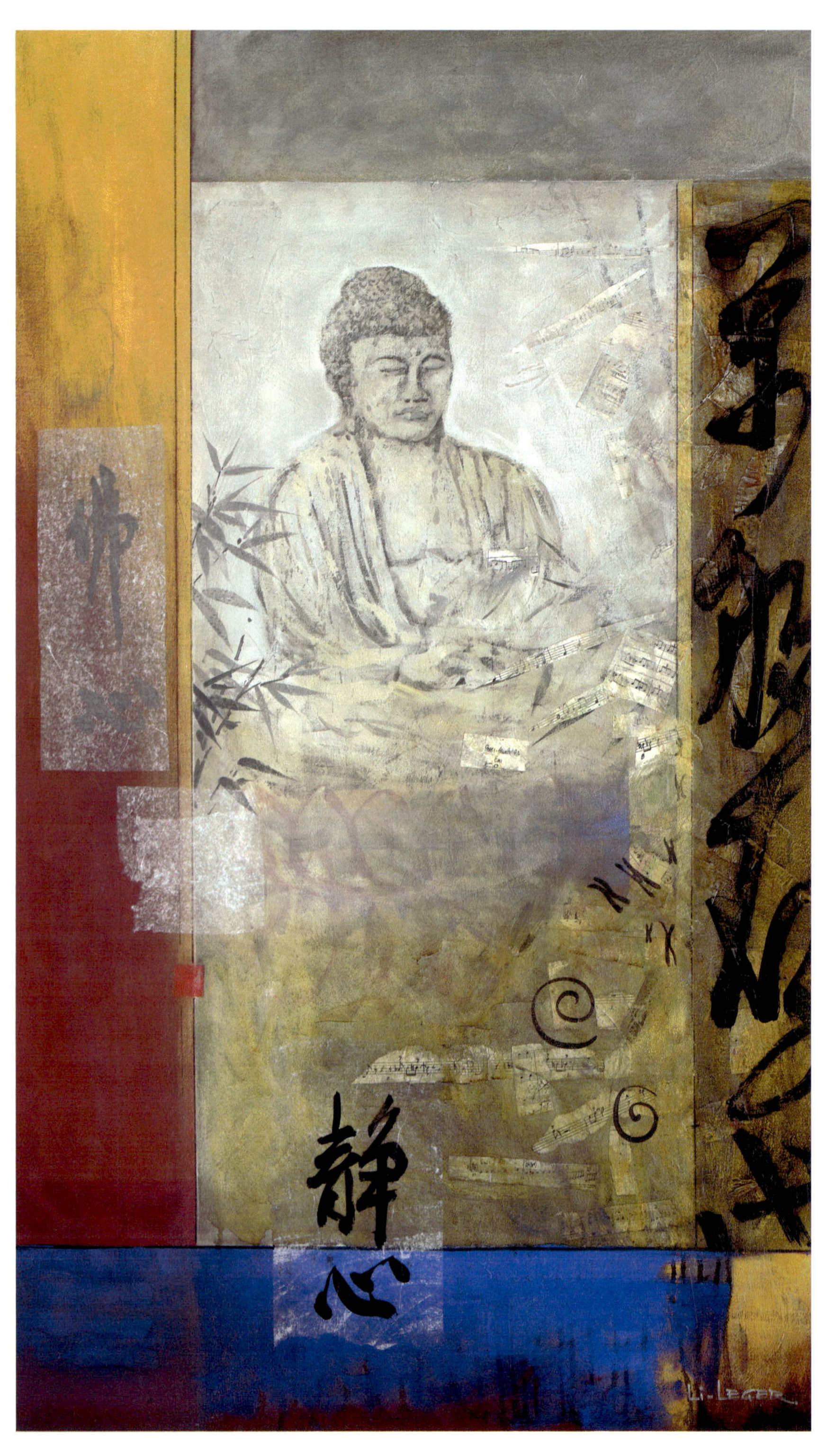

Under the Bodhi Tree I
Acrylic on canvas
40" x 24", 2001
Private Collection

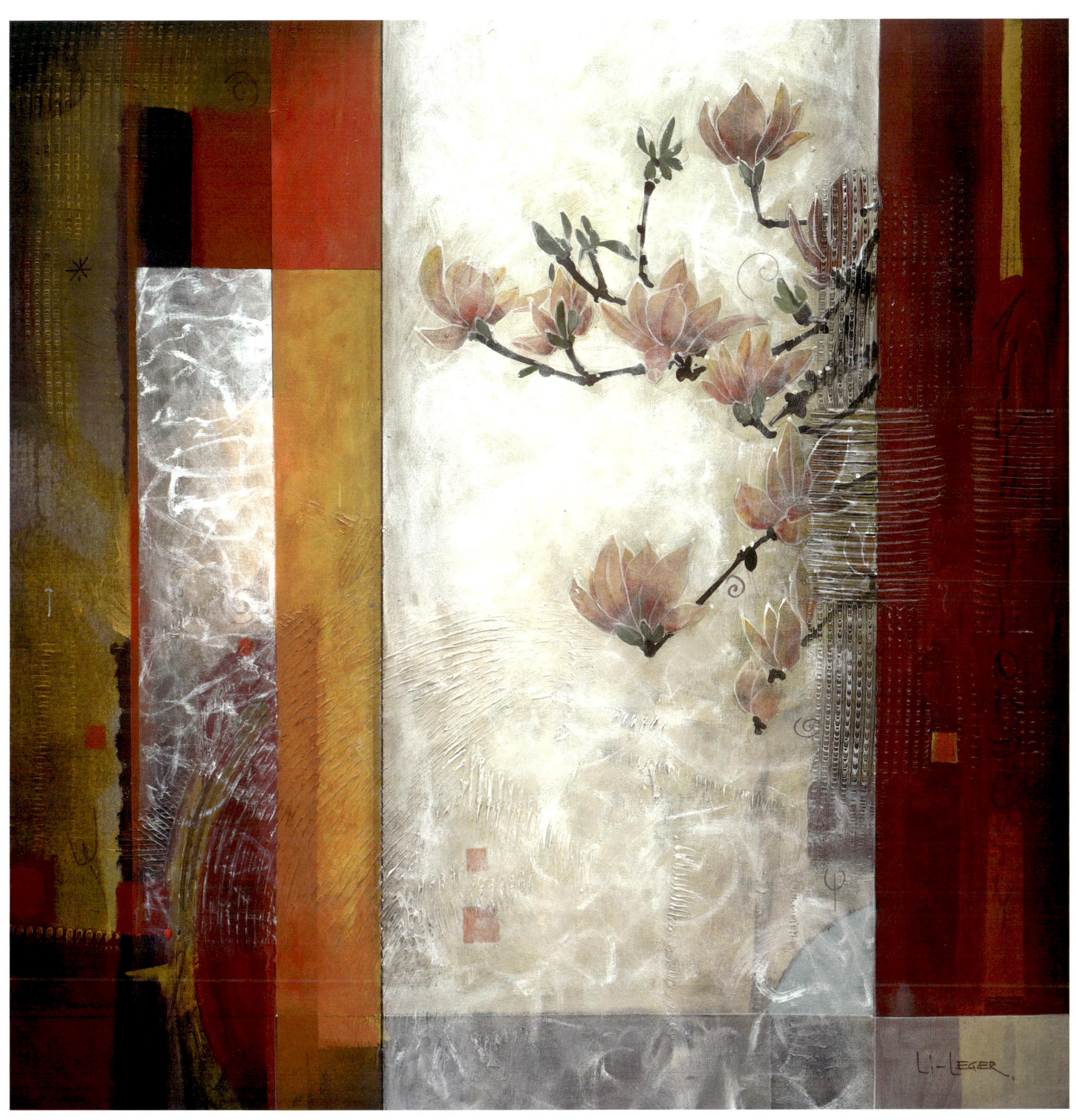

Manhattan Garden
Acrylic on canvas
40" x 40", 2002
Collection of Nancy
and Alan Wasserkrug

*Man needs color to live; it's just as
necessary an element as fire and water.*

— FERNAND LEGER

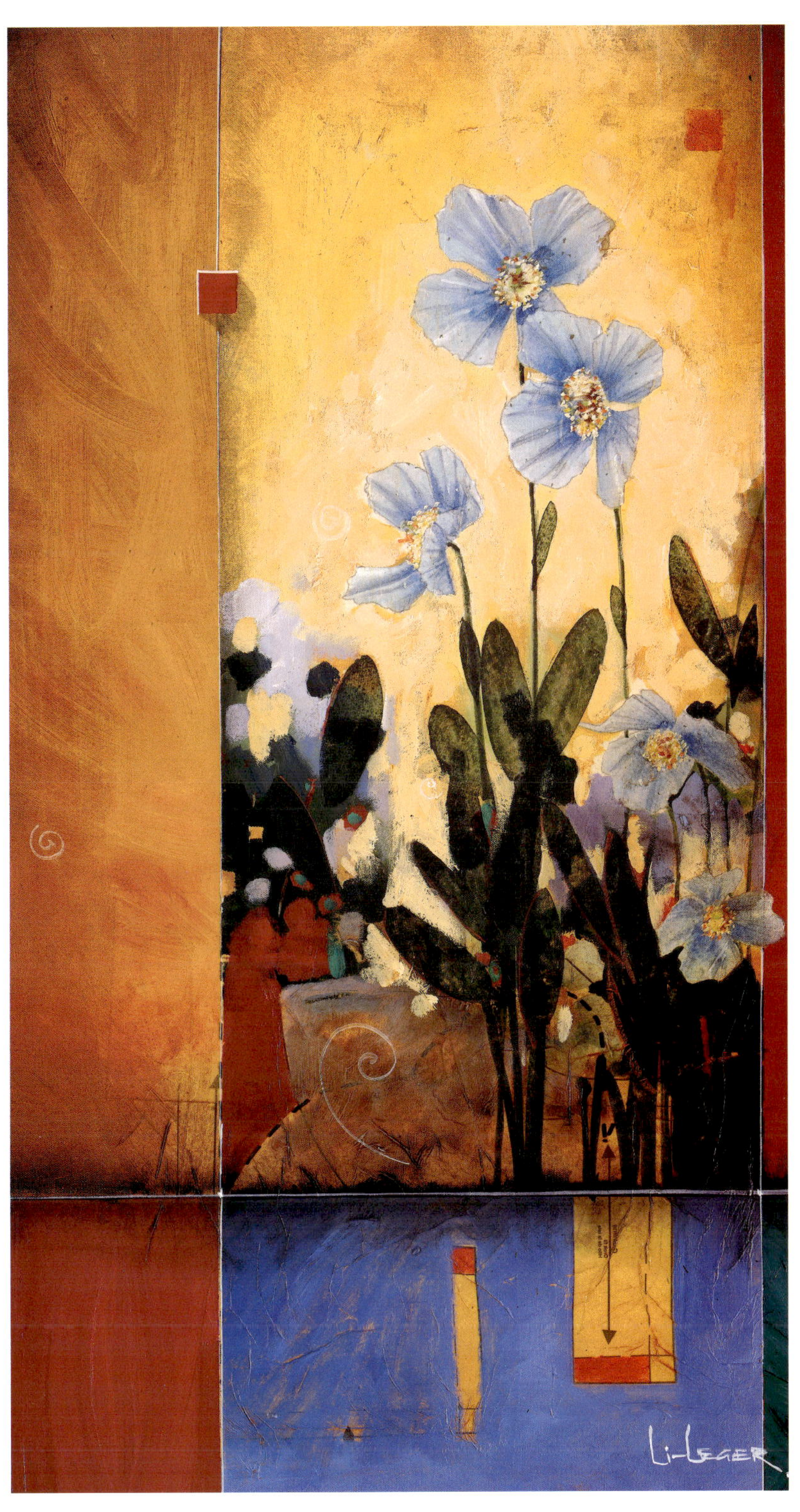

Himalayan Poppy Trek
Acrylic on canvas
20" x 36", 2004
Private Collection

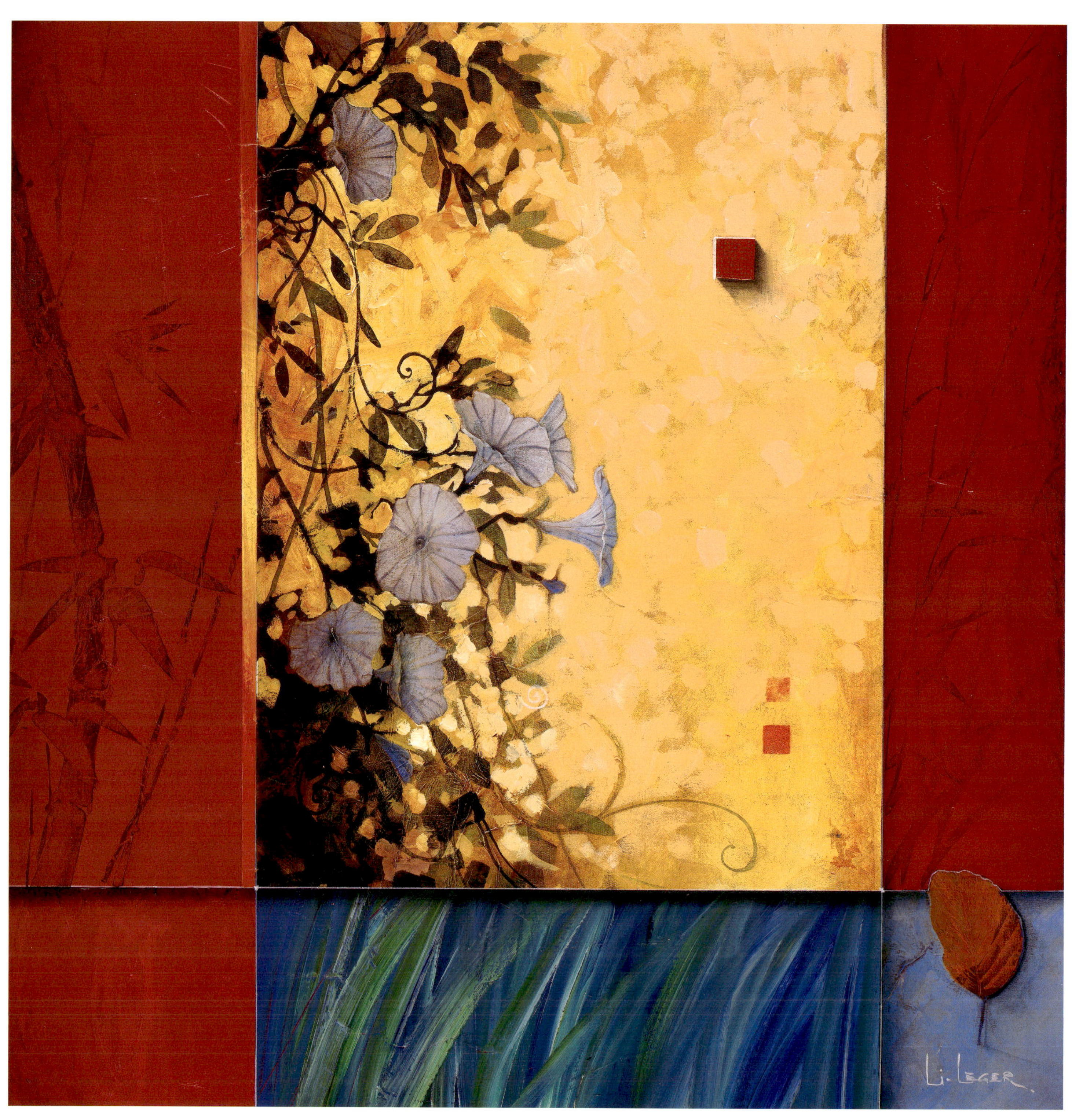

Painter's Garden III
Acrylic on canvas
40" x 40", 2005
Courtesy of
Canada House Gallery

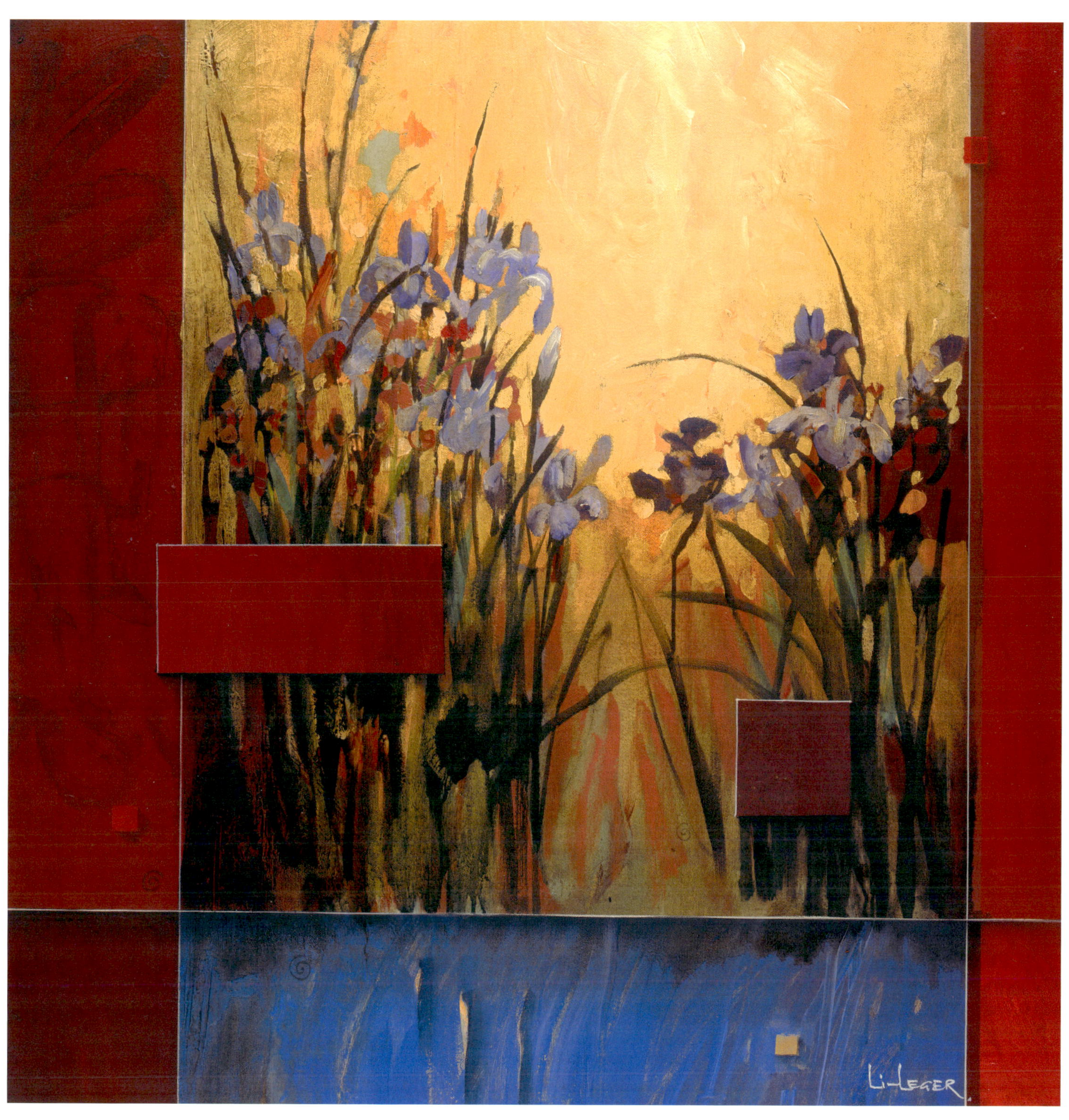

Iris Sunrise
Acrylic on canvas
40" x 40", 2002
Private Collection

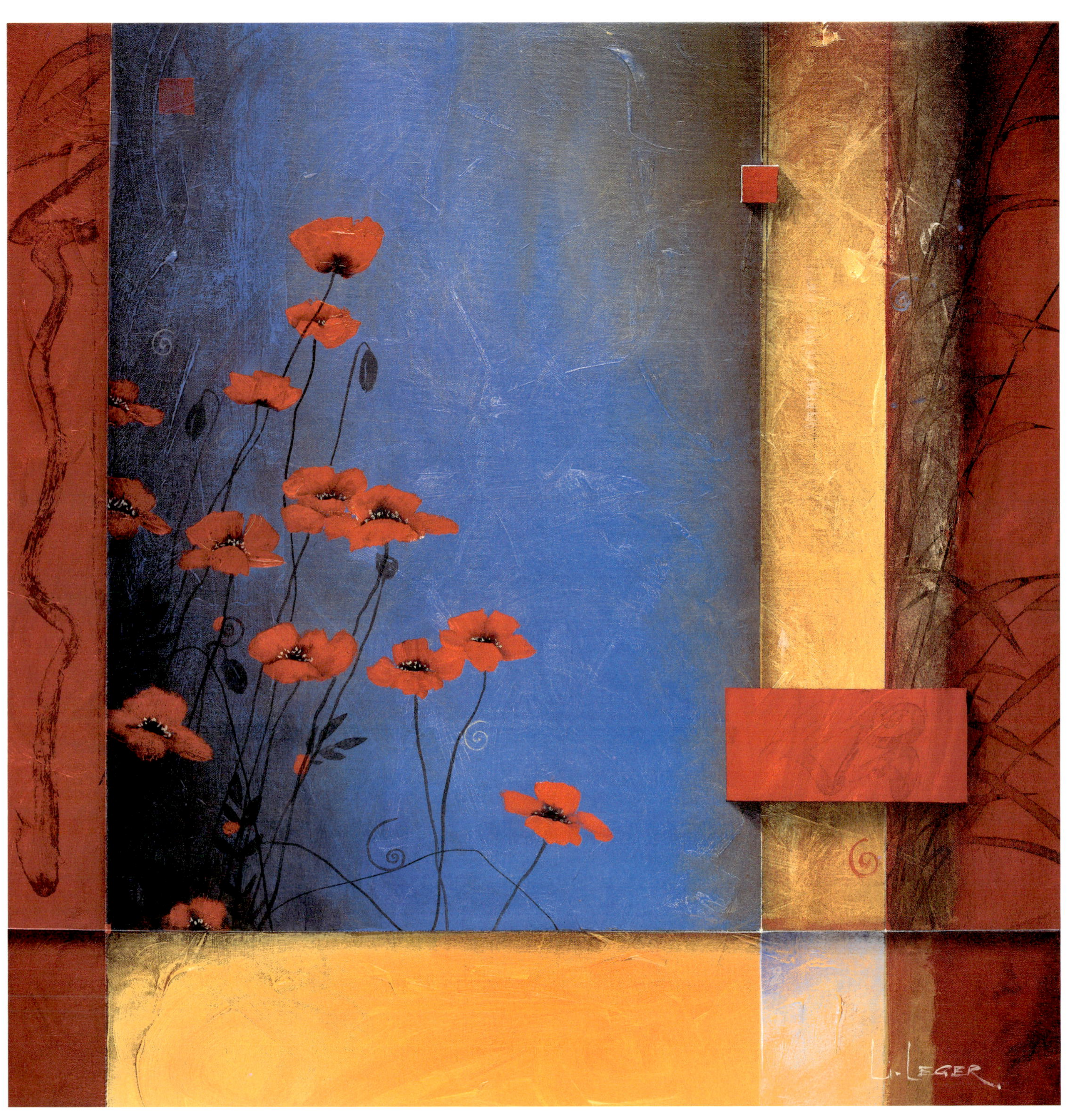

Mystic Journey
(Poppy Dance)
Acrylic on canvas
40" x 40", 2002
Private Collection

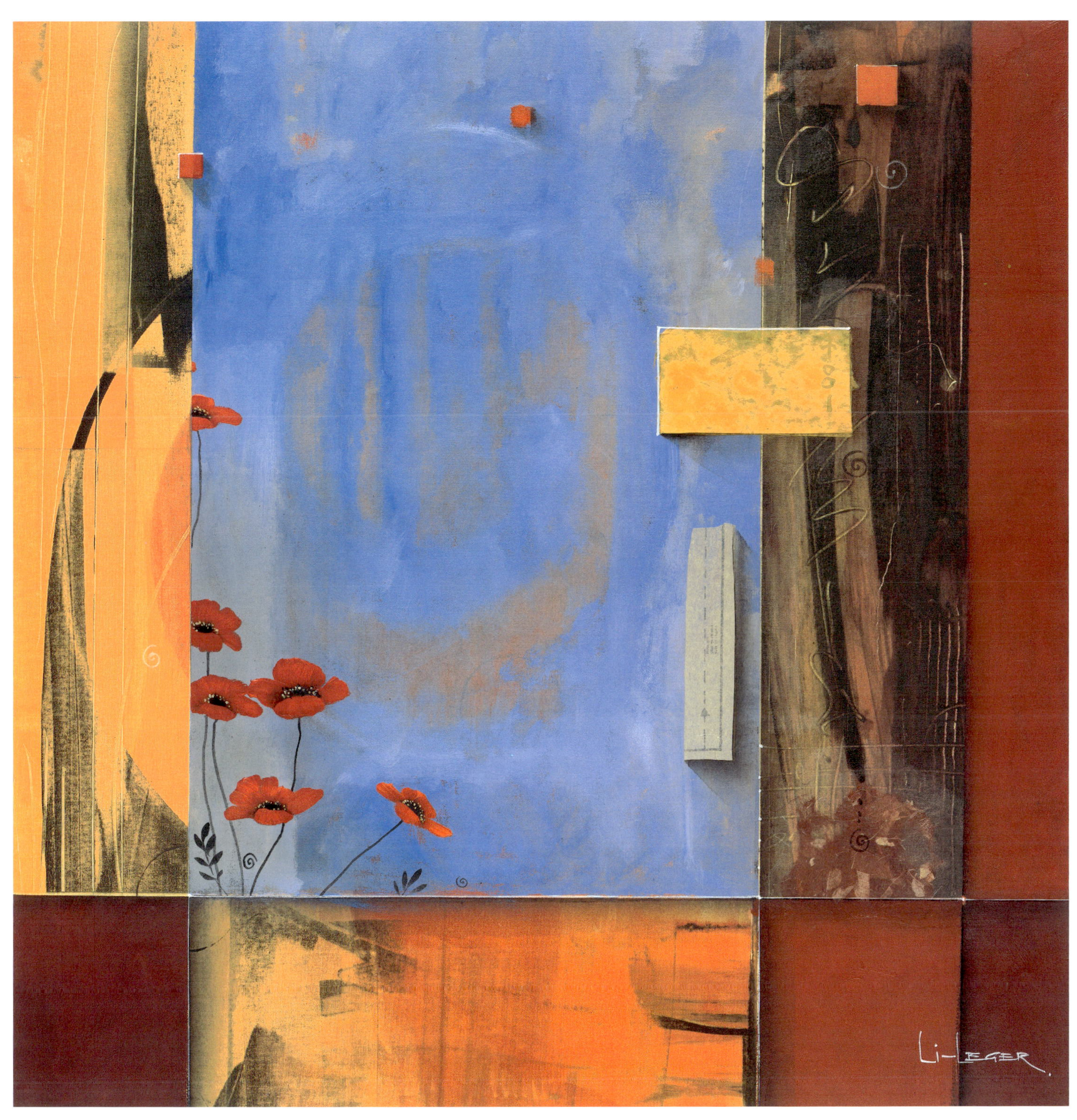

Jardin Mysterieux
Acrylic on canvas
40" x 40", 2002
Collection of Mark
& Teresa Ankenman

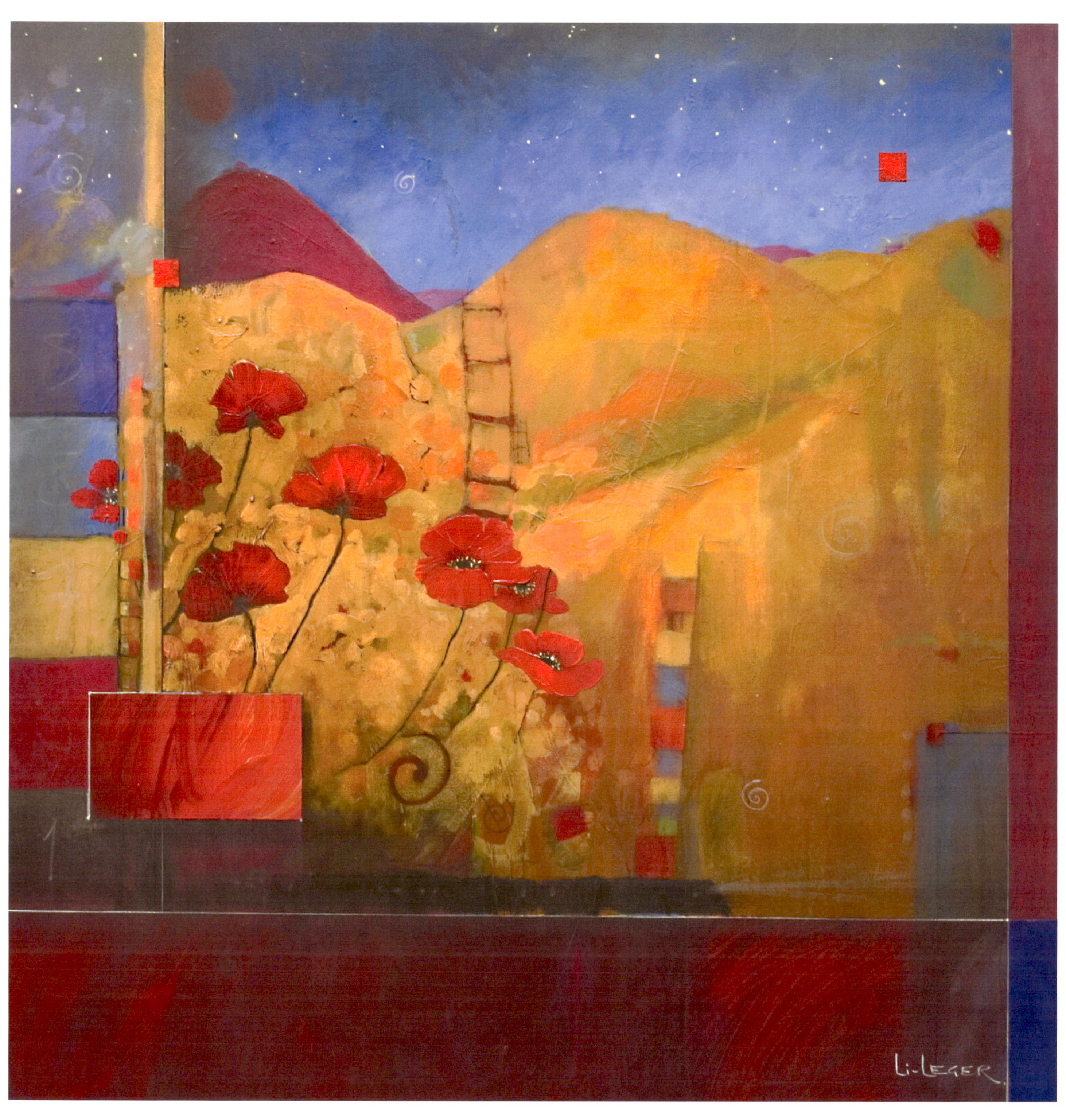

Night Train II
Acrylic on canvas
40" x 40", 2003
Private Collection

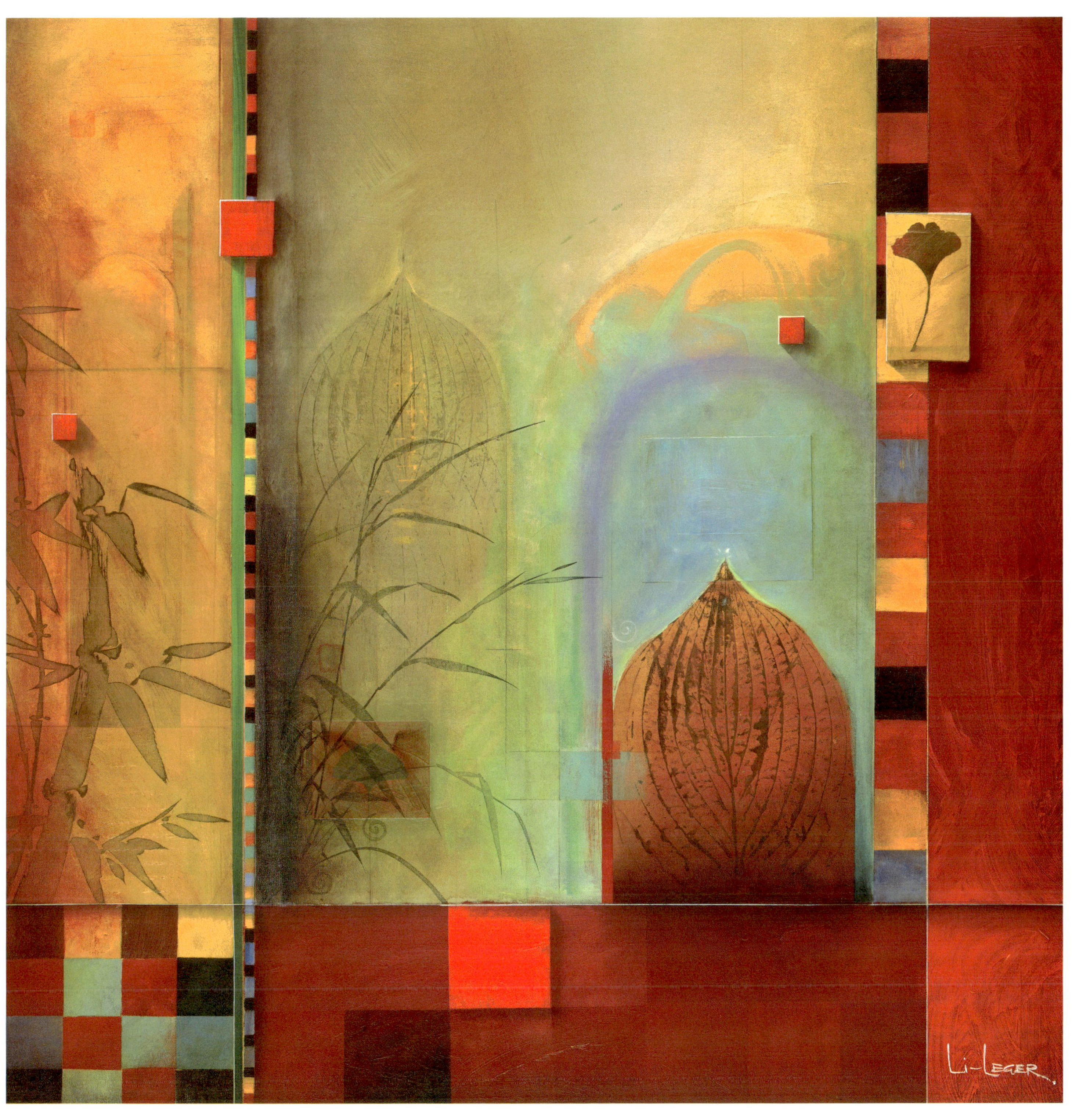

After the Hammam
Acrylic on canvas
40" x 40", 2004
Collection of the Artist

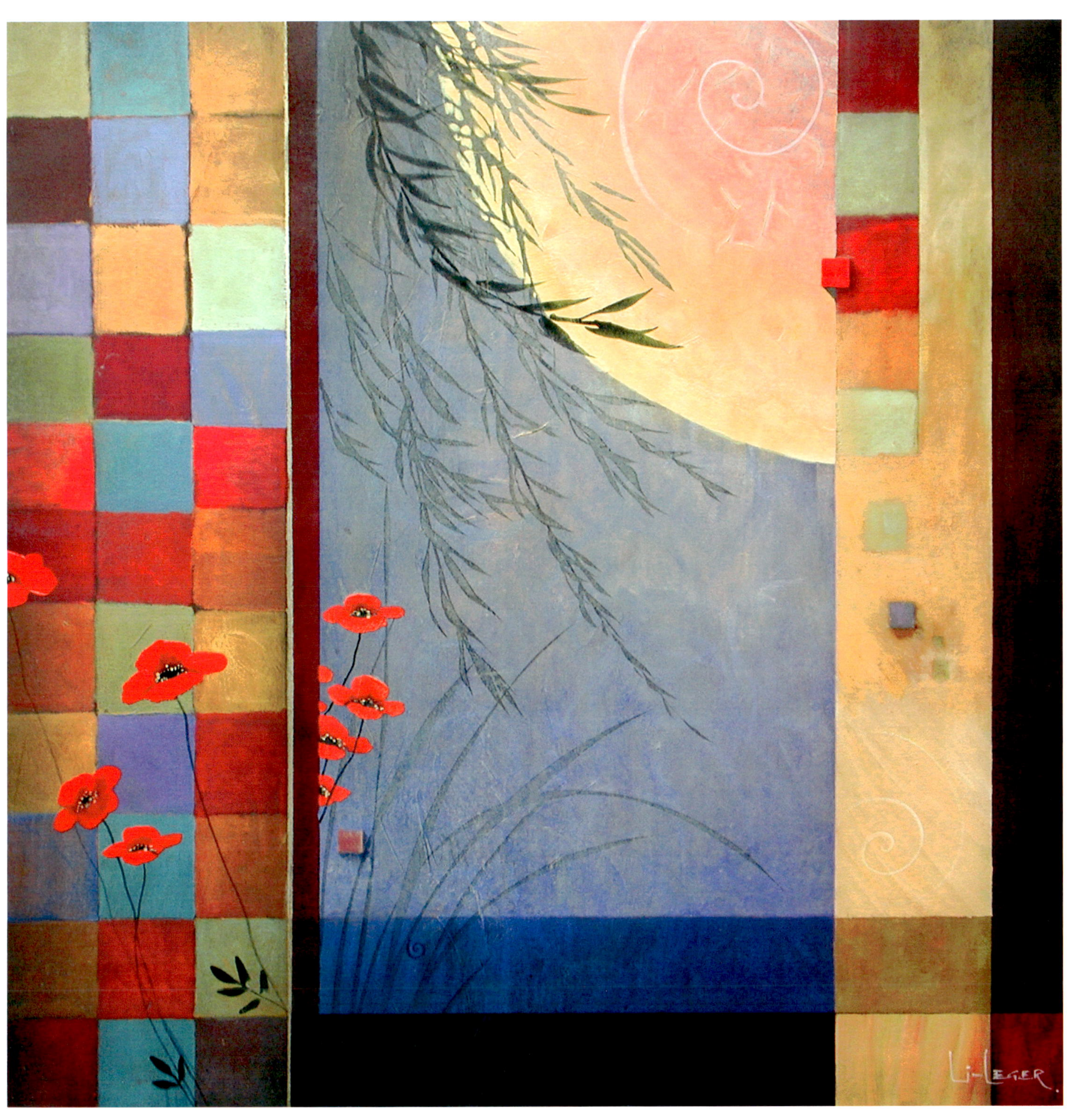

Full Moon – Willow Tree
Acrylic on canvas
40" x 40", 2003
Private Collection

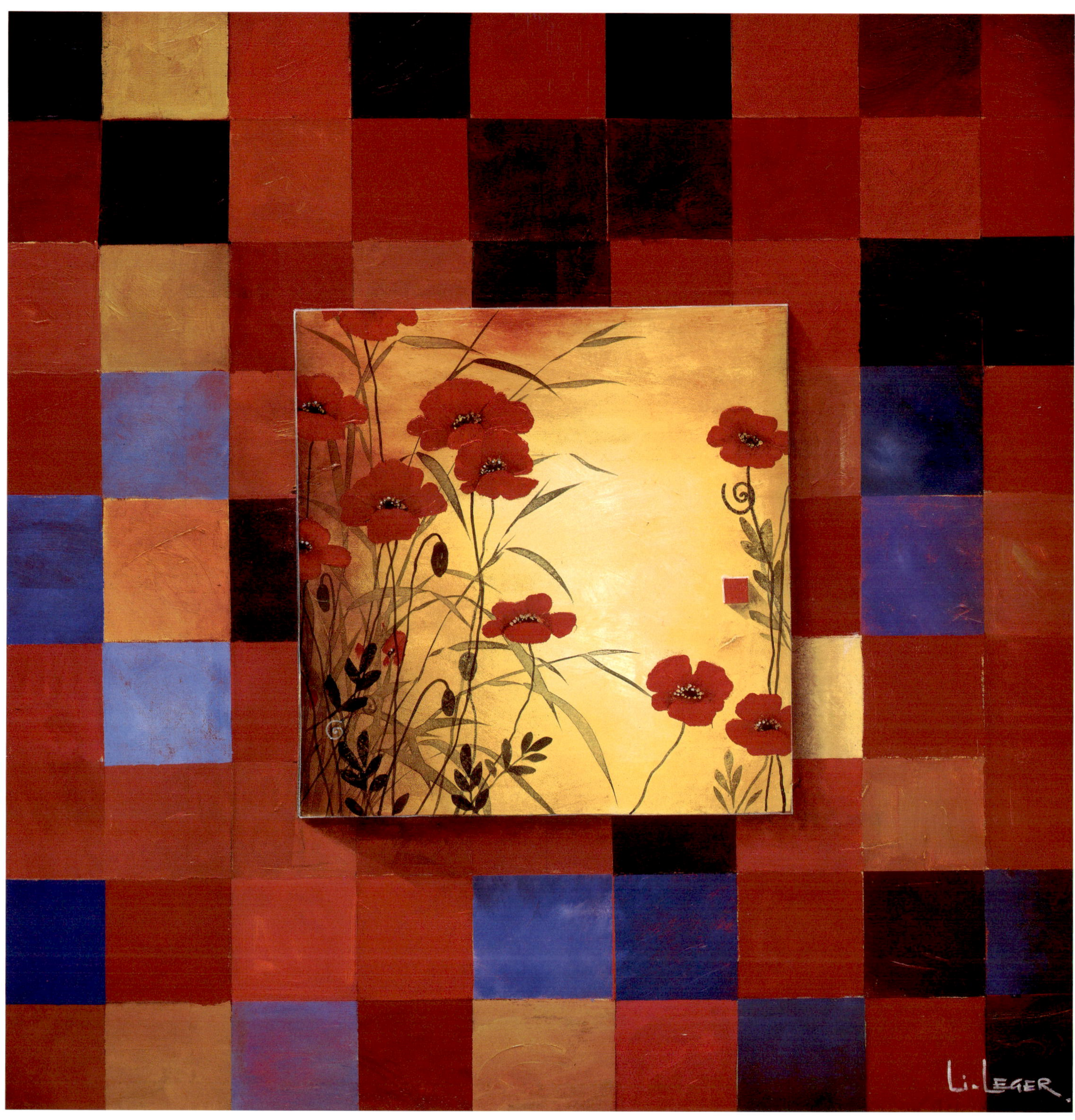

Poppy Patterns
Acrylic on canvas
40" x 40", 2005
Courtesy of
Canada House Gallery

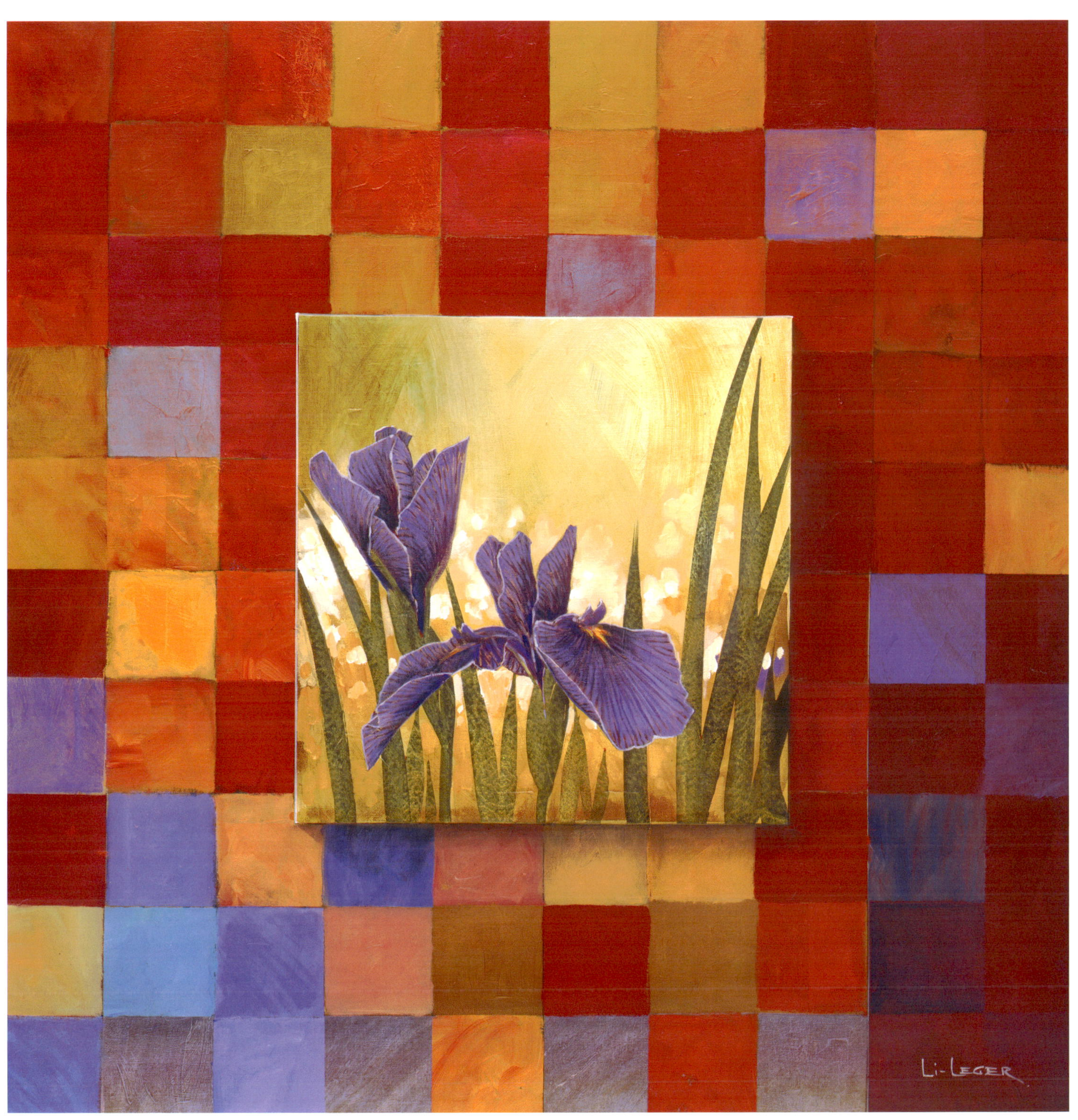

Mirrored Garden
Acrylic on canvas
40" x 40", 2005
Courtesy of
Canada House Gallery

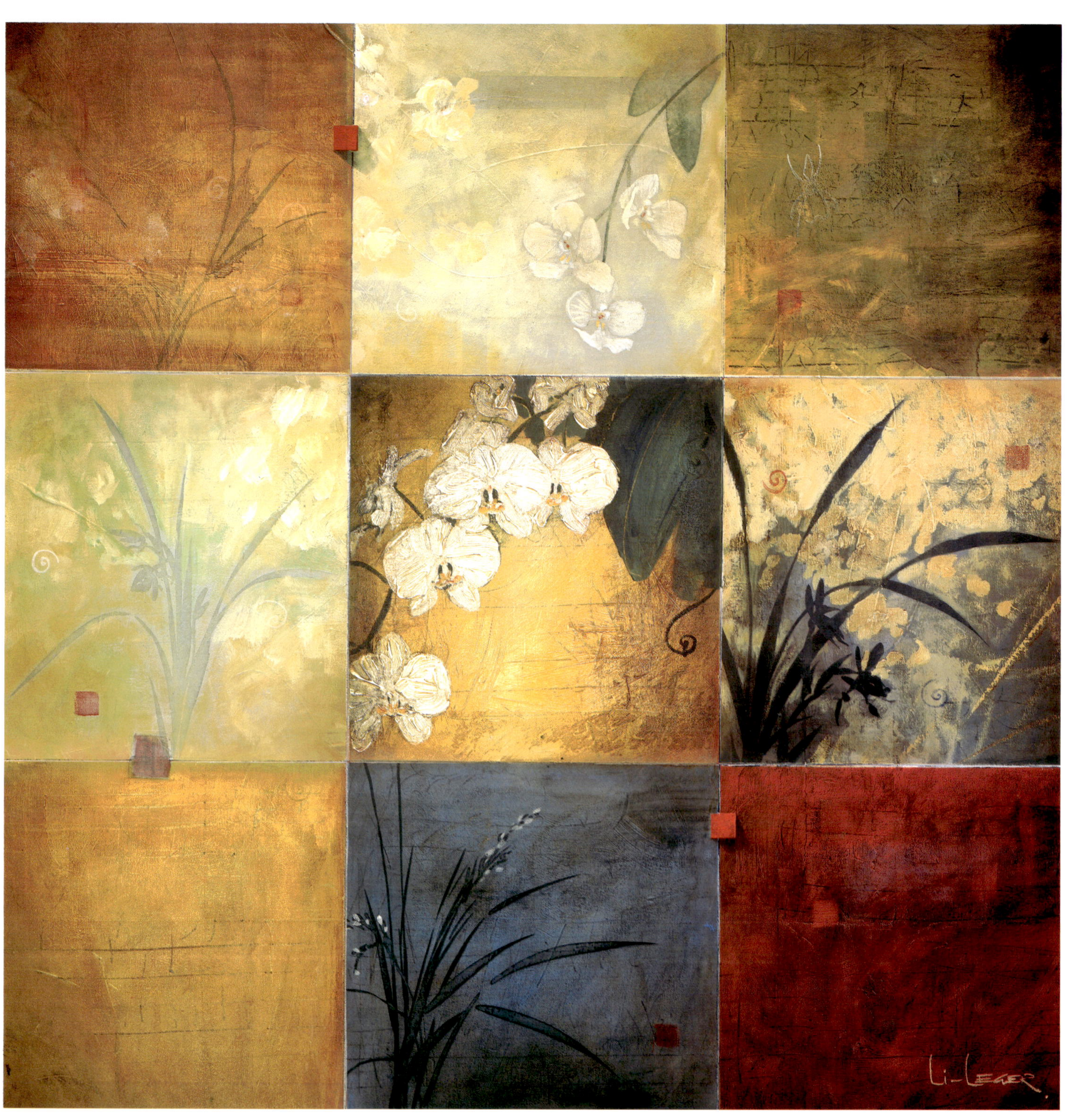

Orchid Nine Patch
Acrylic on canvas
40" x 40", 2004
Private Collection

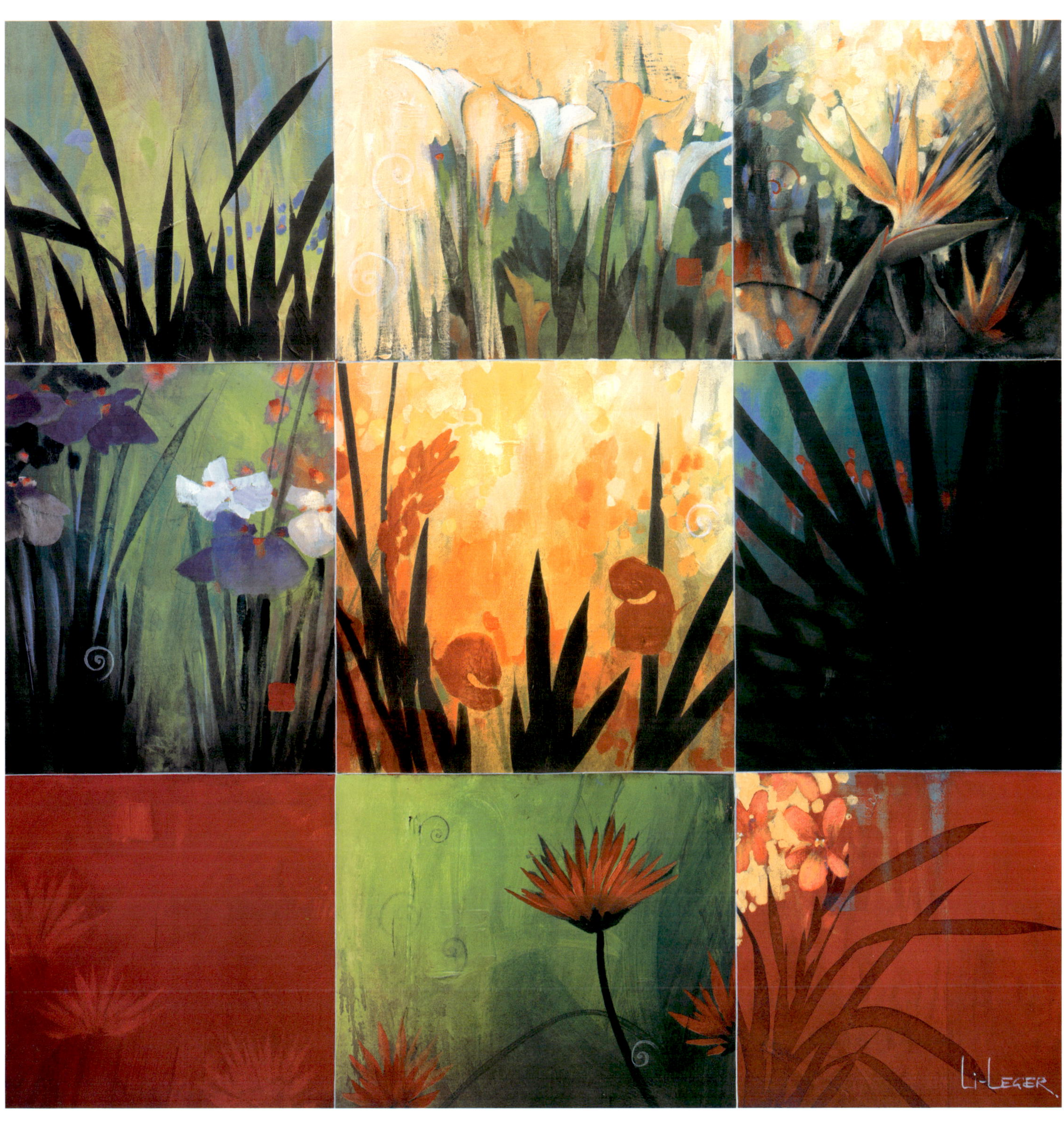

Tropical Nine Patch
Acrylic on canvas
40" x 40", 2004
Collection of the Artist

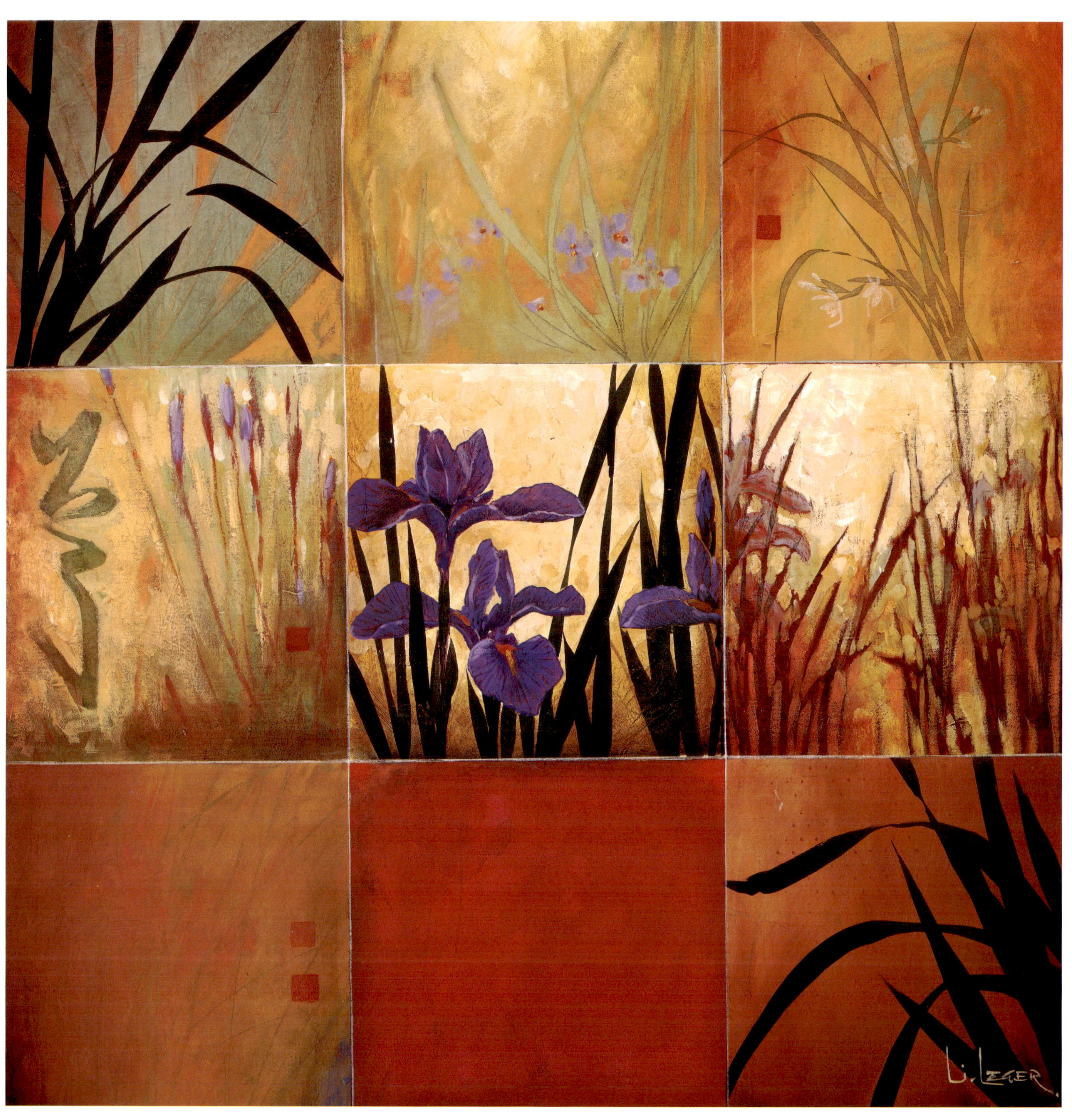

Iris Nine Patch III
Acrylic on canvas
40" x 40", 2003
Private Collection

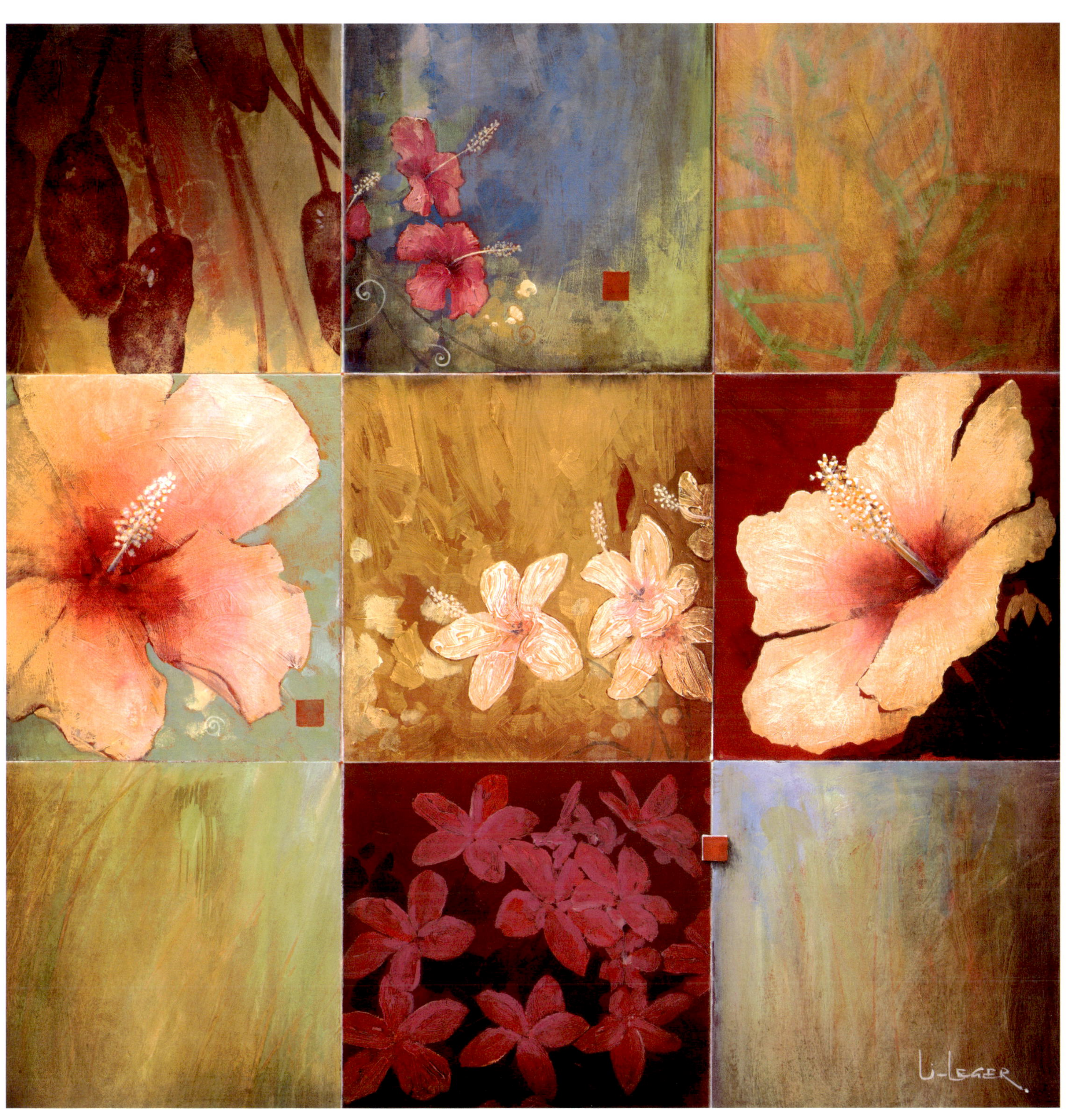

Tropical Nine Patch II
Acrylic on canvas
40" x 40", 2004
Collection of the Artist

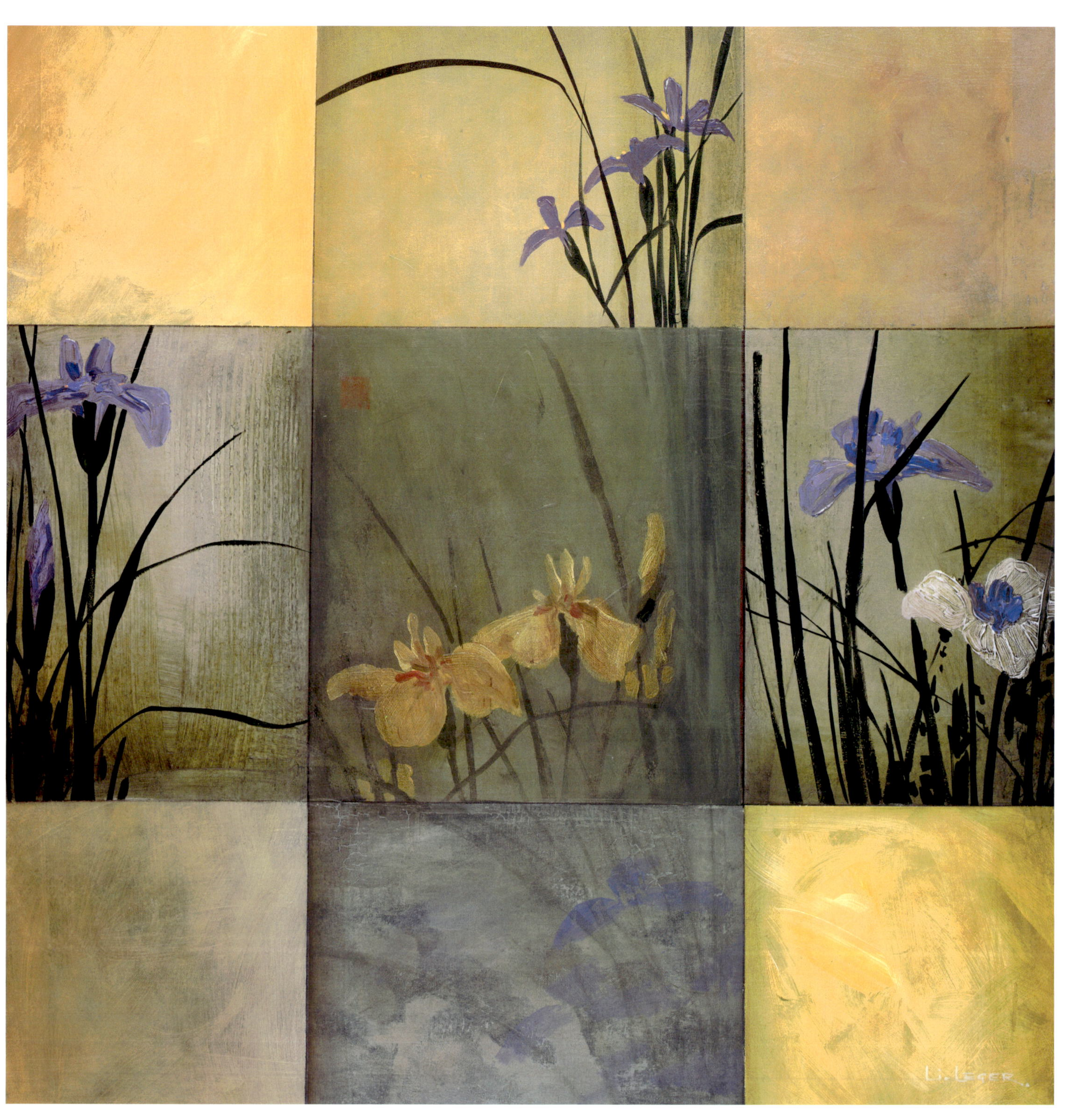

Iris Nine Patch
Acrylic on canvas
40" x 40", 2002
Private Collection

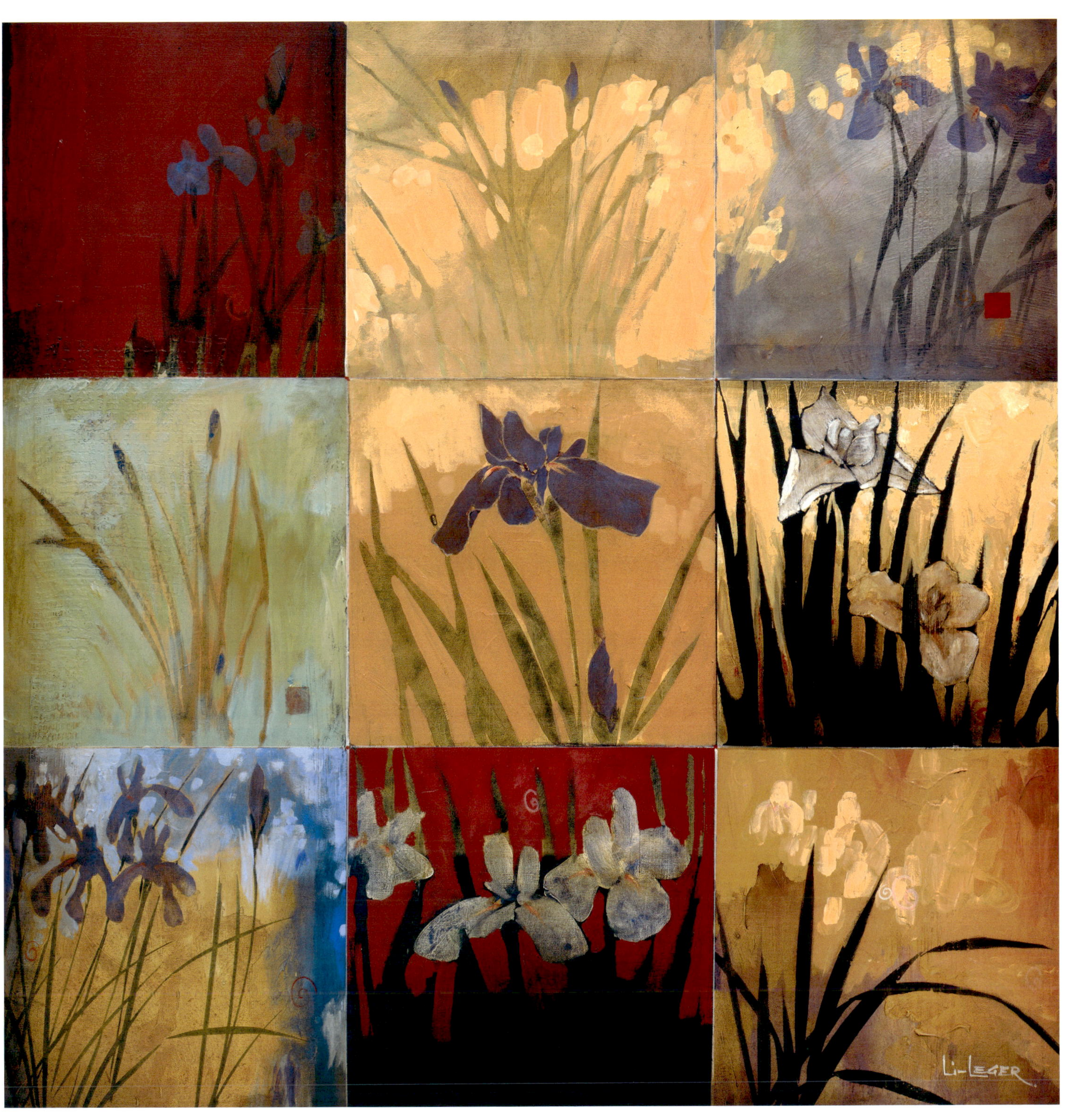

Iris Nine Patch II
Acrylic on canvas
40" x 40", 2003
Private Collection

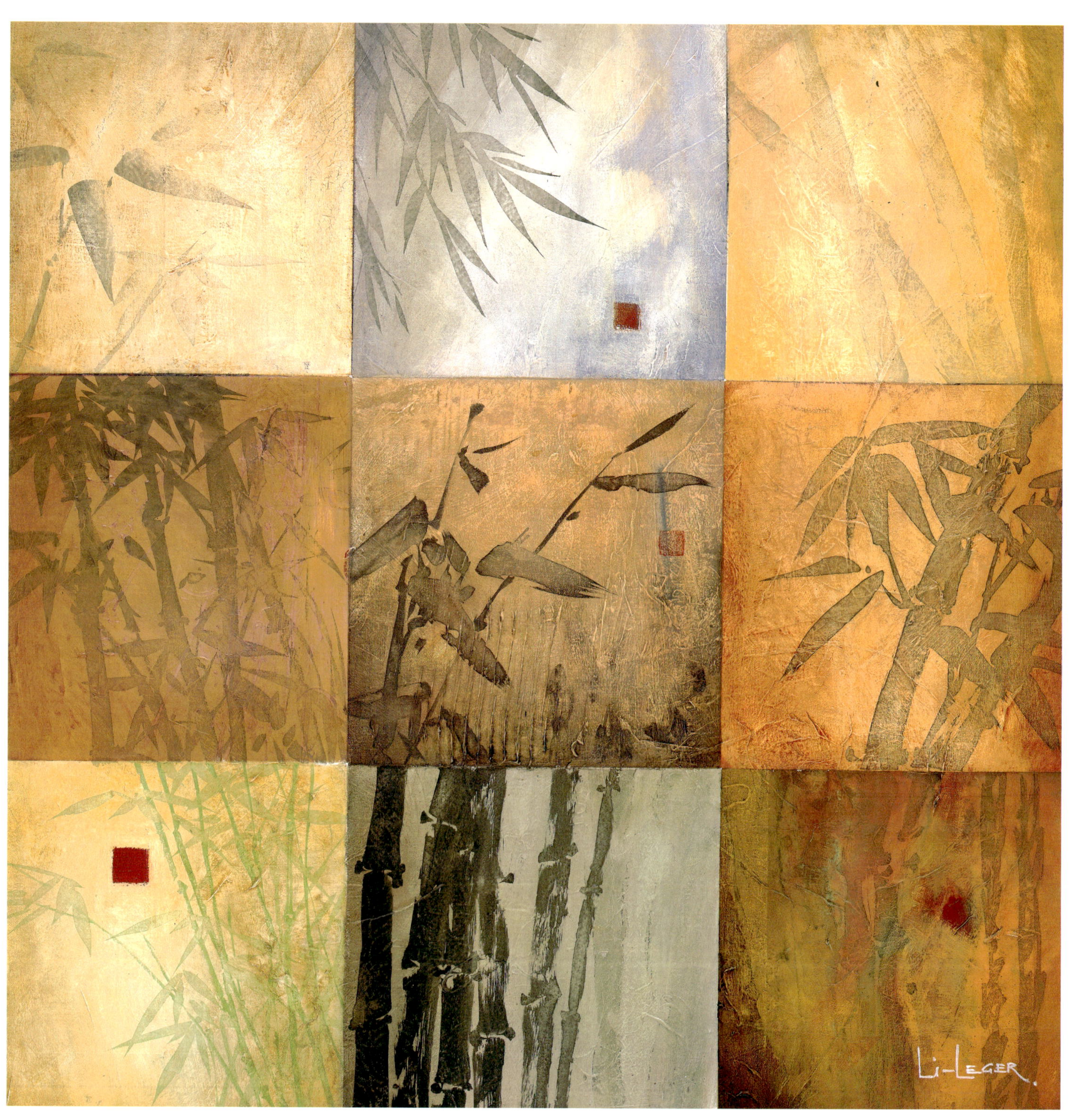

Bamboo Nine Patch
Acrylic on canvas
40" x 40", 2005
Collection of the Artist

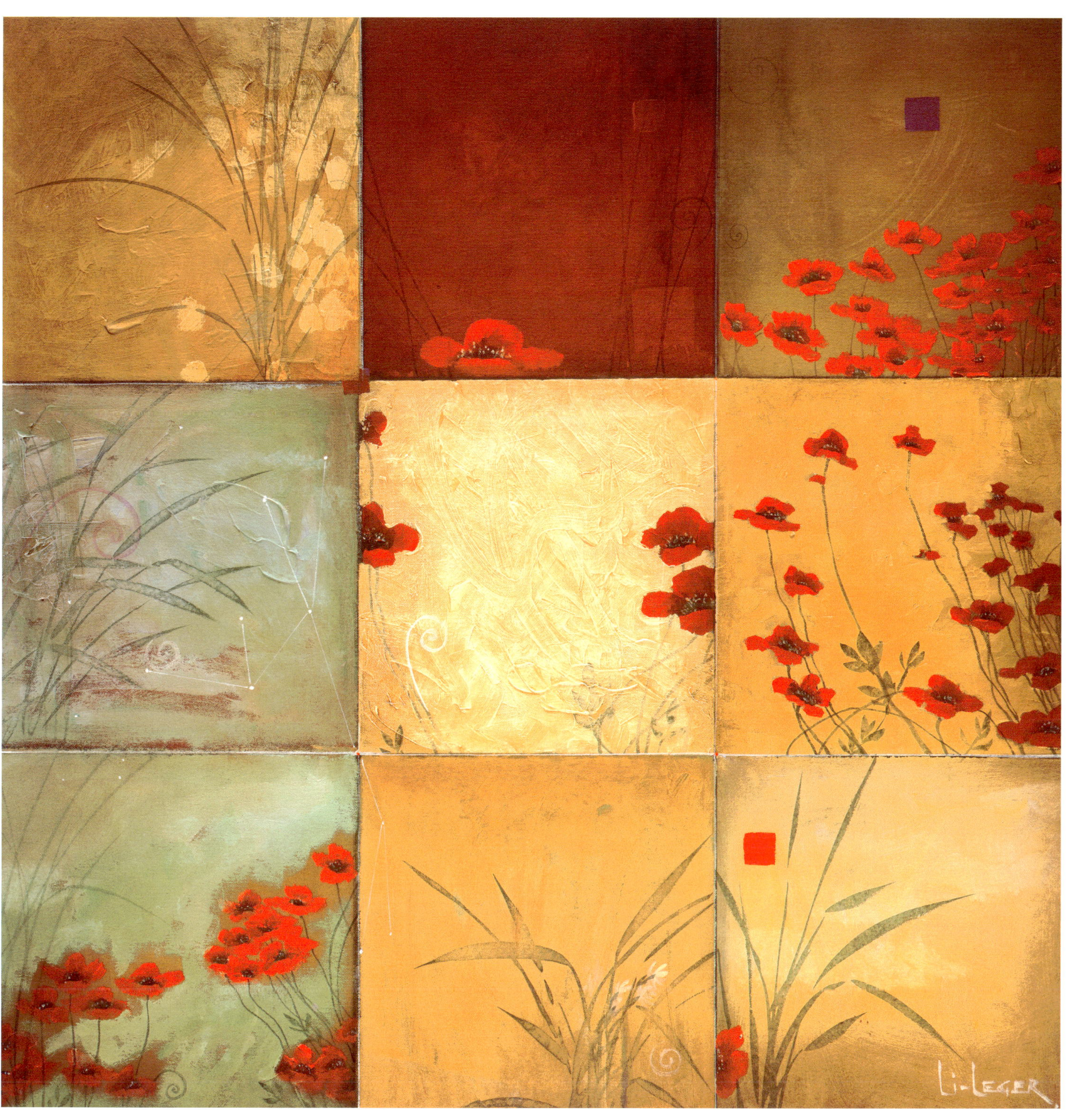

Poppy Nine Patch
Acrylic on canvas
40" x 40", 2004
Collection of
Tracy Morrison
and Brooke Wade

There is no must in art because art is free.

— WASSILY KANDINSKY

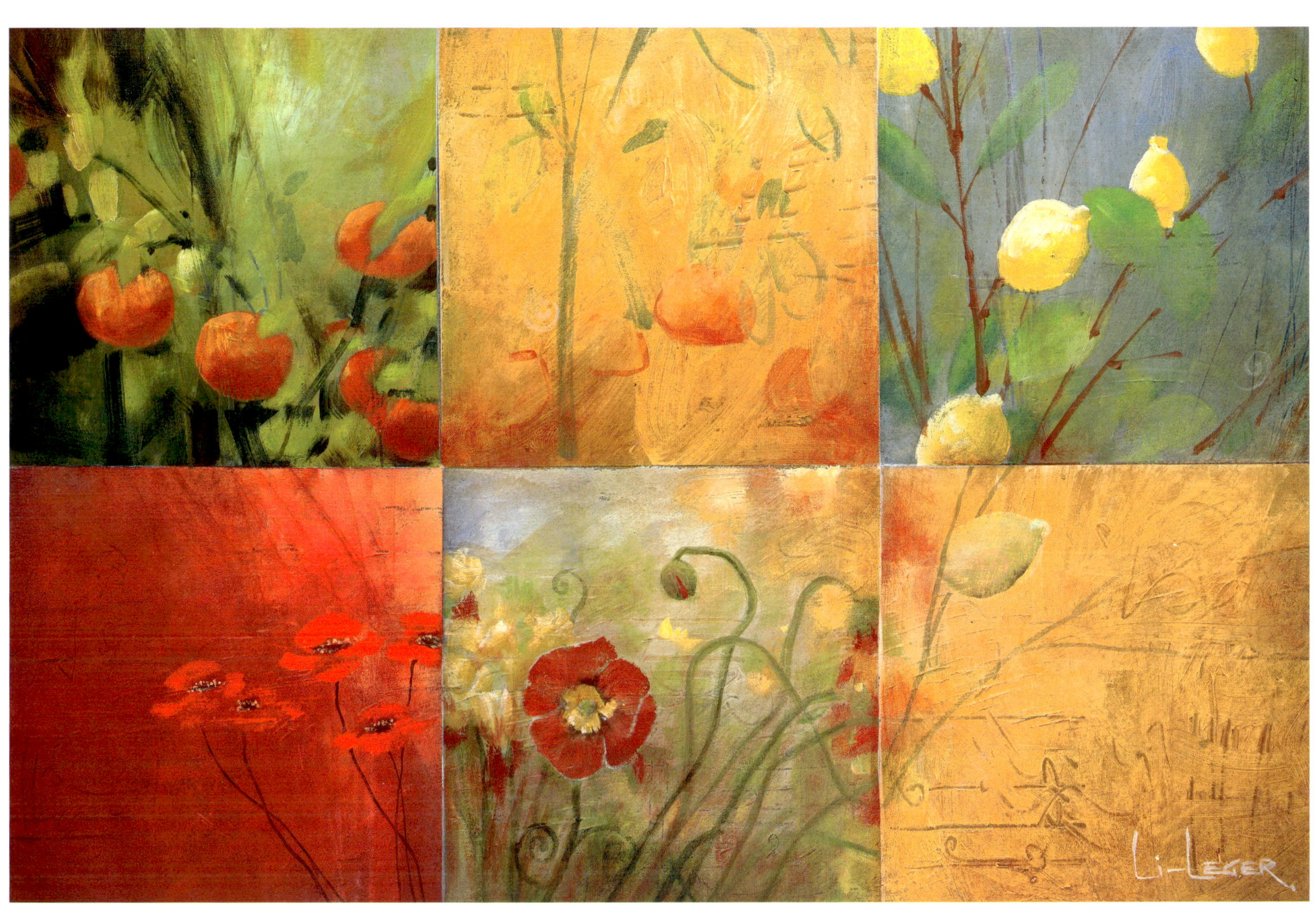

Citrus Delight
Acrylic on canvas
24" x 40", 2004
Collection of Amy
and Peter Mabie

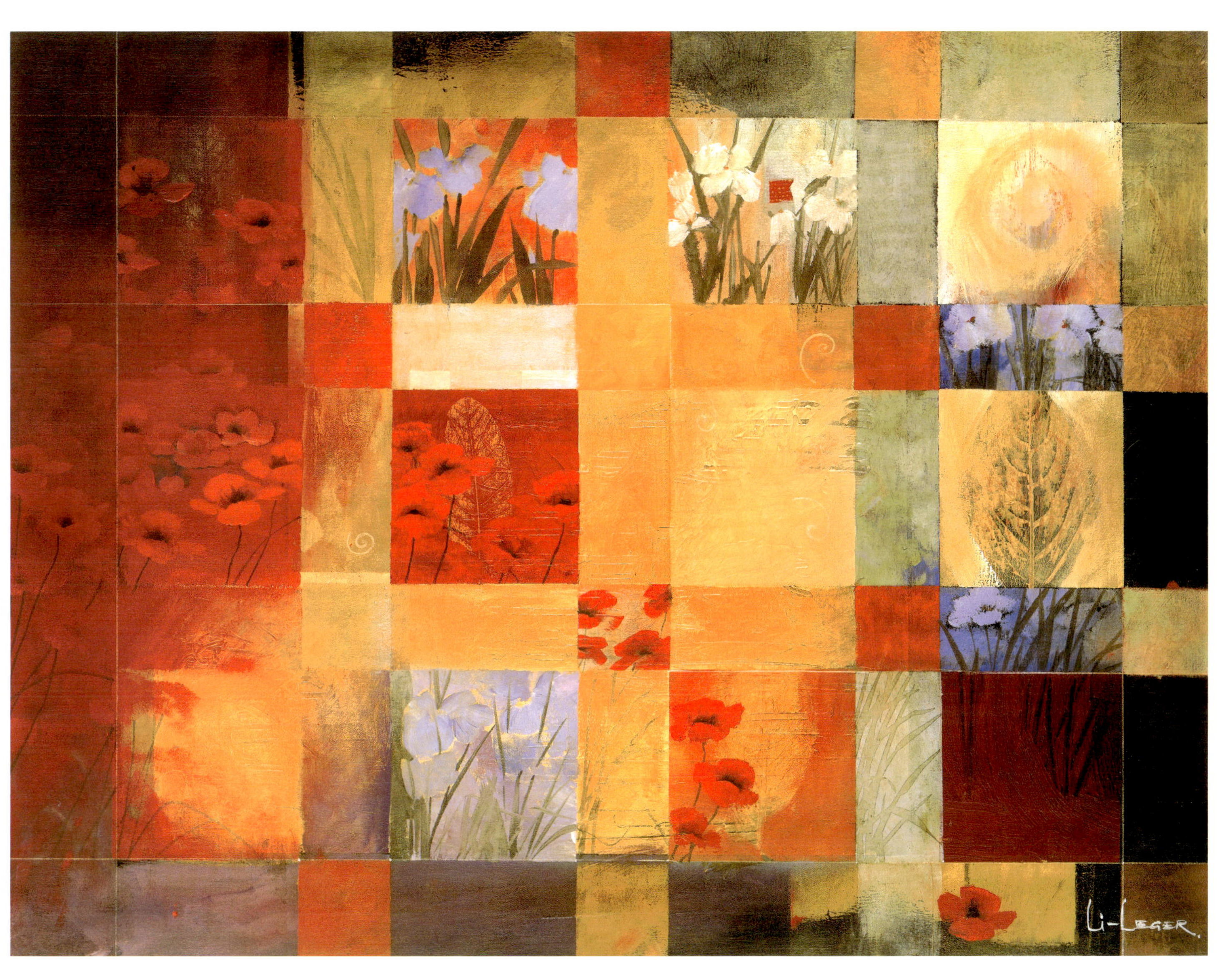

42 Views of my Garden
Acrylic on canvas
30" x 40", 2004
Collection of the Artist

Color is all. When color is right, form is right. Color is everything, color is vibration like music; everything is vibration.

— MARC CHAGALL

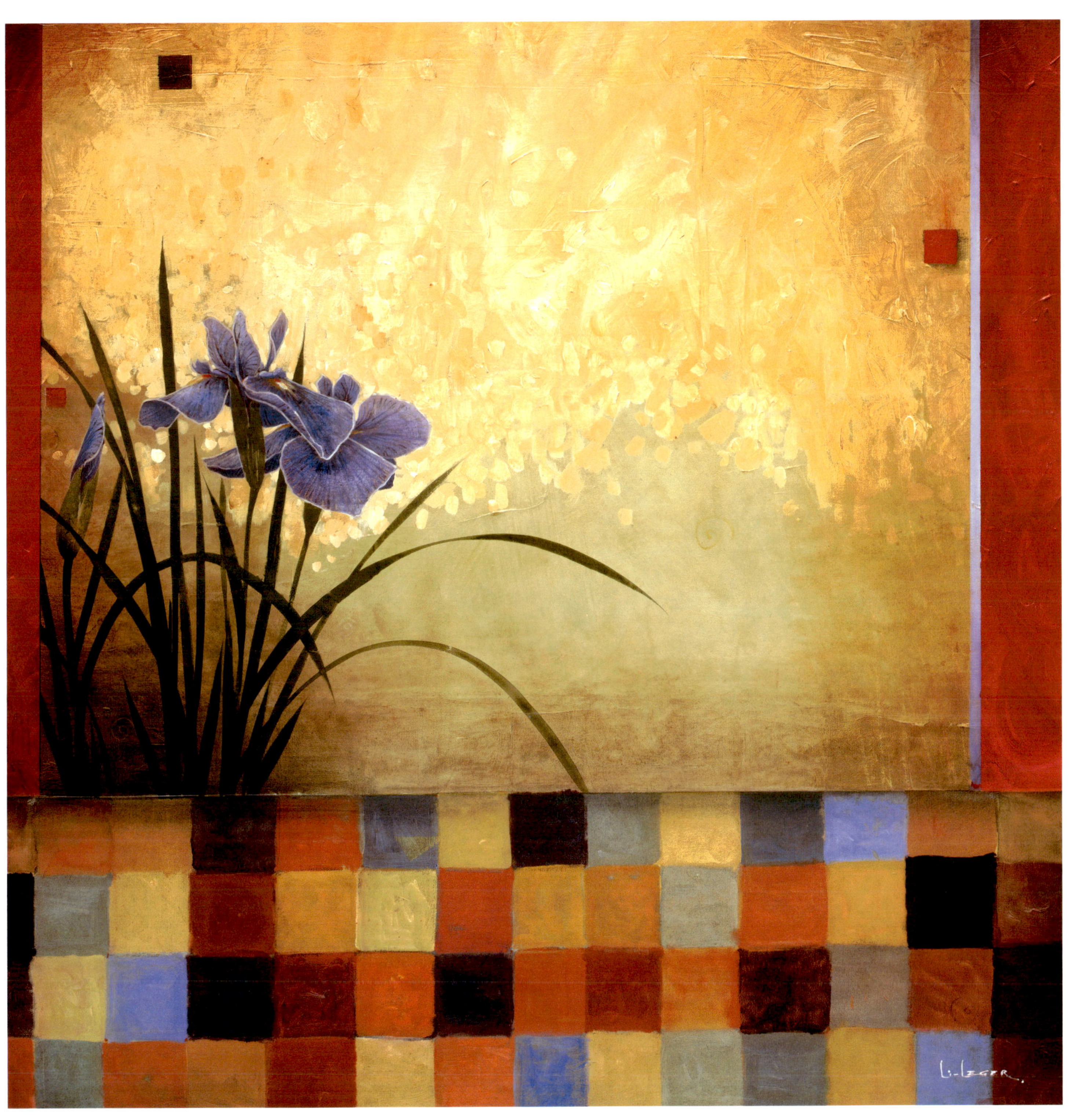

Iris Quilt
Acrylic on canvas
54" x 54", 2002
Collection of the Artist

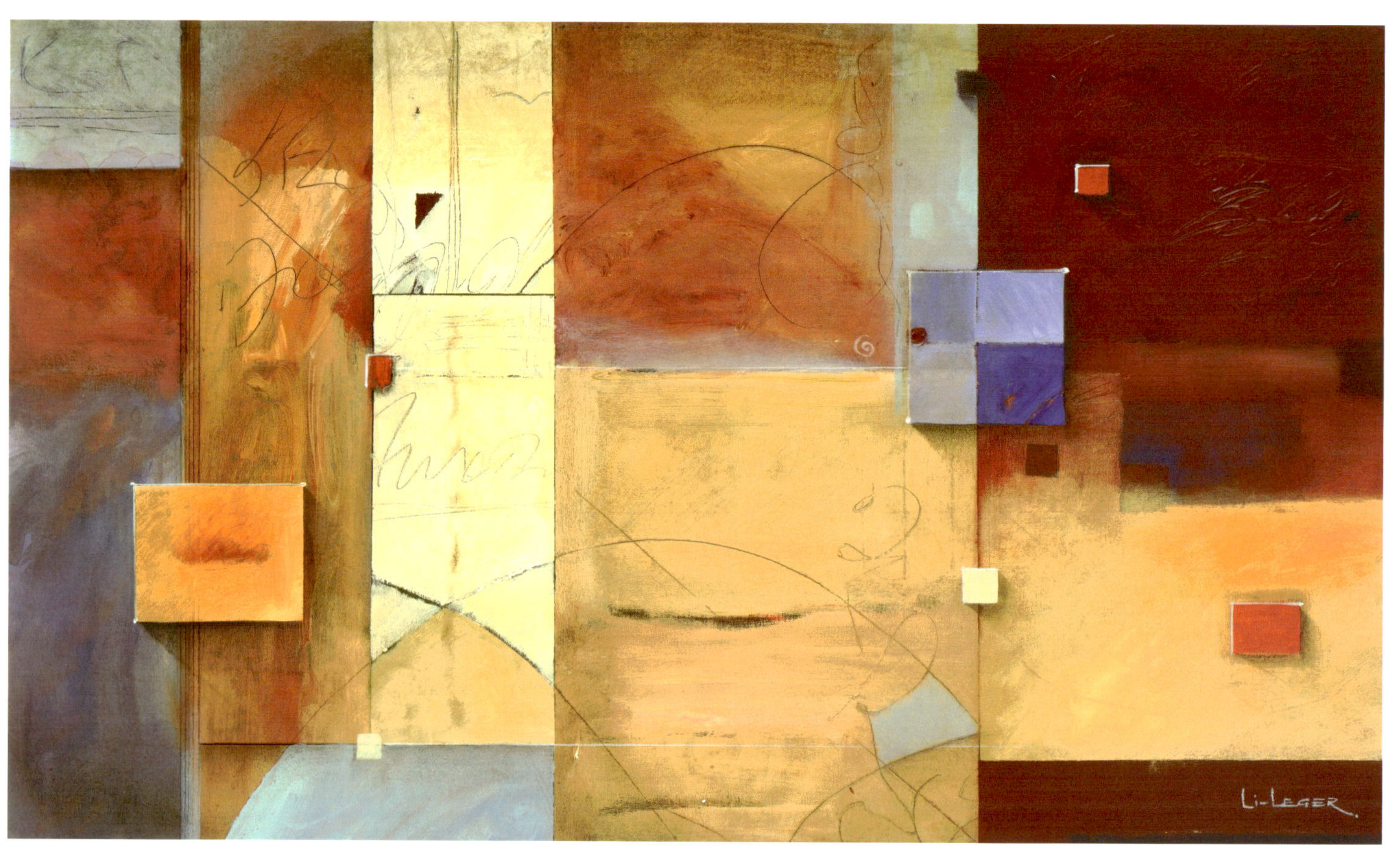

Poet's Cause
Acrylic on canvas
24" x 36", 2003
Private Collection

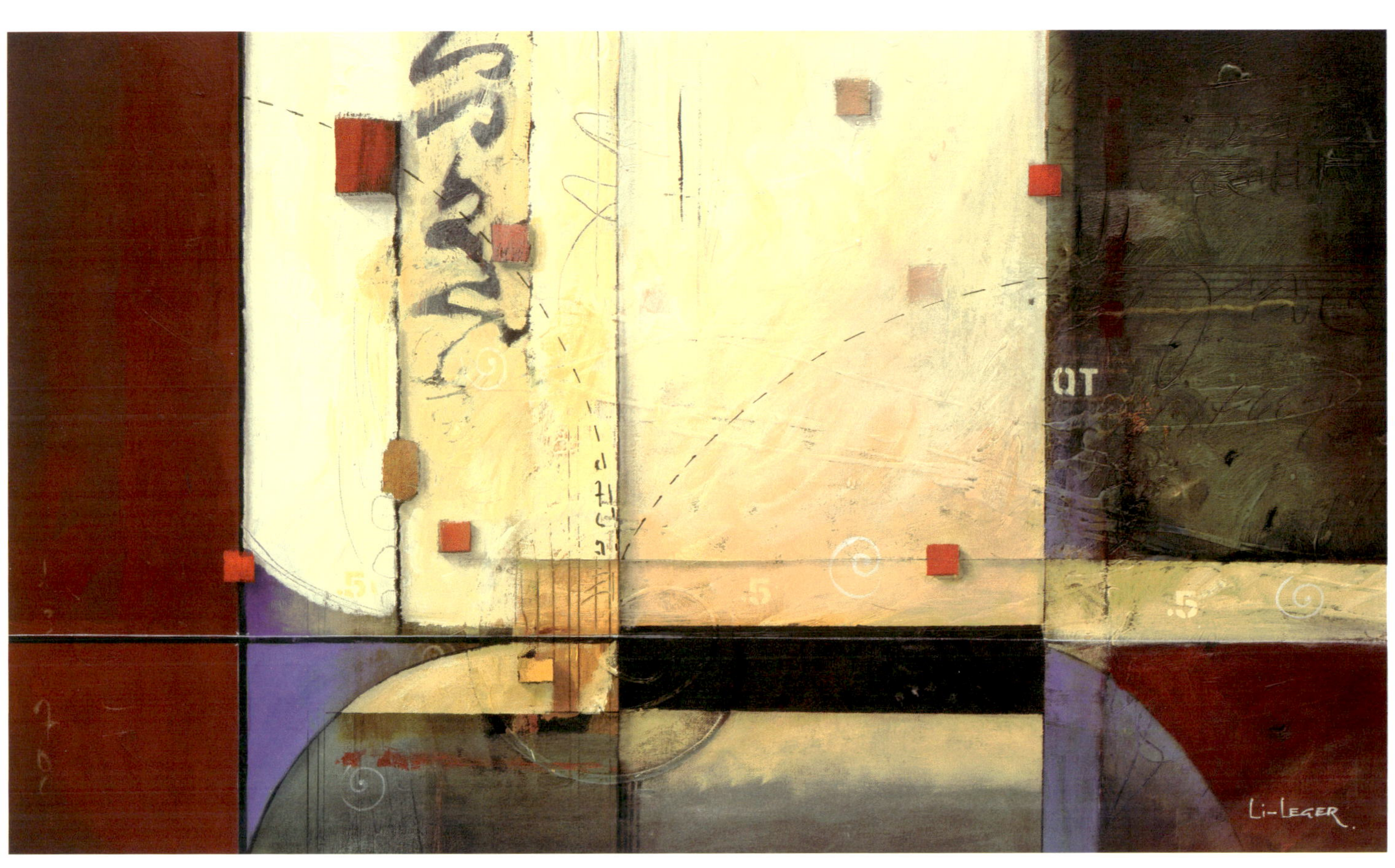

Ocean Voyage
Acrylic on canvas
24" x 36", 2003
Private Collection

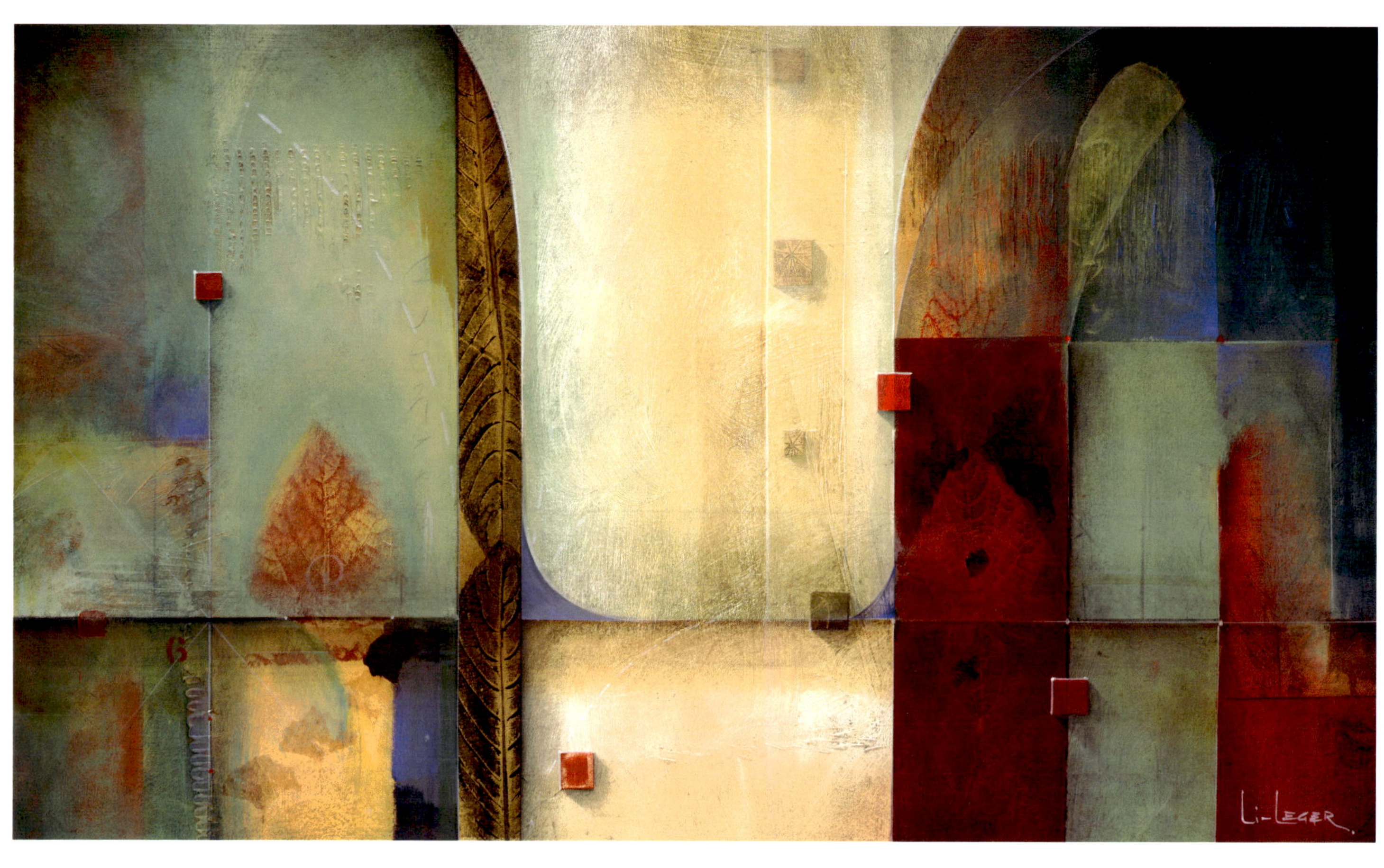

Orchestration
Acrylic on canvas
24" x 40", 2003
Collection of the Artist

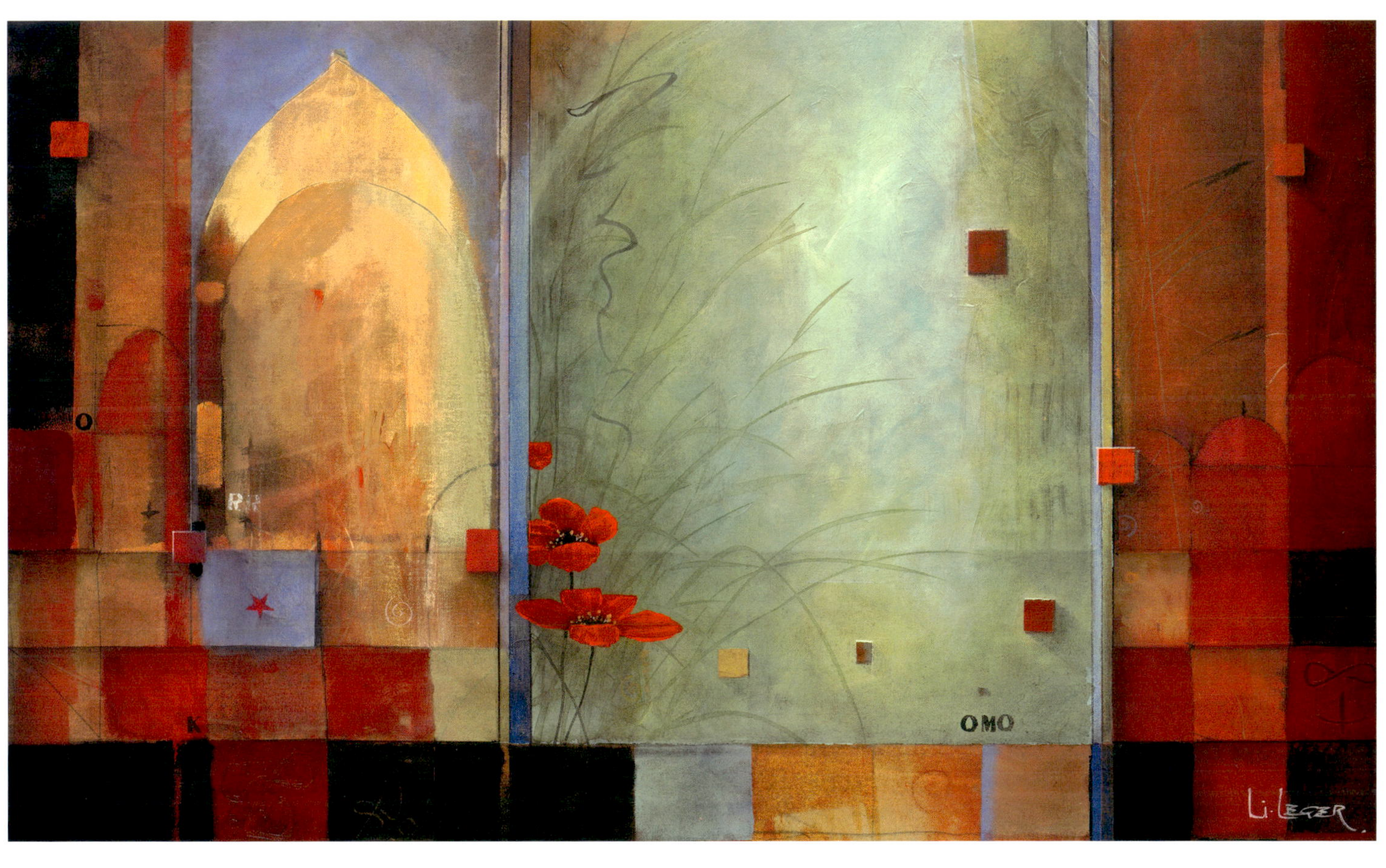

Passage to India
Acrylic on canvas
24" x 40", 2003
Collection of Gary
and Claire Conrad

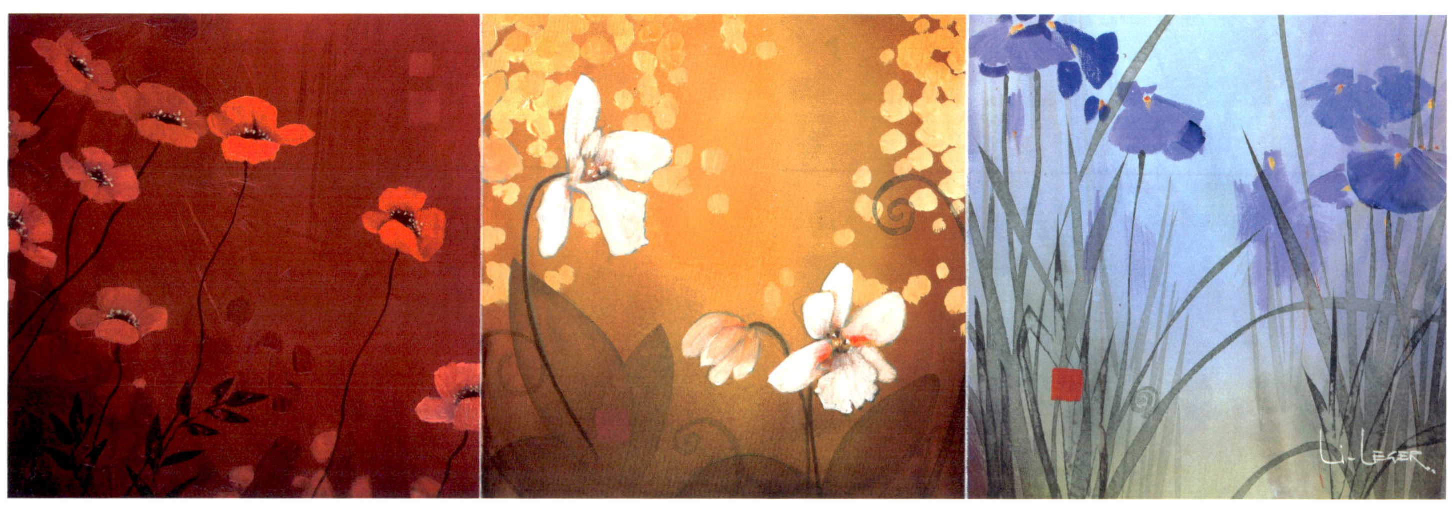

Serene Dream
Acrylic on canvas
16" x 48", 2003
Collection of
Alan and Carmela Chan

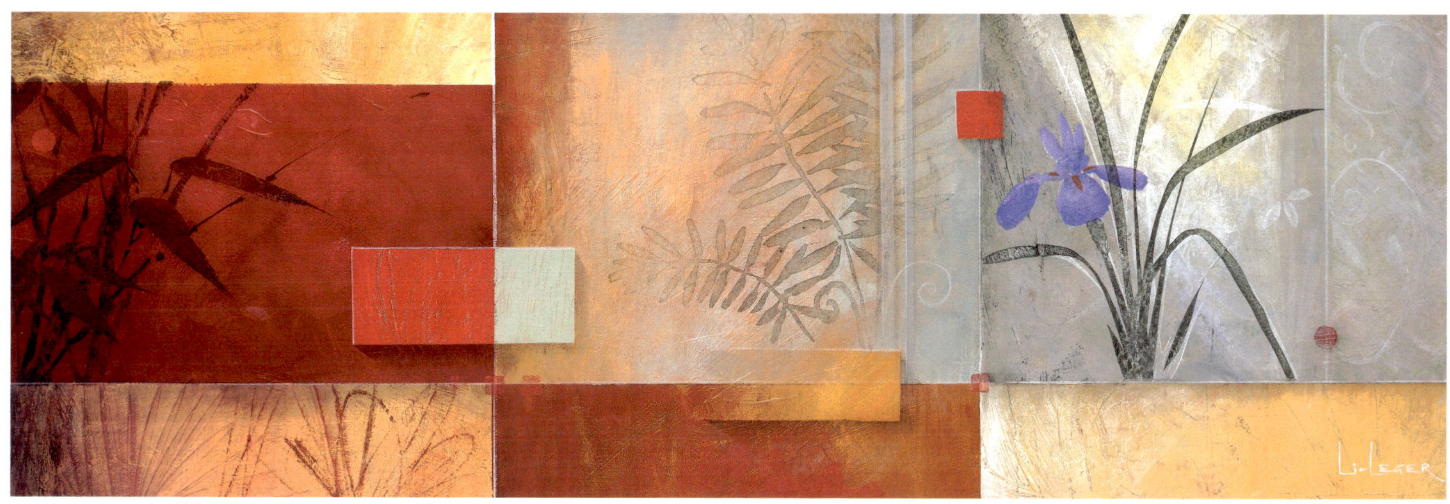

Niki's Spa
Acrylic on canvas
16" x 48", 2004
Courtesy of
Canada House Gallery

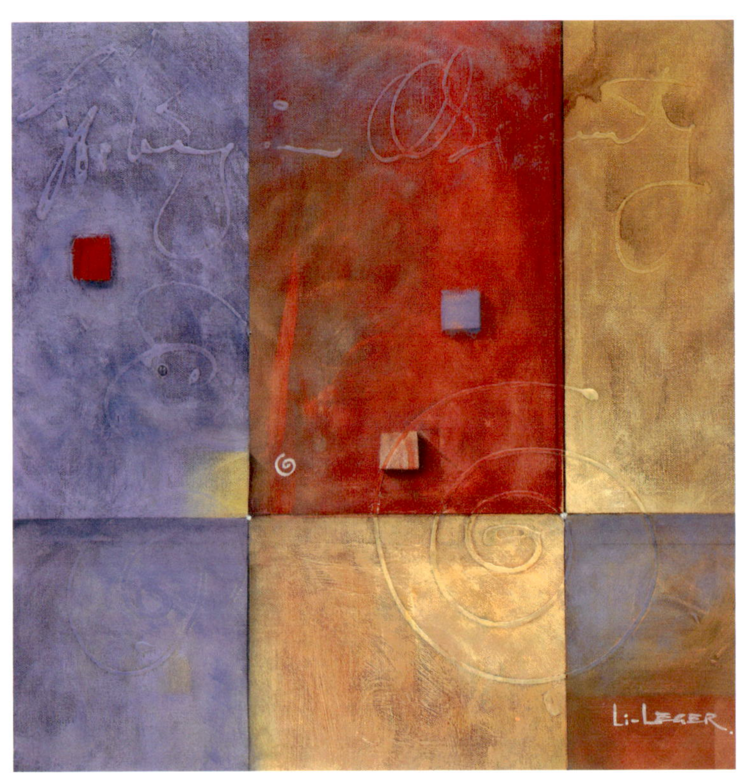

Water Garden II
Acrylic on canvas
24" x 24", 2003
Private Collection

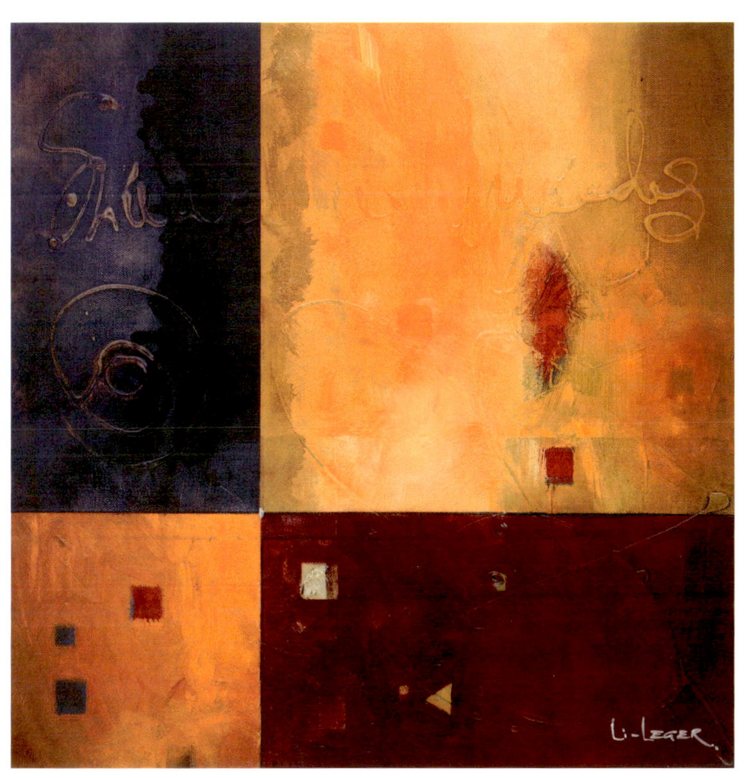

Water Garden I
Acrylic on canvas
24" x 24", 2003
Private Collection

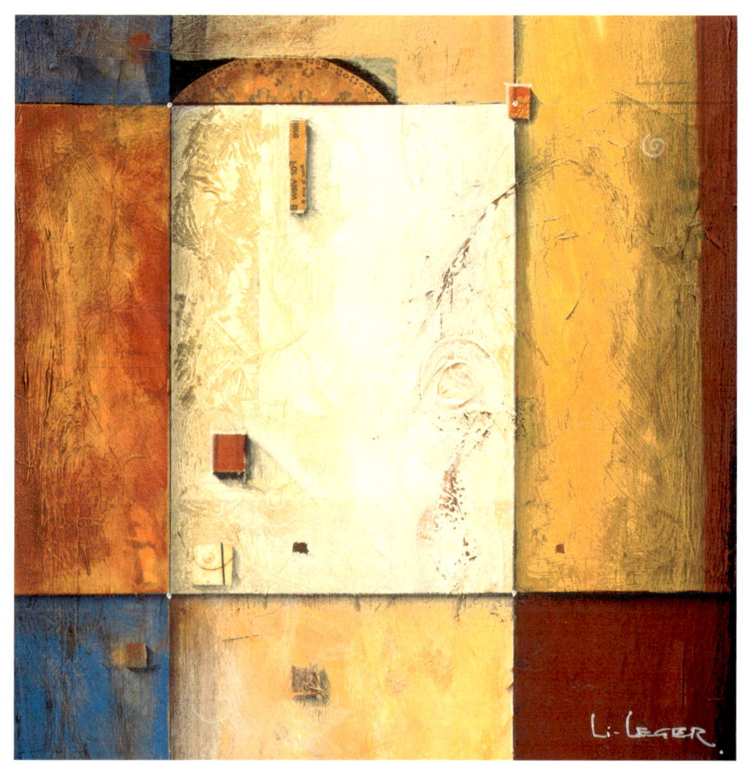

Antiquities
Acrylic on canvas
24" x 24", 2003
Private Collection

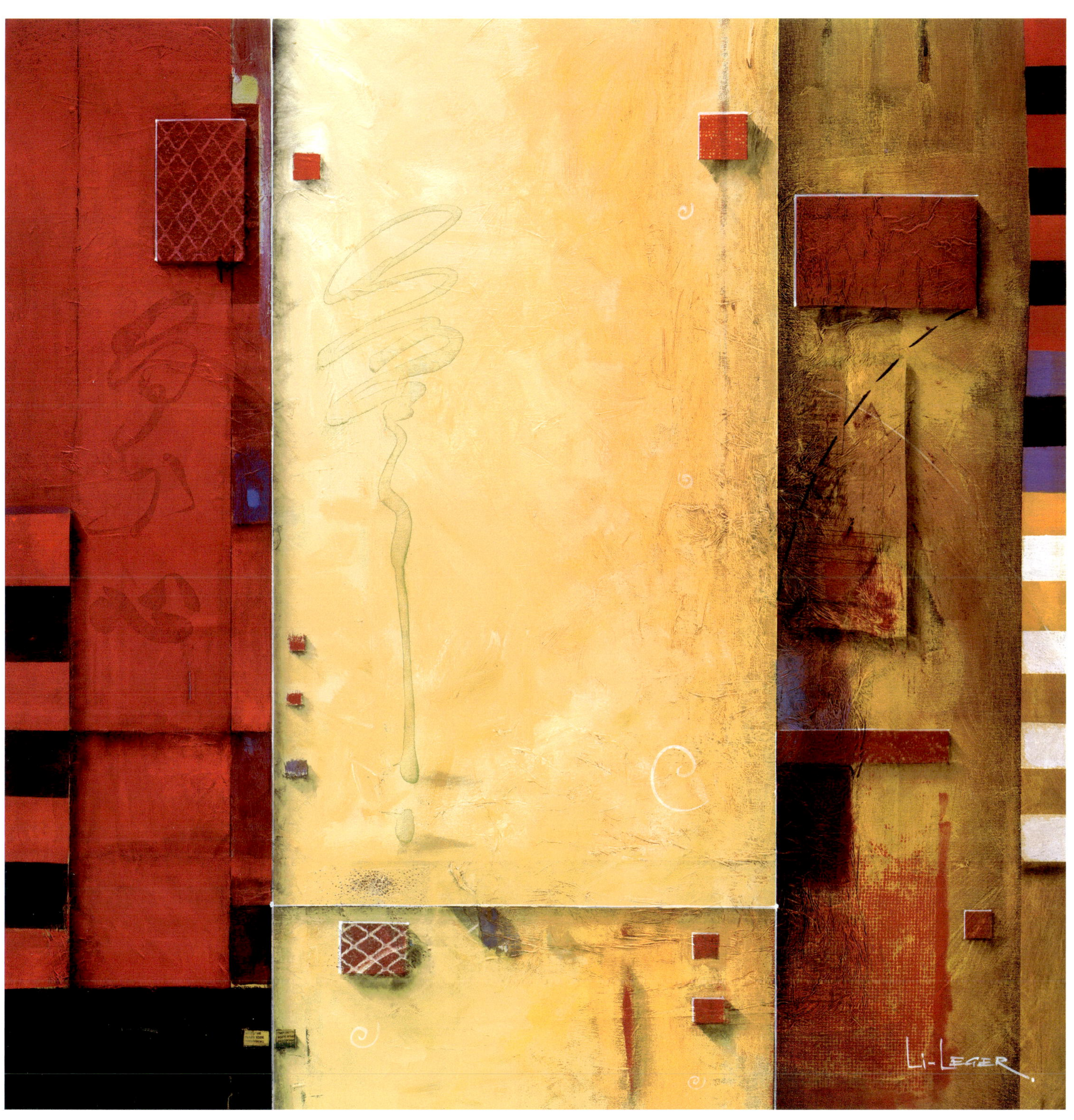

Joie de Vie
Acrylic on canvas
40" x 40", 2003
Private Collection

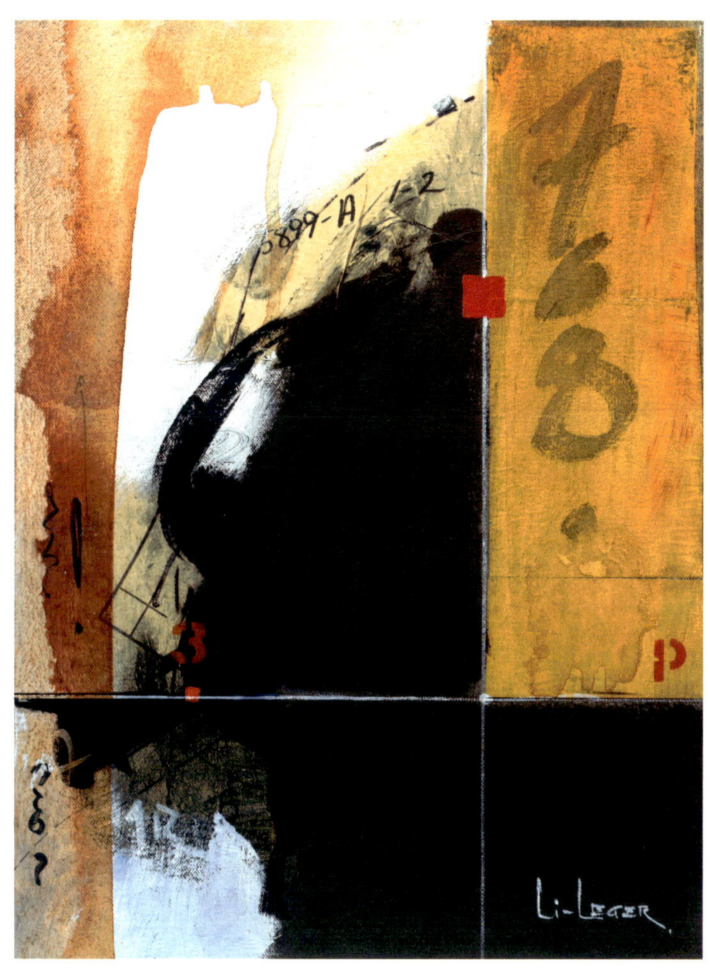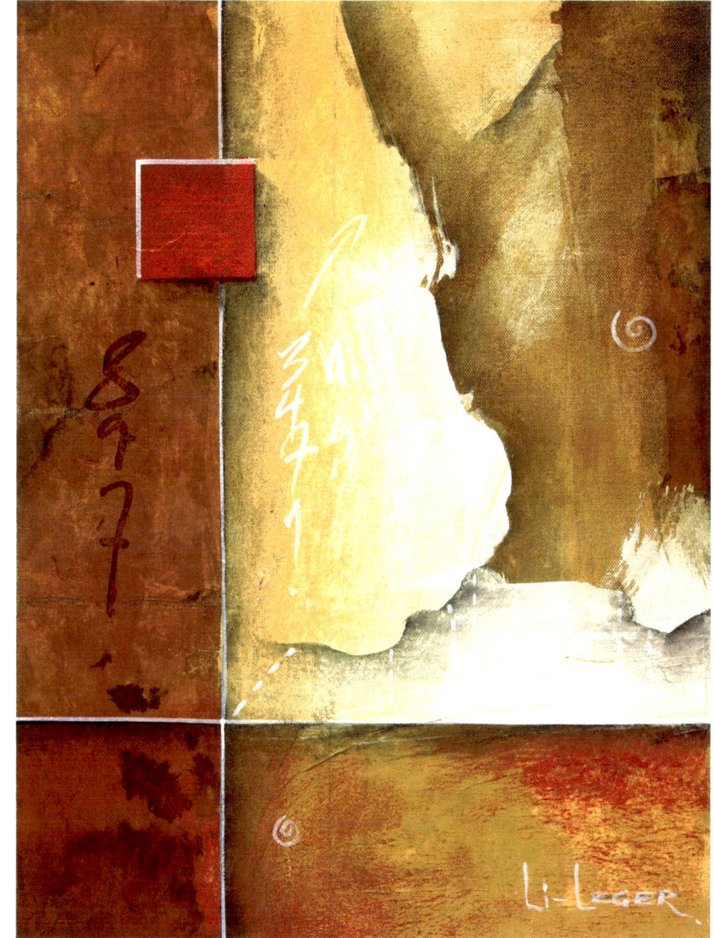

Intention
Acrylic on canvas
16" x 12", 2003
Collection of the Artist

Pompeii Patterns
Acrylic on canvas
16" x 12", 2003
Courtesy Canada House
Gallery

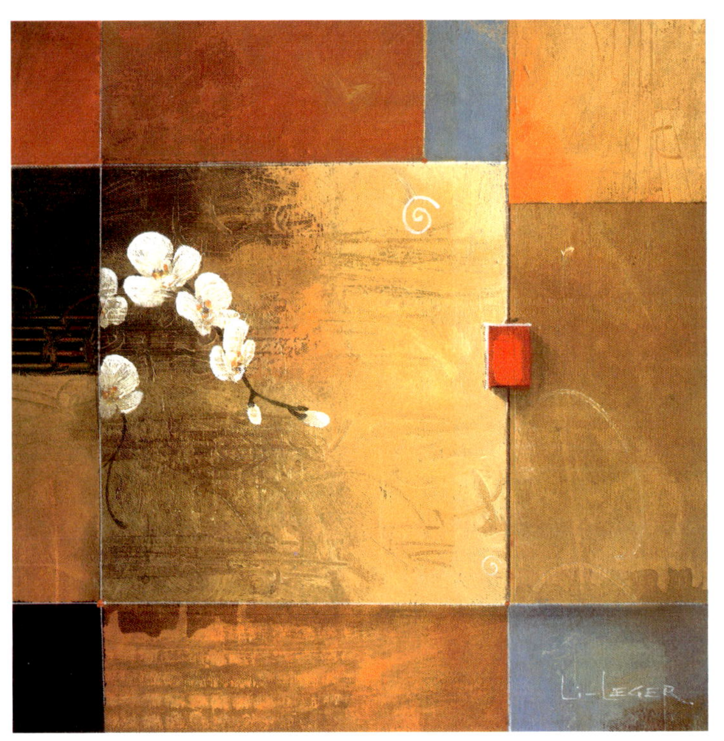 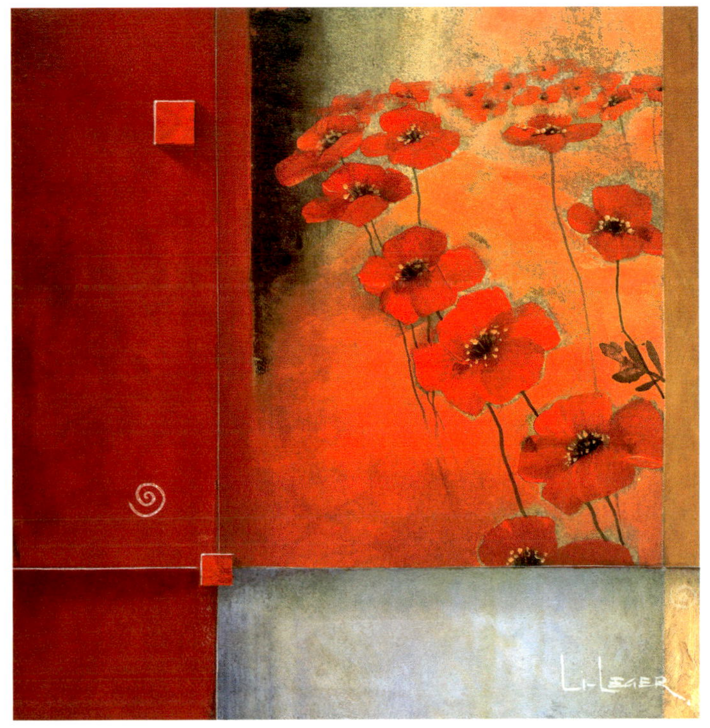

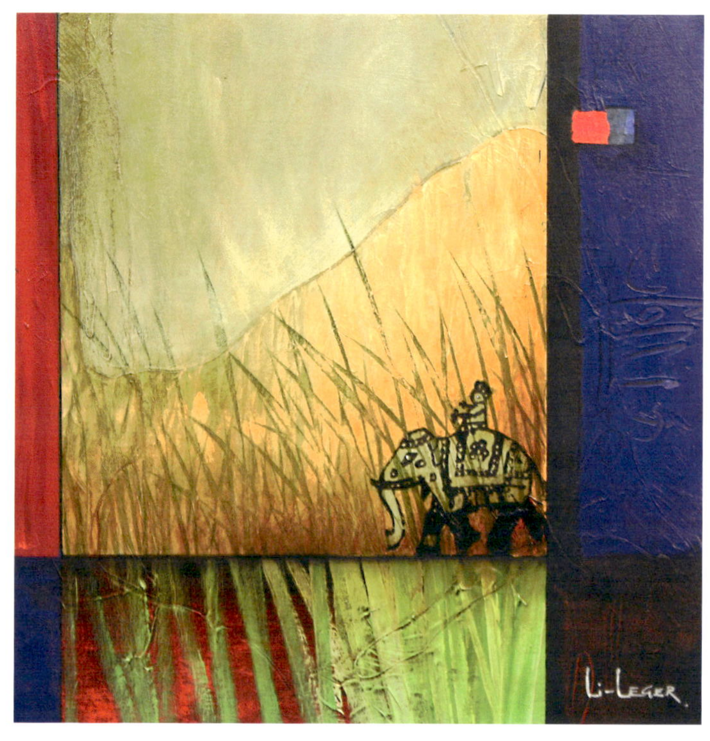

**More Travels with
Ganesh**

Acrylic on canvas
24" x 24", 2004
Collection of
Steve Wiseman
and Leslie Wicholas

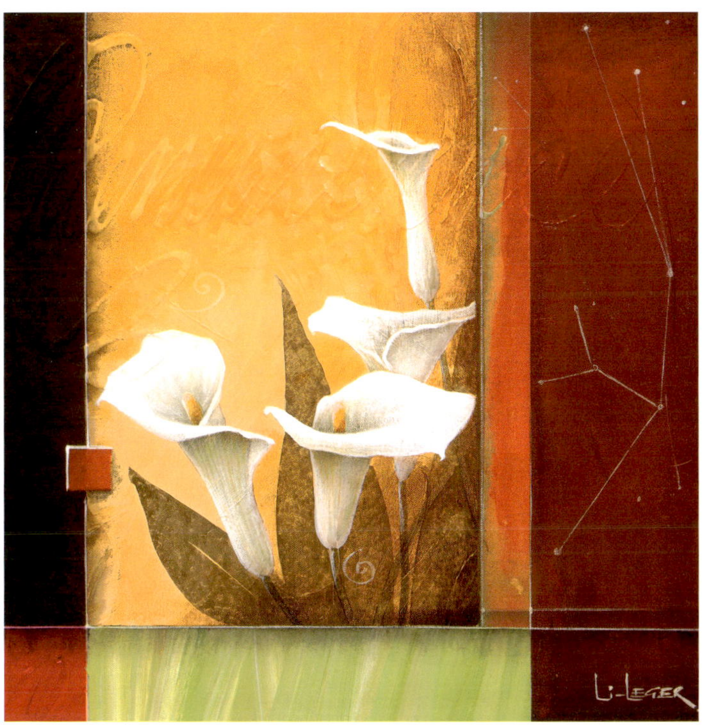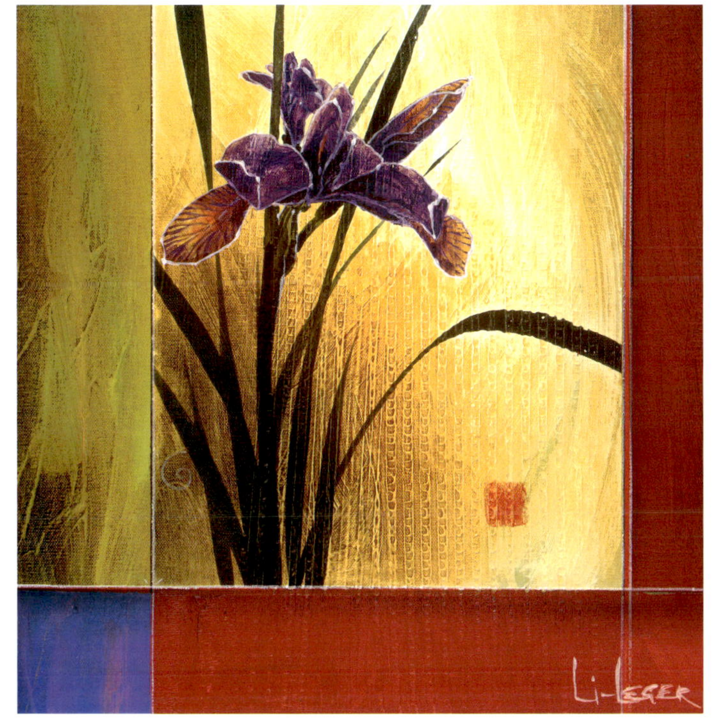

Reminiscence
Acrylic on canvas
16" x 16", 2004
Private Collection

Iris Interlude
Acrylic on canvas
16" x 16", 2004
Collection of
Arefeh Rouhi

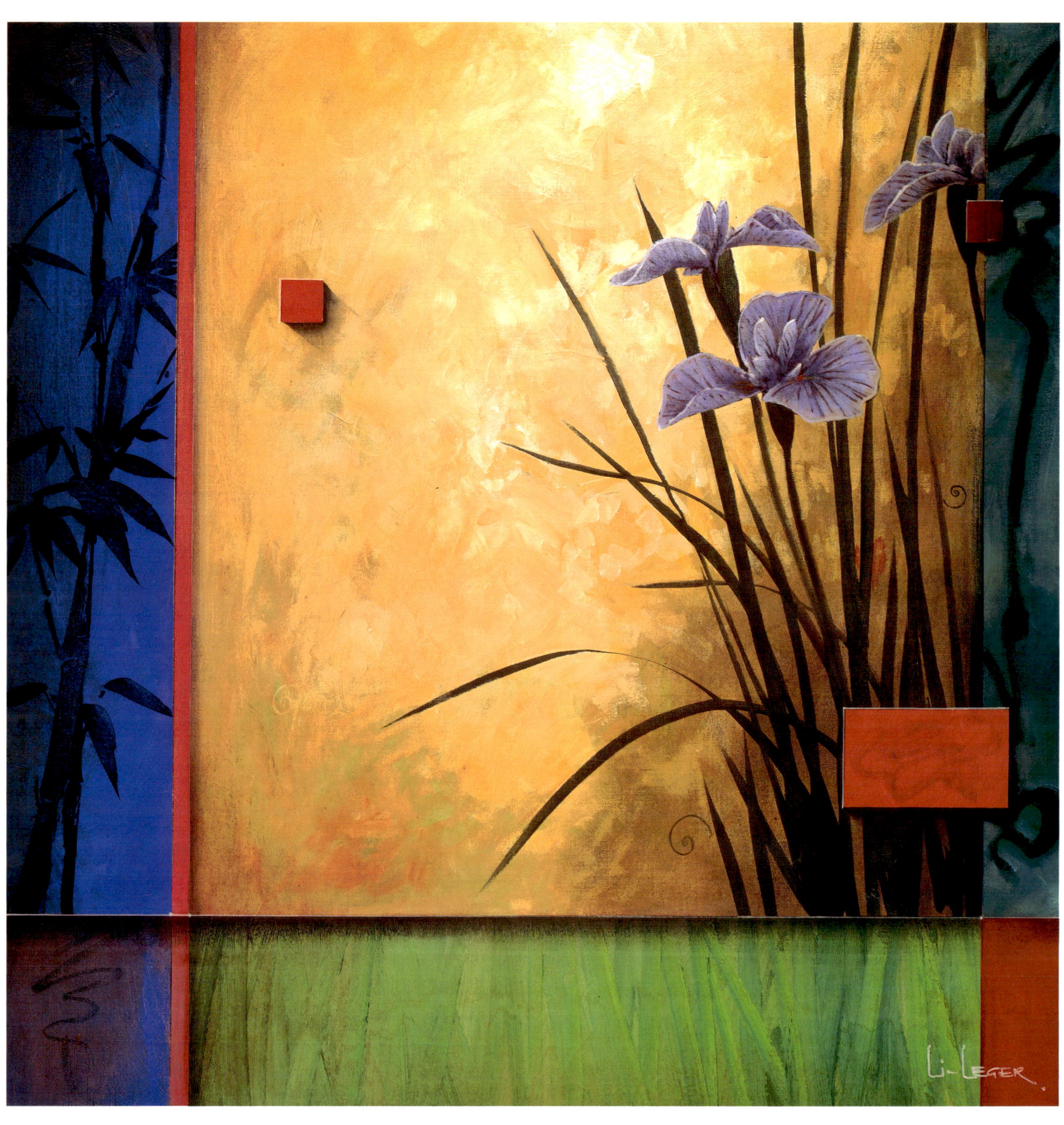

Japanese Iris Garden
Acrylic on canvas
40" x 40", 2004
Courtesy of
White Rock Gallery

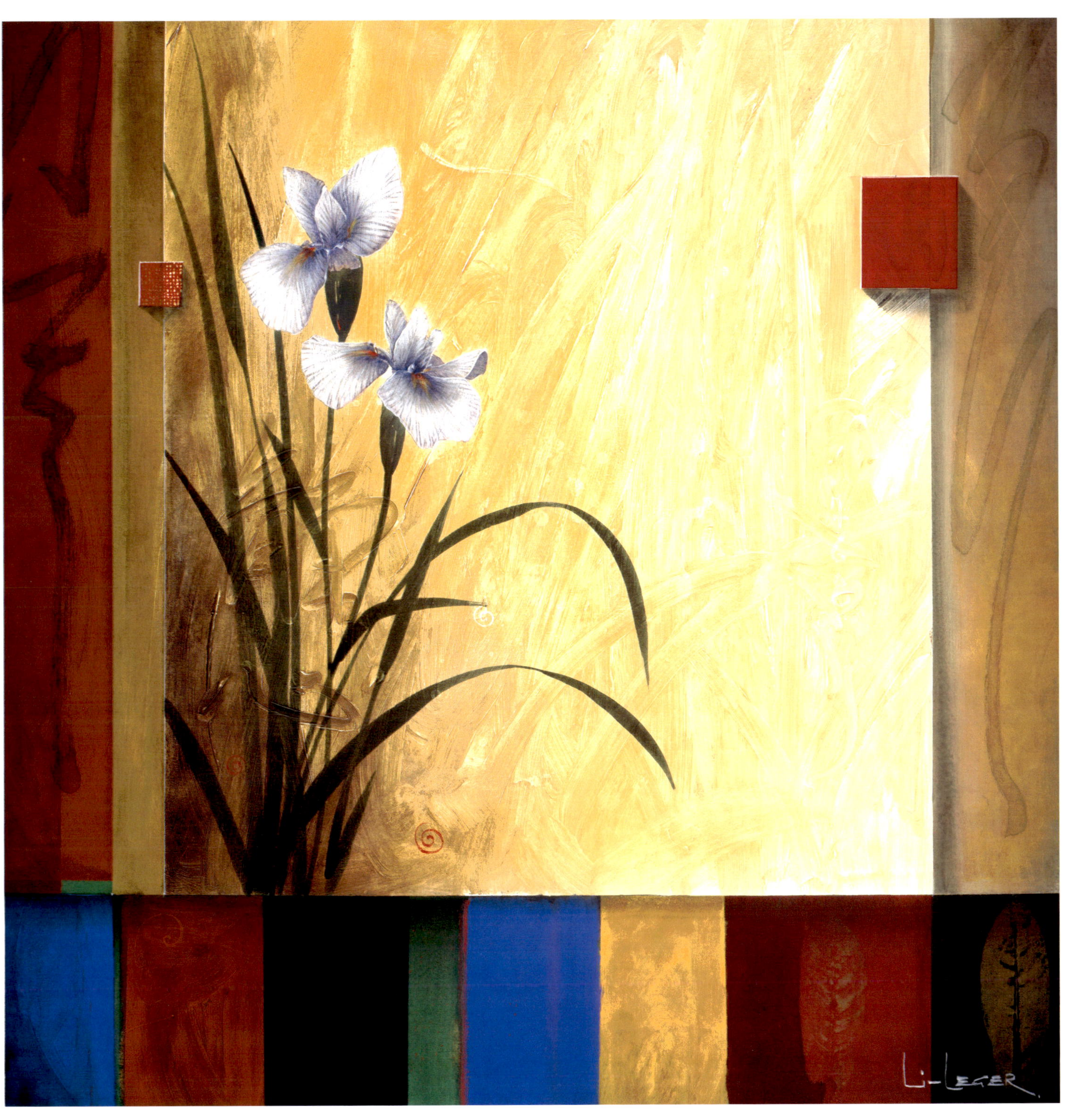

Meditation Iris
Acrylic on canvas
40" x 40", 2004
Collection of Justin
and Julia Tee

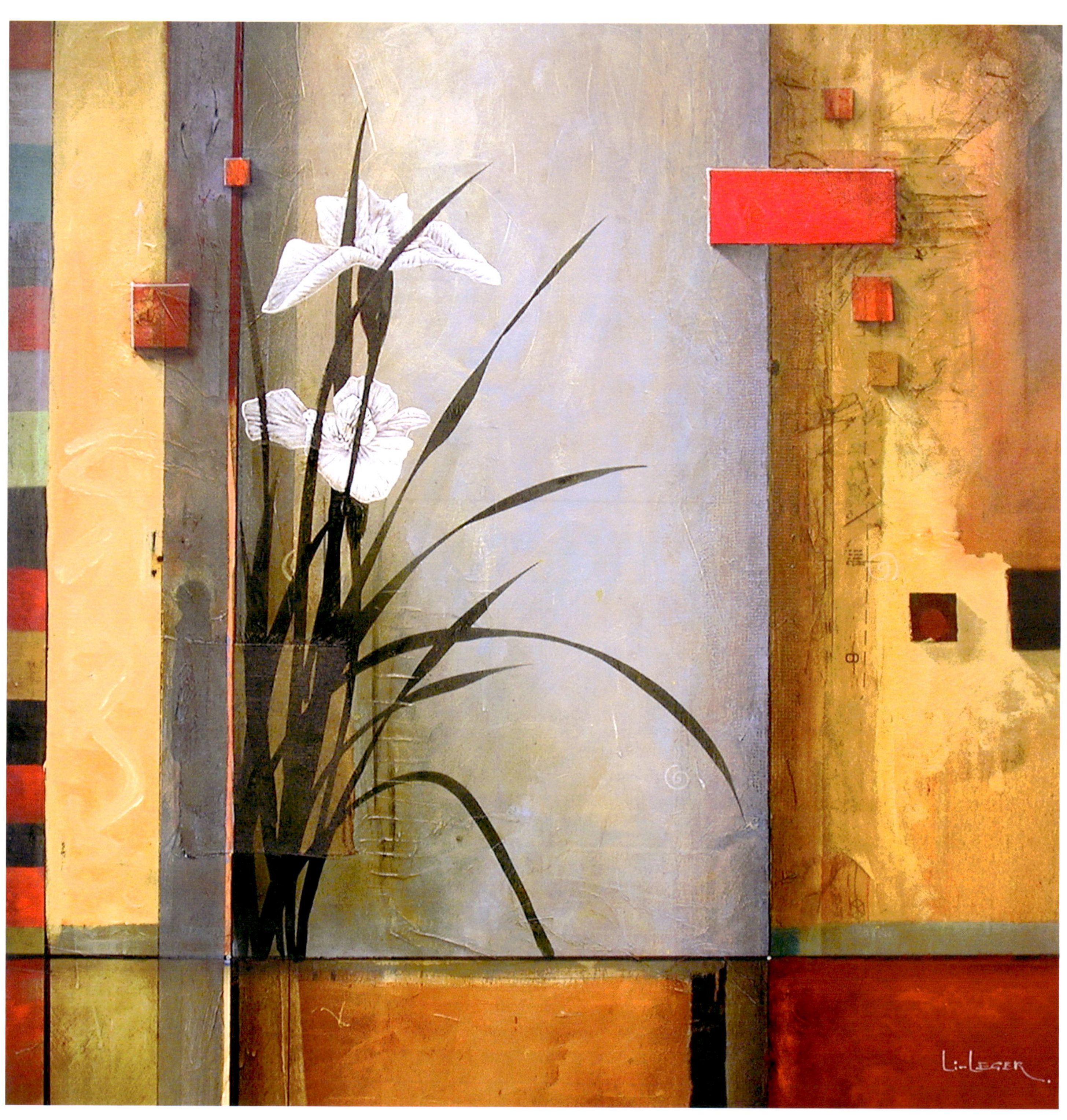

Open Window Irises
Acrylic on canvas
40" x 40", 2002
Private Collection

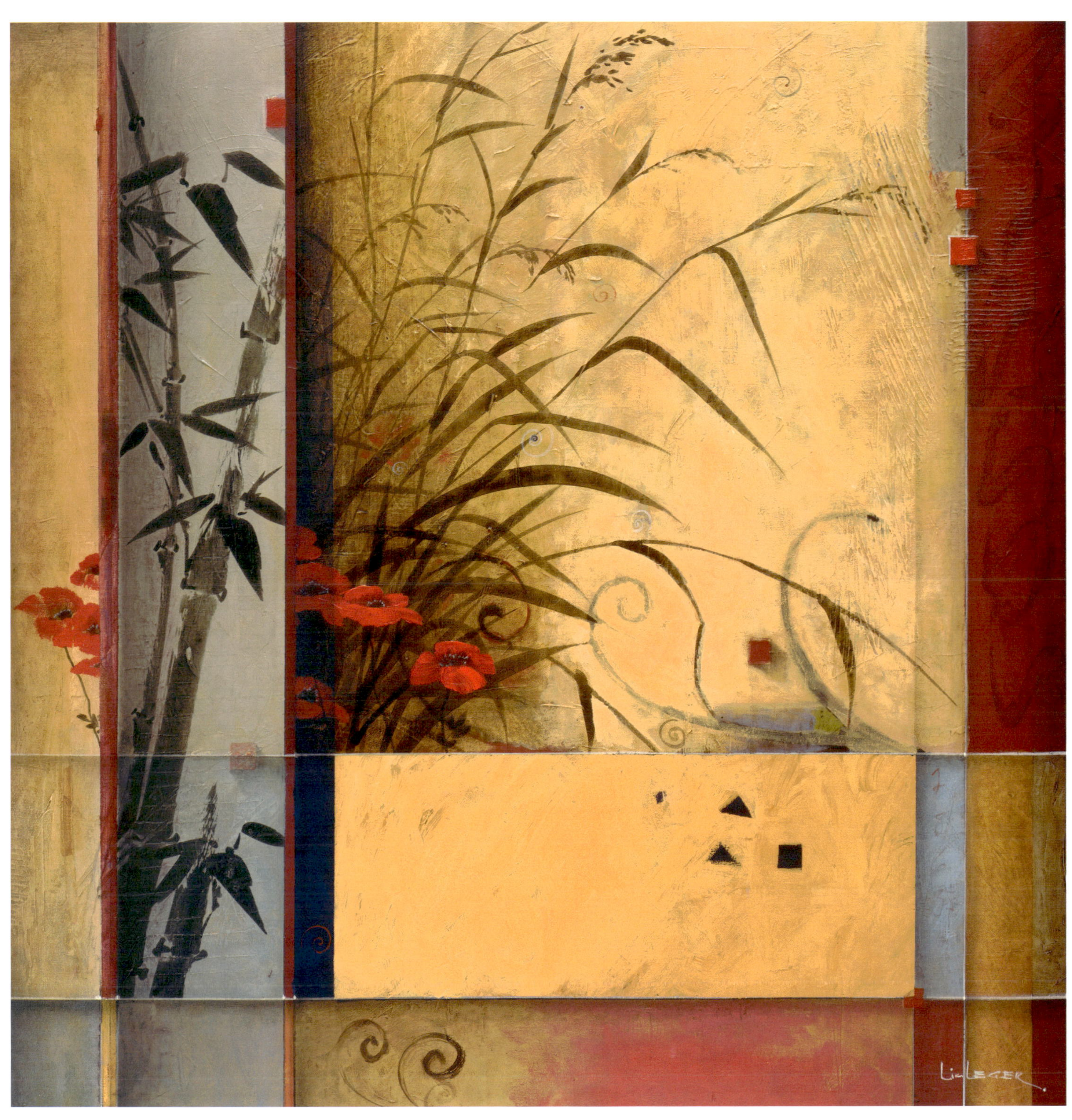

Bamboo Division
Acrylic on canvas
40" x 40", 2001
Private Collection

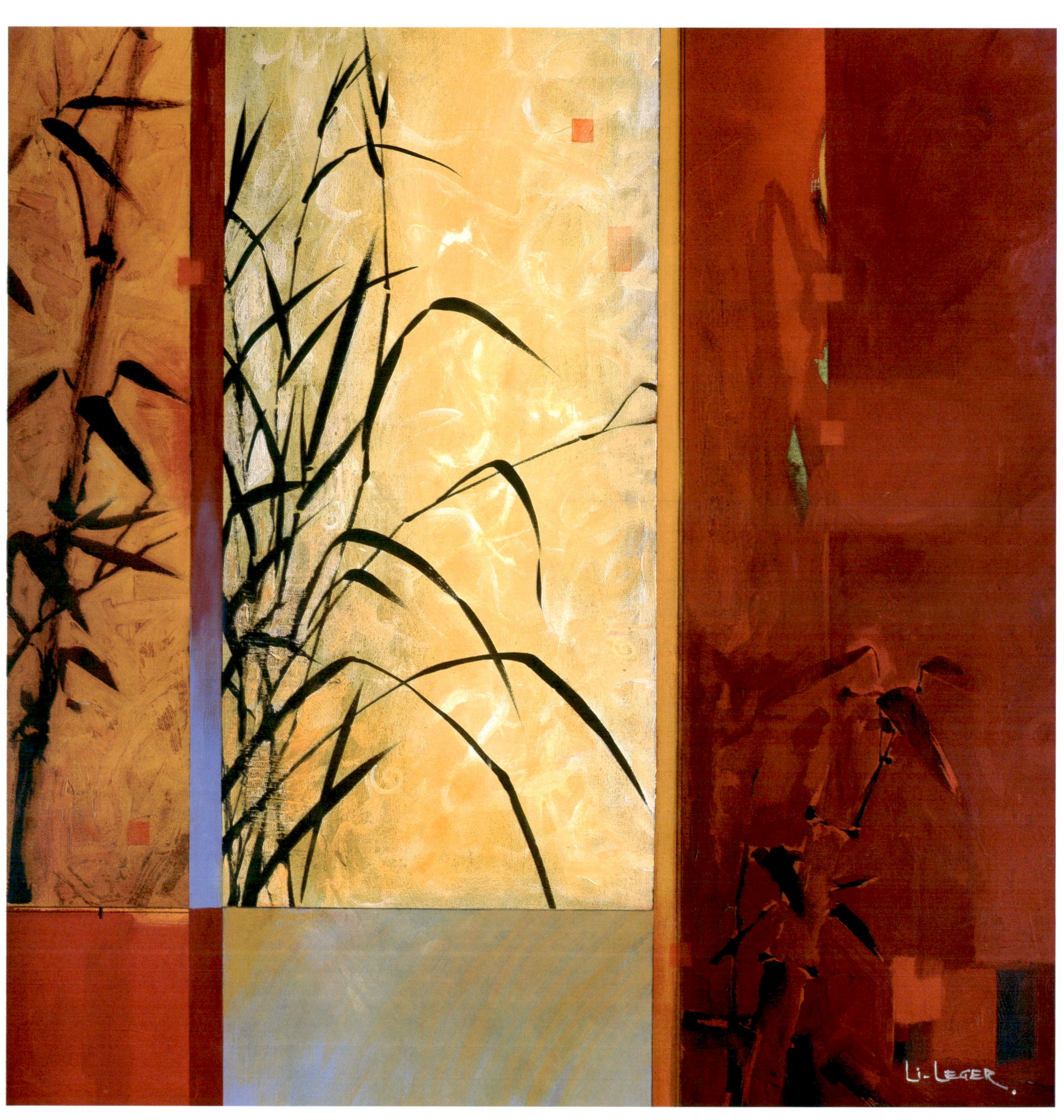

Bamboo Garden
Acrylic on canvas
40" x 40", 2002
Private Collection

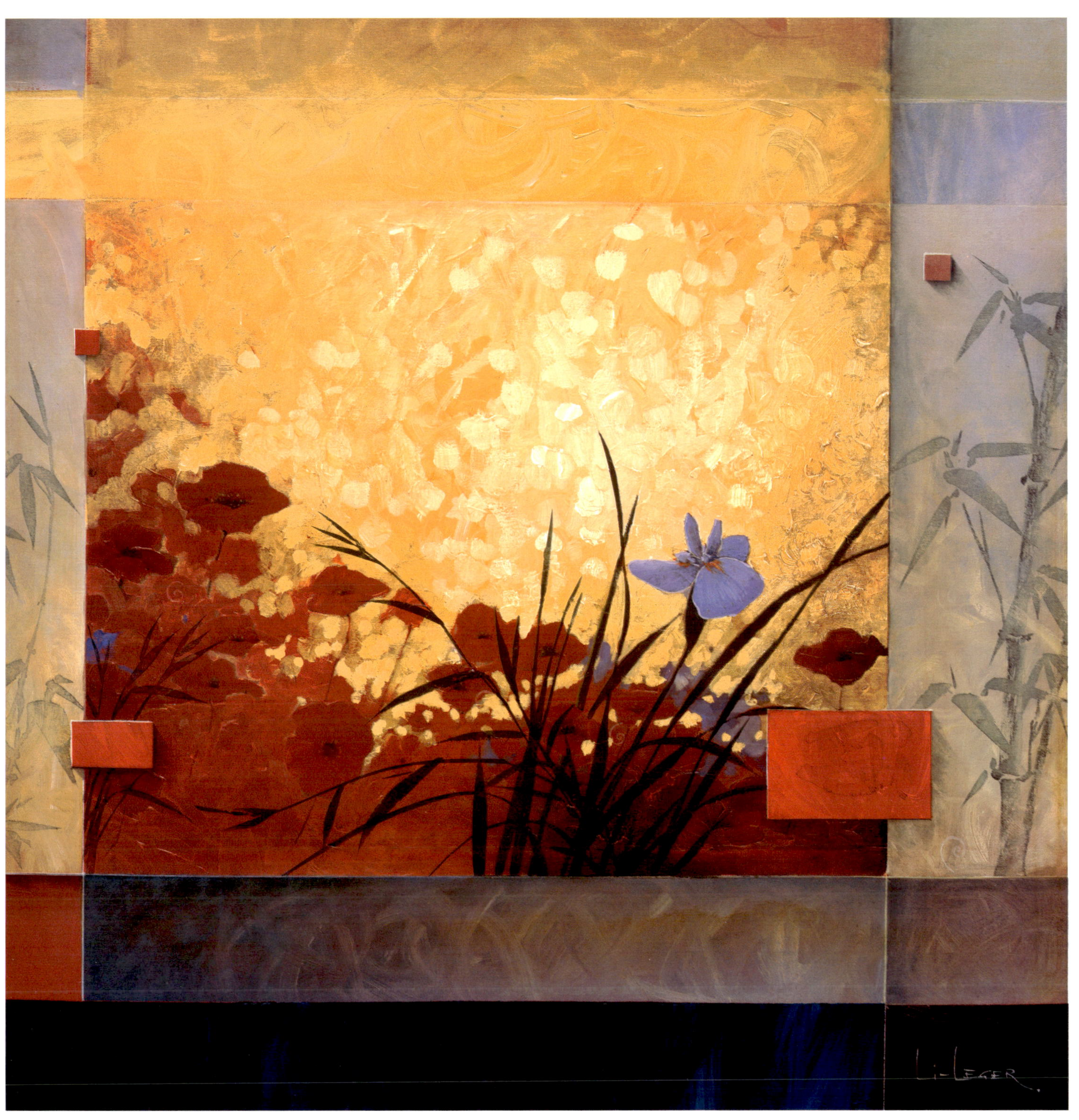

Singing Garden
Acrylic on canvas
40" x 40", 2004
Collection of Paul
and Susan Sugarman

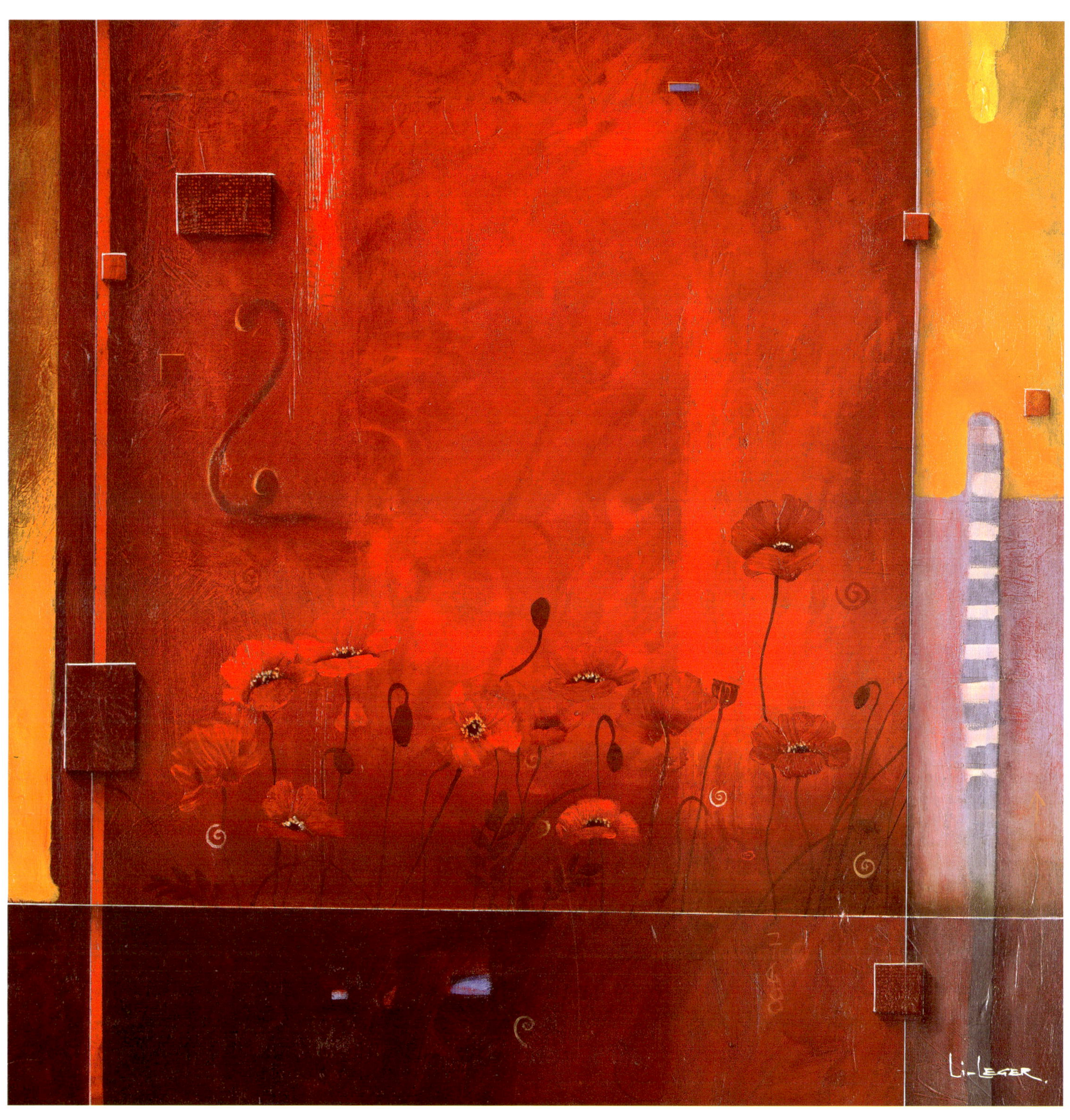

Le Rêve Rouge de Jardin
Acrylic on canvas
40" x 40", 2003
Collection of
Cora Li-Leger

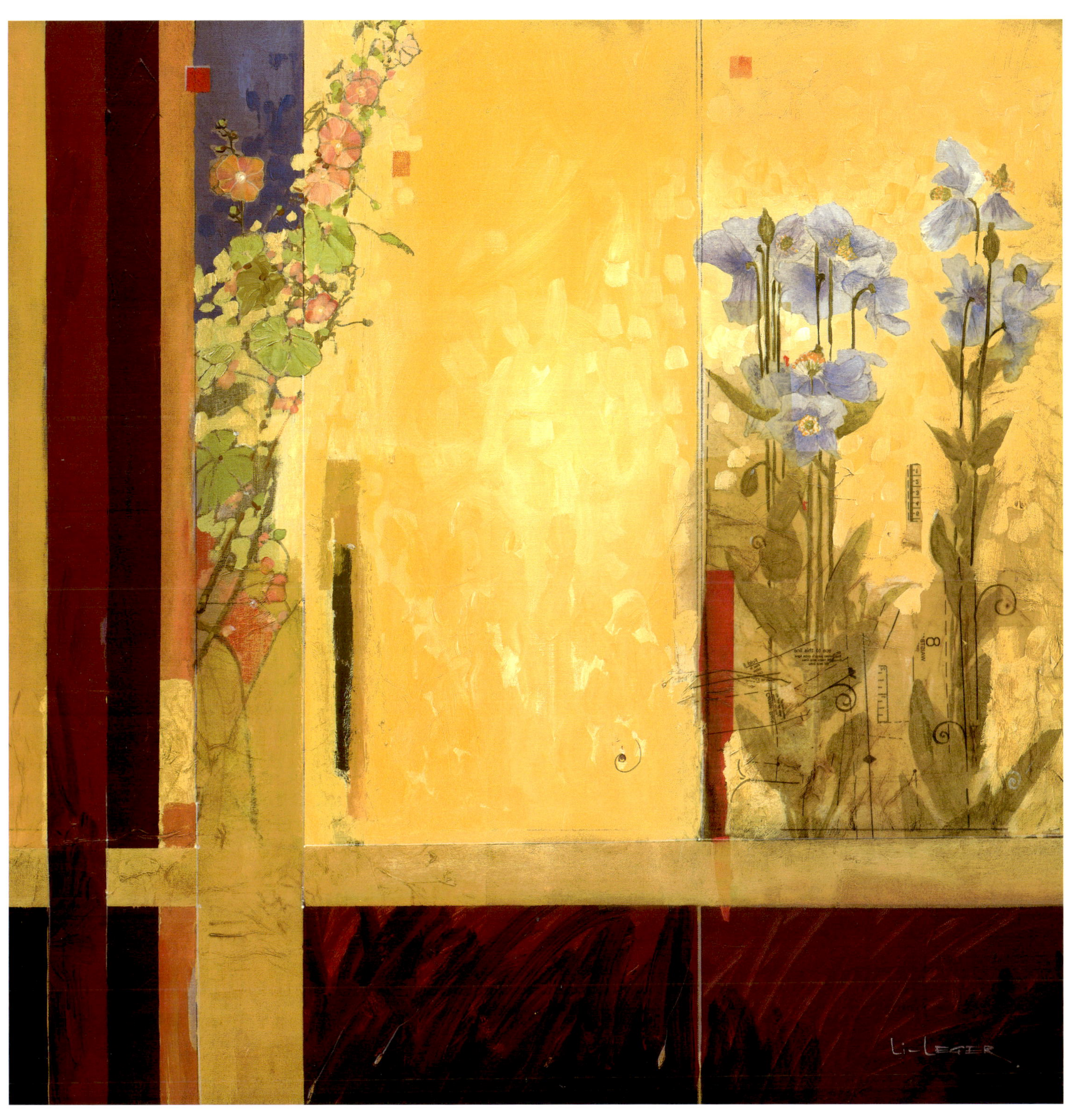

Himalayan Memory
Acrylic on canvas
40" x 40", 2002
Private Collection

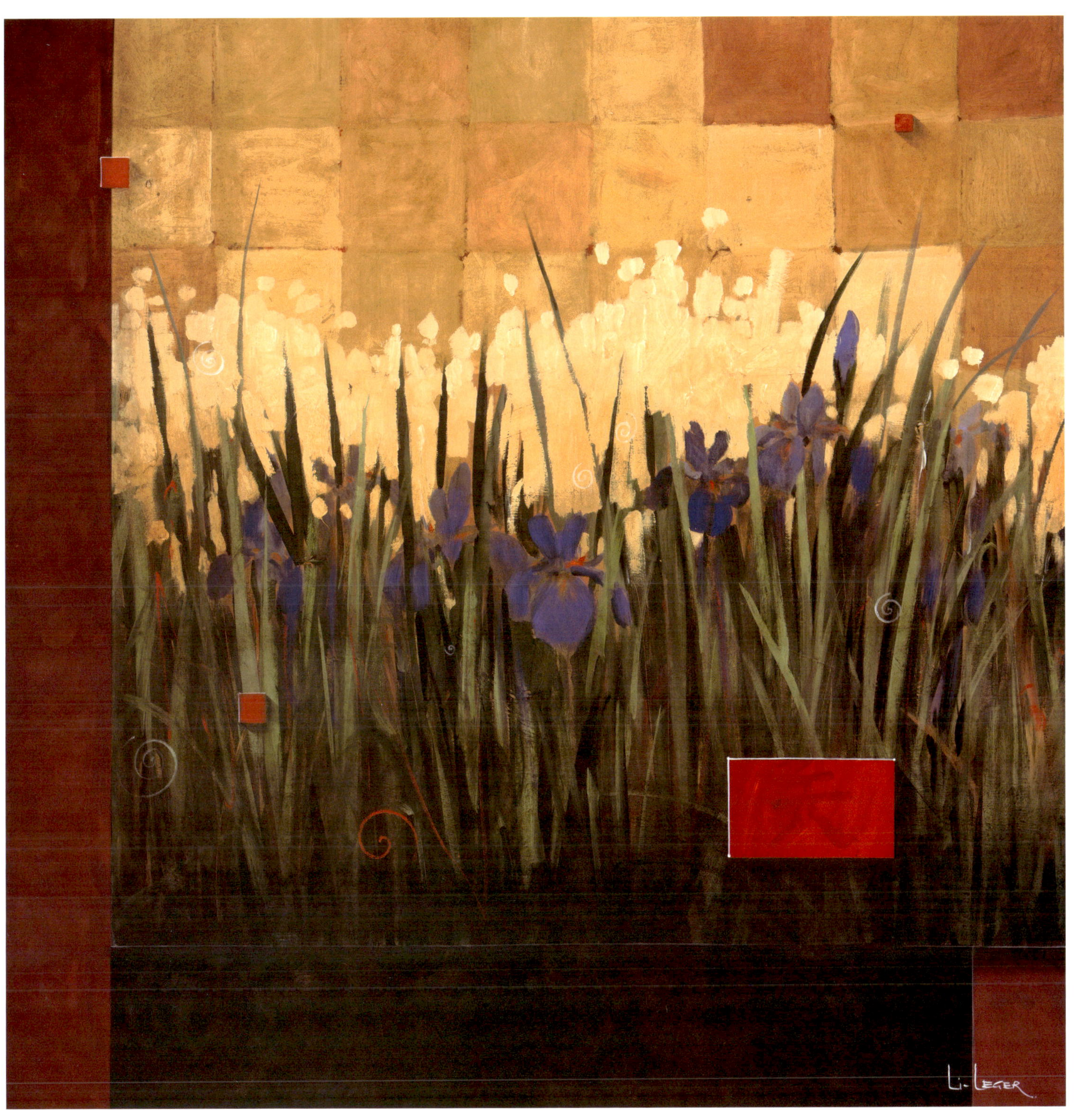

The Heavenly Art
of Gardening
Acrylic on canvas
54" x 54", 2003
Private Collection

1948   Donald Stephen Leger born in North Vancouver, British Columbia.

Father Alfred Leger owned a cement factory. Mother Marie Leger, a registered nurse, painted as a hobby.

1954-66   Family moved to Maple Ridge, BC. Attended public school.

1966   Before graduating from high school, hitchhiked with a schoolmate across Canada, working at odd jobs such as picking tobacco in Ontario. Saved enough money to travel on to Europe for 3 months.

1969-70   Studied painting at the Vancouver School of Art, Vancouver, BC.

Studied brush painting with a Chinese Master in Vancouver.

1971   Traveled around the world, visiting Europe and Asia.

Spent time in India. Began to study Hindu philosophy and practice meditation. Began to paint in a surrealist style.

1972-75   Studied biology and plant ecology at Simon Fraser University, Burnaby, BC.

Did field work for Environmental Research Consultants.

Became interested in drawing and painting from nature.

1975   Studied painting with Terry Frost at the Banff Centre School of Fine Arts, Banff, Alberta. Met Cora Li, an art student from the United States…three weeks later married and moved to the Okanagan Valley in the Interior of British Columbia.

1976-77   Studied bird illustration with Frank Beebe, a retired natural history artist for the BC Provincial Museum.

Studied intaglio printing at Okanagan College, Kelowna, BC.

1978   Moved to Victoria, BC. Continued to develop detailed paintings from nature.

1980   Moved to Burke Mountain, near Vancouver, BC. Cultivated first flower garden.

Exhibited work at Marion Scott Gallery, Vancouver, BC.

Canadian Art Prints began to publish reproductions of paintings.

1981   Produced first serigraphs.

1981-89   Participated in numerous group and solo exhibitions throughout North America.

Traveled several times to Asia. Explored the countryside and looked at classical and contemporary Asian art, while visiting Taiwan, Hong Kong, China, and Japan. Met artists in China.

1984   Son Noah born.

1986   Daughter Erica born. Family moved to South Surrey, BC.

Cultivated a lush perennial garden with a small pond, from which images will be used in numerous works of art.

1988   Met Matt Petley-Jones. Began to exhibit work at the Petley Jones Gallery, Vancouver, BC.

1992   Produced first series of etchings through New Leaf Editions, Granville Island, Vancouver, BC; Elizabeth Tapper, Seattle, Washington; and Gina Chase in artist's studio.

1994   Traveled to France, Italy and Germany, studying master paintings in the major museums.

Made a pilgrimage to Murnau, Germany to see the works of Wassily Kandinsky, an important influence and inspiration.

1996-97   Served on the Public Art Policy
           Development Committee, Surrey, BC.

1997   Produced first monoprints, incorporating
           collage and found material in the imagery.

1998   Cora began to train as an art therapist. Don
           read about the approaches of art therapists
           London, McNiff and Nachmanovich, which
           inspired further spontaneous art exploration.

           Began to make improvisational paintings,
           combining bold saturated colour, ambigu-
           ous space, calligraphy, found objects and
           images from nature.

1999   Awarded grand prize, Daniel Smith
           Printmaking Competition, Seattle,
           Washington.

           Awarded first prize, Canadian Duck Stamp
           Competition, Ottawa, Ontario.

2000   Traveled in Catalonia, Spain. Particularly
           inspired by Antonio Gaudi's mosaics.

2001   Winn-Devon Art Group distributed paint-
           ings and reproductions throughout the
           United States.

2002   The Li-Leger's commissioned Ankenman
           Architects to build a new house on their
           South Surrey property, which incorporated
           the garden as an integral part of the living
           space. The garden was expanded and a
           larger pond developed. The garden contin-
           ued to provide sources of imagery for
           paintings.

2003   Traveled to Southeast Asia, visiting
           Thailand, Vietnam, and Laos. Met artists
           in Hanoi, Vietnam.

2000-05   Continued to develop paintings, incorpo-
           rating studies of Indian miniatures,
           Buddhist art, Indonesian batik stamps,
           Chinese painting, calligraphy and collage.

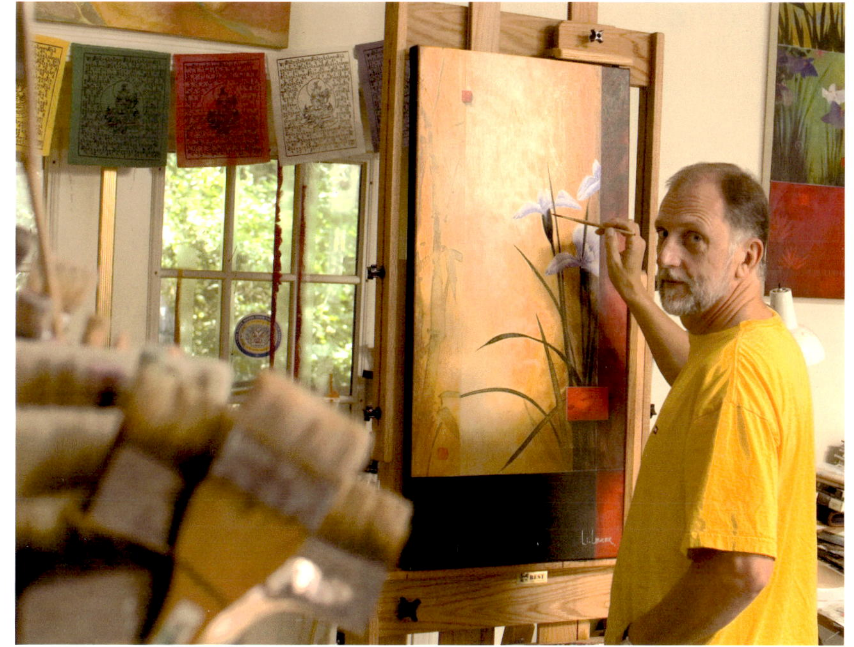

On the Beach, monoprint on Arches paper, 20" x 32", 1998
Collection of the Artist

SOLO EXHIBITIONS

1988 – 05   **Recent Paintings**, Petley Jones Gallery, Vancouver, BC

2005   **Tranquility**, Canada House Gallery, Banff, Alberta

2004   **Visions Of "Mind" – Paintings from the Garden**, Petley Jones Gallery, Vancouver, BC

2004   **Exotica**, Canada House Gallery, Banff, Alberta

2003   **Sanctuaries**, Galerie d'Art Michel Bigué, St-Sauveur, Québec

2002   **East Meets West Anew**, Hambleton Gallery, Kelowna, BC

2002   **Interpretations of Spirit and Tranquility**, White Rock Gallery, White Rock, BC

1998   **Don Li-Leger Monoprints & Etchings**, Marshall Clark Gallery, Tsawwassen, BC

1994 – 95   **Looking at You, Looking at Me**, Surrey Art Gallery, Surrey, BC

1994   **New Works,** Petley Jones Gallery, Vancouver, BC

1987   Canadian Pavilion, Epcot Center, Orlando, Florida

1984   Surrey Art Gallery, Surrey, BC

1981   Houston/Farris Gallery, Vancouver, BC

1978 – 80   Marion Scott Gallery, Vancouver, BC

1978   Kelowna Art Gallery, Kelowna, BC

SELECTED PUBLICATIONS, ARTICLES & REVIEWS

GROUP EXHIBITIONS

2005 **The Art and Act of Drawing in Three Exhibitions**, Surrey Art Gallery, Surrey, BC

2000 – 05 Petley Jones Gallery, Vancouver, BC

2002 – 05 White Rock Gallery, White Rock, BC

2001 – 05 NY Art Expo, Winn Devon Art Group, New York, NY

2004 **Art Blooms**, Canada House Gallery, Banff, Alberta

2002 **Journey**, Surrey Art Gallery, Surrey, BC

1999 **Small Prints '99**, Oak Park, Illinois

1993 – 94 **Wetlands and Waterfowl**, Wildlife Habitat Canada, Canadian Museum of Nature, Ottawa, Ontario

1991 **Beautiful BC**, Diane Farris Gallery, Vancouver, BC

1991 Duck Stamp Competition, Wildlife Habitat Canada, Beckett Gallery, Hamilton, Ontario

1990 Conservation Art Exhibition, The Nature's Trust, Vancouver, BC

1989 **Carmanah: Artistic Visions of an Ancient Rainforest**, Vancouver, BC

1983 – 84 **Birds in Art**, Leigh Yawkey Woodson Art Gallery, Wausau, Wisconsin

National Geographic Society, Washington, DC

Denver Museum of Natural History, Denver, Colorado

Houston Museum of Natural Science, Houston, Texas

1982 **Spirit of the Wild**, World Wildlife Fund, Toronto, Ontario

Babic, Marisa. "Where beauty meets bounty." *The Now*, 8 December 2001, p. 3.

Brown, Alex. "Li-Leger: redefining Asian fusion." *The Peace Arch News*, September 2002, page unknown.

Brown, Alex. "The intimacy of prints." *The Peace Arch News*, 26 November 1997, pp. A28, A30.

Brown, Alex. "Portraits of Surrey." *Surrey/North Delta Leader*, 11 August, 1993, p. A14.

Coulson, Kate "Spacious Simplicity: The Art of Don Li-Leger", Pacific Rim Magazine, Volume 2, Issue 7, 2005, pp.21-23.

Davison, Liane and Brian Foreman, *Journey*. Surrey: Surrey Art Gallery, 2002.

Davison, Liane, and Tim Fitzharris. *Looking at You, Looking at Me Paintings of Wildlife by Don Li-Leger*. Surrey: Surrey Art Gallery, 1994 – 1995.

Radford, Kathy. "Don Li-Léger Vision en fusion." *Magazin'Art*, 13e année, no. 2, (hiver/Winter 2000/2001), pp. 74-76.

Radford, Kathy. "Don Li-Léger Fusing Visions." *Magazin'Art*, 13e année, no. 2, (hiver/Winter 2000/2001), pp. 104-106.

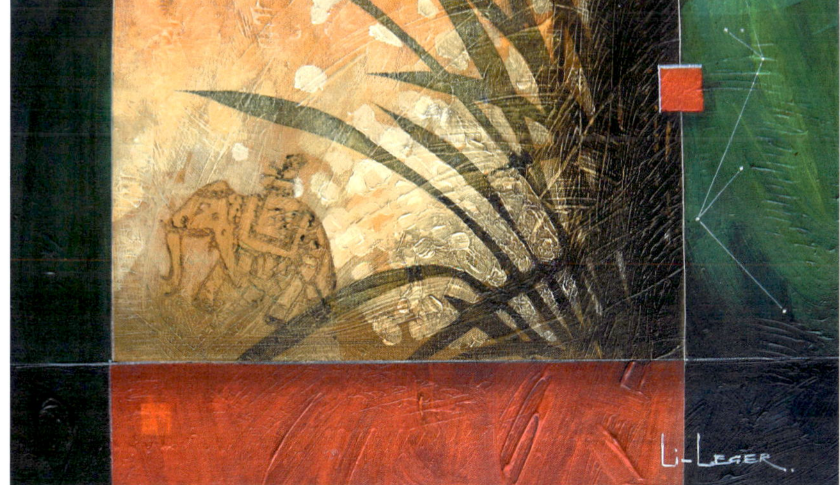

Travels with Ganesh, acrylic on canvas, 16" x 20", 2004, Collection of Tracy Morrison and Brooke Wade